DEMOCRACY'S GOOD NAME

Also by Michael Mandelbaum

The Nuclear Question: The United States and Nuclear Weapons, 1946–1976 (1979)

The Nuclear Revolution: International Politics Before and After Hiroshima (1981)

The Nuclear Future (1983)

Reagan and Gorbachev (Co-author, 1987)

The Fate of Nations: The Search for National Security in the Nineteenth and Twentieth Centuries (1988)

The Global Rivals (Co-author, 1988)

The Dawn of Peace in Europe (1996)

The Ideas That Conquered the World: Peace, Democracy, and Free Markets in the Twenty-first Century (2002)

The Meaning of Sports: Why Americans Watch Baseball, Football, and Basketball and What They See When They Do (2004)

The Case for Goliath: How America Acts as the World's Government in the Twenty-first Century (2006)

DEMOCRACY'S GOOD NAME

THE RISE *and* RISKS *of the* WORLD'S
MOST POPULAR FORM *of* GOVERNMENT

MICHAEL MANDELBAUM

PUBLICAFFAIRS New York

Published in the United States by PublicAffairs™, a member of the
Perseus Books Group.

Designed by Timm Bryson

A Cataloging-in-Publication data record for this book is available from
The Library of Congress

ISBN-13: 978-1-58648-514-6
ISBN-10: 1-58648-514-8

10 9 8 7 6 5 4 3 2 1

To Thomas B. and Hadassah Brooks Morgan
and in memory of John P. and Lorraine W. Frank:
champions of democracy;

and to Anne Mandelbaum, with my love and admiration.

CONTENTS

ACKNOWLEDGMENTS

I am grateful to the Carnegie Corporation of New York, which gave me a grant for the 2003–2004 academic year under the auspices of the Carnegie Scholars Program, during the term of which I completed work on a previous book, *The Case for Goliath: How America Acts as the World's Government in the Twenty-first Century*, and began the writing of this one. I am particularly indebted, for many contributions to my work over the years, to the Corporation's President, Vartan Gregorian; to its President Emeritus, David A. Hamburg; to the Chair of the Carnegie Scholars Program, Patricia Rosenfield; and to Deana Arsenian and David C. Speedie III.

I benefited from the opportunity to explore some of the ideas in this book in the op-ed pages of *Newsday* and am grateful to James Klurfeld, the editor of the newspaper's editorial page, and to Noel Rubinton, the former editor of its op-ed page, for making this possible. I also learned a great deal from conversations with Thomas L. Friedman of *The New York Times* about many of the subjects addressed in the pages that follow.

The peerless literary agent, Morton L. Janklow, encouraged me to write about democracy and ably represented the book that resulted. I am grateful to the superb team at PublicAffairs, its founder and editor-at-large Peter Osnos, its publisher Susan Weinberg, Morgen VanVorst, Laura Stine, and Whitney Peeling, for their skillful supervision of the publication process. Anna Borshchevskaya provided helpful research assistance. Sheila Lewis gave me invaluable assistance, as well.

My greatest debt is to my wife, Anne Mandelbaum, who took time out from her own work to edit this book and who has given me her wise counsel, her unwavering and indispensable support, and her love for more than three decades.

INTRODUCTION

The last quarter of the twentieth century witnessed one of the most remarkable developments in all of recorded history: the rise of democracy around the world. In 1900, only ten countries were democracies. By mid-century the number had increased to thirty, and twenty-five years later it remained there. By 2005, 119 of the world's 190 countries were democracies. This global democratic surge has a strong claim to being the single most important political development in a century hardly lacking in momentous events and trends.

As it spread, democracy's reputation also soared. By the beginning of the twenty-first century, that reputation was a golden one. Democracy had a good name, the best of any form of government. It had such a good name, in fact, that every other political system was widely considered inferior to it. Non-democracies came to be seen as unfortunate and ill-fated departures from what was universally acknowledged to be the best political system.

Yet this was not always the case. Democracy's good name has not, historically, been the norm. For almost all of recorded history, until well into the nineteenth century, the word "democracy" had a negative connotation. The form of government to which it referred was regarded as dangerous, destructive, and entirely undesirable. Democracy had a low reputation even where its elements flourished earliest, in Great Britain and the United States.

Moreover, even as they spread in the twentieth century, democratic practices brought with them consequences incompatible with the good name democracy came to enjoy. In the 1930s, an electoral process in Germany brought to power Adolf Hitler, who presided over the worst atrocity, the Nazi Holocaust, and launched the bloodiest armed conflict, World War II, in all of human history. In the wake of the Cold War, when democracy had vanquished its major challenger, communism, the movement toward more democratic politics was accompanied in some places by terrible violence—in the Balkans, for example.

In the post–Cold War period, moreover, the concerted efforts of the world's most powerful democracy, the United States, to implant its own form of government in other countries failed in Somalia, Haiti, and the Balkans; and where the United States tried hardest, in Iraq, the result, even with a series of free elections and the presence of 140,000 American troops, was a dismayingly high level of violence.

Why did democracy enjoy such an extraordinary rise and acquire such a glowing reputation in the last quarter of the twentieth century, and what are the dangers and difficulties that have accompanied its worldwide adoption? Answering those questions is the purpose of this book. The key to the answers lies in an understanding of the nature of the democratic form of government.

What the world of the twenty-first century calls democracy is, in fact, a fusion of two political traditions that, for most of recorded history, were not only separate and distinct from each other but were seen by virtually all those who took an interest in politics as entirely incompatible. Democracy's two parts are liberty—individual freedom—and popular sovereignty—rule by all the people. Well into the nineteenth century, the term "democracy" commonly referred to only one of them—popular sovereignty—and a regime based on popular sovereignty was regarded, for historical and logical reasons, as certain to suppress liberty. Economic liberty, especially private property, religious freedom, and political rights of the kind guaranteed by the first ten amendments to the American Constitution, it was widely believed, could not survive the rule of the people.

In the latter part of the nineteenth century and the early decades of the twentieth, contrary to this received wisdom, liberty and popular sovereignty were successfully fused in a few Western countries. It is this hybrid political form, which acquired the name that previously belonged to popular sovereignty alone, that swept over the world in the last quarter of the twentieth century and earned democracy the good name it enjoys in the twenty-first.

If it was wrong to believe that liberty and popular sovereignty could never be joined together, however, it was right to fear that rule by the people without liberty would be dangerous. Popular sovereignty in the absence of liberty can lead, and has led, to the tyranny of the majority over the minority. In the nineteenth century, the champions of liberty feared that the people, once empowered, would seize or destroy the property of the wealthy few. In the twentieth and twenty-first centuries, the tyranny of the majority has often taken a different form: the oppression, sometimes including mass expulsion and even murder, by a more numerous ethnic, racial, or religious group of a less numerous and therefore more vulnerable one. Popular sovereignty without liberty has also led to large-scale violence of a more familiar and better organized kind: war.

During the Cold War, the United States devised, although it never used, chemical weapons known as "binary nerve gases," which were composed of two chemicals each of which was harmless alone but became lethal when mixed together. Modern democracy is just the opposite: benign when its two component parts are combined, potentially toxic when one—popular sovereignty—appears without the other. Because it is easier to establish than liberty, popular sovereignty all too often has appeared alone, creating the risks that democracy—or, more accurately, *partial* democracy—poses, including in the Balkans in the 1990s and Iraq in the first decade of the twenty-first century.

Still, in many other places, the virtuous combination of rule by the people and the protection of individual freedom has taken root, which is why democracy, rightly, enjoys such a good name. The most important, and most hopeful, political fact of the twenty-first century is that the rise of democracy is the rule, while the risks its rise poses are the exception. This book is about both.

The rise of modern democracy begins with the successful merger of its two component parts. Chapter 1 of *Democracy's Good Name* describes the circumstances of their merger and the obstacles to the spread of liberty and popular sovereignty that remained even after they had been fully established in a few countries.

Democracy did eventually spread, largely because the countries where it flourished became unusually successful and therefore served as attractive models for others to emulate. In particular, Great Britain in the nineteenth century and the United States in the twentieth became militarily the most powerful and economically the most prosperous of all the sovereign states of the international system. The two be-

longed to the winning coalition in each of the three global
conflicts of the twentieth century: World Wars I and II and
the Cold War. These extraordinary successes made a strong
impression on others. Countries, like individuals, learn from
what they observe. For countries, as for individuals, success
inspires imitation. The course of modern history, as the
book's second chapter describes, made democracy seem well
worth emulating.

While the power of the democratic example created a widespread desire for democracy, especially in the last quarter of
the twentieth century, the desire for a democratic political system does not, by itself, create the capacity for establishing one.
This is where the risks of democracy arise. Genuine democracy, and in particular liberty, requires supporting institutions.
These cannot function properly unless the people operating
them have the necessary skills and habits, which are underpinned by a particular set of values. Institutions, skills, and values all take time to develop. They cannot be created quickly.
But how can they be created at all?

Their principal source, and therefore, along with the democratic example, the second major cause of democracy's remarkable twentieth-century rise, is the free-market economy. Even
governments hostile to democracy, such as the Communist
regime in China, have adopted the free-market system of economic management because it is the system that most effectively produces economic growth. The working of a free
market, in turn, promotes democratic politics and especially
liberty in a number of ways, which chapter 3 discusses.

The core of a market system is private property, which is itself a form of liberty. The wealth that the free market generates
underwrites the kind of political participation that democratic
government requires. The free market builds the network of

organizations and groups independent of the government—businesses, trade unions, professional associations, clubs, and the like—that is known as civil society, which is itself indispensable to a democratic political system. A free-market economy, moreover, cultivates the skills and attitudes that, when transferred from economic to political life, foster democracy.

The worldwide spread of democracy counts as very good news indeed for international relations, according to one extensively studied and widely embraced proposition, which holds that democracies tend to conduct peaceful foreign policies and seldom, if ever, go to war with one another. The widely shared belief that this is so helps to account for democracy's glittering good name.

Chapter 4 assesses the validity of this proposition. It finds that the presence of popular sovereignty, in the absence of liberty, can actually increase the chances of armed conflict. Moreover, pressures for democracy can prompt undemocratic governments seeking to resist them to carry out bellicose foreign policies in an attempt to consolidate their power. This is a prominent feature of politics in the Arab Middle East. In such cases, an undemocratic government's fear of being replaced by a democracy also increases the chances of war. Nor does the simultaneous presence of liberty and popular sovereignty offer complete protection against terrorism. In some ways, full-fledged democracy heightens the threat of terrorism because terrorists find it easier to operate in democratically governed countries than in undemocratic ones.

Nonetheless, on balance, war and terrorism are less likely to emanate from democracies than from dictatorships. In general, a more democratic world will be a more peaceful place. This makes a matter of some consequence to people everywhere the question that the fifth chapter of *Democracy's Good Name* addresses, a question that has become one of the major issues of international public policy for the twenty-first century: what are the prospects for the further spread of popular sovereignty and especially of liberty?

For a variety of reasons, direct efforts to implant democracy in undemocratically governed countries are not likely to succeed. The indirect promotion of democracy, by contrast, will likely have a powerful impact in the years ahead, just as it did in the nineteenth and twentieth centuries. The powerful pull toward democracy that stems from the economic and political successes of countries with this form of government, combined with the push in the same direction created by the workings of the free-market economy, can be expected to affect all undemocratic countries, of which the most important for the future of international politics and the global economy are Russia, China, and the Arab countries. The final chapter assesses the social and political forces pressing for, and those resisting, the advent of democracy in each. While it is not possible to be certain when, or indeed whether, democracy will come to any of them, it is possible to identify the way this is likely to happen—if it happens at all.

Pressure on undemocratic governments to make way for democratic politics will persist as long as the worldwide forces pressing for democracy persist. These forces will operate as long as the democratic form of government remains robust where it began and where its roots are deepest—in its Western stronghold. While challenges to the democracies surely lie ahead, and while the risks democracy brings with it will remain, there is no good reason, the concluding chapter finds, to believe that countries whose political systems feature individual liberty and popular sovereignty will prove unable, or less able than undemocratic countries, to meet these challenges. If, and as, the democratically governed countries of the West do meet the challenges of the future, therefore, democracy will keep its good name and its rise will continue well into the twenty-first century.

I

The Origins of Democracy

"If you establish a democracy, you must in due time reap the fruits of a democracy. You will in due season have great impatience of the public burdens, combined in due season with great increase of the public expenditures. You will in due season have wars entered into from passion and not from reason. You will in due season find your property is less valuable and your freedom less complete."

—Benjamin Disraeli, to the
House of Commons, 1830[1]

The Triumph of Democracy

On January 20, 2005, George W. Bush was inaugurated for the second time as President of the United States. Like all his predecessors in that office going back to George Washington in 1789, he delivered an inaugural address. Its subject was the spread of democracy around the world, a cause for celebration where it had already occurred and the object of American hopes and, as Bush promised, American exertions where it had not.

The speech was in keeping with the purposes of the inaugural addresses of the past. It concerned a large, important subject. Its theme—the value of democracy for all people—commanded wide support in the United States. "Americans of every party and background, Americans by choice and by birth," Bush said, "are bound to one another in the cause of freedom."[2] In the President's view, that theme justified the major initiatives he and his colleagues had already undertaken—the removal of oppressive governments in faraway Afghanistan and Iraq and the effort to implant democratic regimes in their places—and foreshadowed even more extensive efforts to foster democracy beyond America's borders in the presidential term that was just beginning.

Like the notable inaugural addresses of the past, moreover, this one dealt with a distinguishing feature of the historical moment in which it was given. Abraham Lincoln's second inaugural message in 1865 looked forward to healing the divisions of the terrible Civil War that had engulfed the nation, with the President promising "malice toward none" and "charity for all." Franklin Roosevelt's speech at his first inauguration, in 1933, sought to reassure the nation in the midst of the worst economic crisis in its history that it "had nothing to fear but fear itself." John F. Kennedy's 1961 inaugural address sounded a note of defiant commitment to the global struggle with communism in which the United States was then engaged, vowing to "pay any price, bear any burden, support any friend, oppose any foe" in order to prevail. George W. Bush's choice of subject implied that the global diffusion of democracy was as important for the United States, and the rest of the world, in the first decade of the twenty-first century as the Civil War had been in the 1860s, the Great Depression in the 1930s, and the Cold War in the 1960s.

The presence of democratic governments around the world was certainly a more conspicuous feature of the world of 2005 than it had been thirty years earlier. In the course of the previous three decades, the number of democracies had tripled.[3] The political system that Bush celebrated had taken root in almost every part of the planet. In Southern Europe, Spain, Portugal, and Greece adopted it. In Asia, where democracy was entirely absent until the second half of the twentieth century, South Korea, Thailand, the Philippines, Taiwan, and Indonesia all rid themselves of undemocratic regimes and began to build democratic political structures. During that period, most of the countries of Latin America changed from dictatorial to democratic governance. Communist regimes collapsed across Eurasia from Germany to the borders of China, and democracies emerged in many of the formerly Communist countries and territories. Whereas in 1975, 30 of the world's countries could be counted as democracies, by 2005, 119 of them had democratic political systems.[4]

Stirrings of democracy even appeared in regions previously inhospitable to it. In the Arab Middle East, shortly after Bush's inaugural speech, free elections were held in the midst of a deadly insurgency in Iraq and in the territory of the Palestinian Authority following the death of the corrupt Palestinian leader, Yasir Arafat, and large, peaceful demonstrations in Lebanon forced the retreat of the Syrian army of occupation, one of the main obstacles to democracy, from that country. In three countries that had for most of the twentieth century been part of the Soviet Union—Ukraine in Europe, Georgia in the Caucasus, and Kyrgyzstan in Central Asia—similar demonstrations succeeded in evicting governments with flimsy or nonexistent democratic credentials and replacing them, in the Ukrainian case through a free and fair election, with people more committed to democratic procedures. Indeed, during the President's adult lifetime, "the swiftest advance of freedom ever

seen"[5] had taken place, providing striking evidence for his assertion that "history has a visible direction"[6] and that that direction was toward democracy.

What propelled history in this direction? Why did democracy spread so far and so fast? According to Bush, this was part
of the natural order of things. "Eventually," he said, "the call
of freedom comes to every mind and soul."[7] Freedom is "the
permanent hope of mankind . . . that is meant to be fulfilled."[8]

It was hardly novel for an American President to speak of
democracy as the destiny of mankind: Bush's predecessors regularly did so,[9] because the commitment to and the celebration
of democratic principles saturate American history. Indeed,
the United States was explicitly founded on democratic principles, and advancing those principles, according to Bush, "is
the mission that created our nation."[10] The United States was
the first country to be established on this basis and its founding was therefore a seminal event in the history of democracy.
The era in which it was founded, the late eighteenth century,
was the time when the beginnings of what would be recognized in the twenty-first century as democratic government
first appeared in the world.

America's founders fully expected that the example they
were setting by establishing the new republic would profoundly affect the rest of the world. One of them, Alexander
Hamilton, wrote that "it seems to have been reserved to the
people of this country, by their conduct and example, to decide the important question, whether societies of men are
really capable or not of establishing good government from
reflection and choice."[11] By the first decade of the twenty-first
century that question had evidently been decided in the affir-
mative, in favor of democracy.

Yet Hamilton's expectation calls into question Bush's confidence that democratic government is part of the natural order of human affairs. After all, the final decades of the eighteenth century, when something like modern democracy made its debut on the world stage, came late in human history. Human beings had lived with one another for millennia without organizing their communities in a democratic fashion. Even after governments with democratic characteristics appeared in the world, even after the founding of the United States, other countries did not rush to adopt this form of government.

Hamilton's prediction that the world would follow the American example had largely been fulfilled by the beginning of the twenty-first century, but it was not fulfilled in the nineteenth century or, indeed, for most of the twentieth. In fact, for most of the 200 years after the United States was born, democracy was a rarity, a form of government found only in a minority—and, for most of that time, a small minority—of the world's sovereign states. Nor did democracy endure in every place where it was established. Countries routinely regressed from democracy to dictatorship.[12]

In 1900, only a handful of democracies existed, most of them English-speaking.[13] By 1950, democracy had spread to Western Europe and to two important Asian countries, Japan and India, but almost nowhere else.[14] Even as late as 1975, the American diplomat and historian George F. Kennan—not, to be sure, an enthusiast of democracy but certainly an astute observer of the world and its politics—could write,

> I know of no evidence that "democracy" . . . is the natural state of most of mankind. It seems rather to be a form of government (and a difficult one, with many draw-

backs, at that) which evolved in the 18th and 19th centuries
in northwestern Europe . . . and which was then carried
into other parts of the world, including North America,
where peoples from that northwestern European area appeared as settlers. . . . Democracy has, in other words, a
relatively narrow base both in time and in space; and the
evidence has yet to be produced that it is the natural form
of rule for peoples outside those narrow perimeters.[15]

To account for the global dominance of democracy, therefore, requires, in the first instance, an explanation not of why
it spread so rapidly during the last quarter of the twentieth
century but rather of why it spread so slowly, or indeed at all,
in the two centuries before that.

The beginnings of such an explanation may be found in the
language George W. Bush's second inaugural speech employed. He spoke as if the political system that he was committed to promoting through support for "democratic
movements and institutions in every nation and culture"[16]
were a single, integrated, readily identifiable form of government; and so, in the first decade of the twenty-first century, it
was. Yet it was and is a system of government made up of two
principal components, which President Bush mentioned frequently without, however, noting the distinction between
them. He referred to "liberty" and its synonym "freedom,"
and also to "self-government."

While democratic government, as it has come to be defined
in the twenty-first century, includes both, they are separate
and distinct features of such a political system. Liberty belongs
to individuals; self-government is a property of the community
as a whole. Liberty involves what governments do, or, more accurately, what they are forbidden to do—they are forbidden to

abridge individual freedoms. Self-government, by contrast, has to do with the way those who govern are chosen—they are chosen by all the people. Self-government therefore answers the question of *who* governs, while liberty prescribes rules for *how* those who govern may do so. Liberty refers to the way the machinery of government operates, self-government to the identity of the operators.[17] Not only are these two constituent features of democracy analytically distinct, moreover, they originated in different historical eras and developed in radically dissimilar ways.

THE TWO TRADITIONS

Liberty is what governments cannot prevent individuals from doing. It consists of a series of political zoning ordinances that fence off sectors of social, political, and economic life from government interference. What the contemporary world knows as liberty, or freedom, is an amalgam of several distinct areas of non-interference, which evolved separately from one another, usually out of fierce conflicts among competing centers of power and authority. These conflicts led to truces, the terms of which designated some issues as demilitarized zones—areas of life that would no longer be the subject of contention or governmental intervention.[18]

The conflicts out of which these zones of non-interference emerged go back a very long way: the development of liberty is a theme in European history that can be found in the ancient world. The word "liberty" comes from a term in ancient Rome denoting someone who is not a slave.[19] It was in the Roman Republic that the core of liberty, the principle that government can and should be limited in its reach and its power, first appeared.[20] The modern form of limited government can trace its ancestry to the medieval European system of feudalism, which divided power among monarchs and nobles.[21] For much of its history liberty was associated with the aristocracy. The term connoted privileges of the well-born that the king could not revoke.[22]

The oldest specific form of liberty is the inviolability of private property, which was part of the life of the Roman Republic.[23] Religious liberty emerged from the split in Christendom provoked by the Protestant Reformation of the sixteenth century. The bitter conflicts caused by the Reformation led governments, over the course of several centuries (with Poland and the Netherlands in the lead), to designate faith and worship as matters to be left to the individual conscience, free from the dictates of the government. Political liberty emerged later than the other two forms but is the one to which twenty-first-century uses of the word "freedom" usually refer. It connotes the absence of governmental control of speech, assembly, and political participation.

Liberty requires, and therefore does not appear without, the rule of law.[24] Law is the map of a democratic political system, designating and codifying those areas that are reserved to individuals and are off-limits to government.[25] It spells out the restrictions on the government's power and the social terrain reserved for individual choice and initiative, as well as the rules and procedures for enforcing the restraints and safeguarding the reserved territory. The basic law setting out the fundamental design of a democratic political system is the constitution, and almost all democracies have one.[26]

The history of liberty is protracted and complicated. Its different forms came together in a recognizable, if not exact, version of the way twenty-first-century democracies embody liberty in the second half of the eighteenth century in Great Britain. Unlike the sovereign states of the European continent, Britain had a strong parliament that effectively checked the power of the king.[27] In Europe in the seventeenth century, monarchs had considerably enhanced their powers, leading to what historians have called the "age of absolutism" there. In Great Britain in the course of the seventeenth century, by contrast, a regicide, a civil war, a protectorate supplanting the monarchy, and, after the restoration of the monarchy, the eviction of one king in favor of another king and his queen[28] established limits on the monarch's authority.

Britain also had the most secure property rights and the longest history of respect for such rights.[29] While Britain had an established Protestant Church, other varieties of Protestant worship were tolerated: Catholics and Jews, while not enjoying the full panoply of civic prerogatives available to Protestants, were not persecuted by the government.

As for political liberty, here again Great Britain, from at least the eighteenth century onward, qualified as the freest country in Europe and therefore in the world. Freedom of speech was a particularly noteworthy feature of the country's political life. For partisans of liberty elsewhere such as Voltaire, the French writer and leader of the intellectual movement devoted to reason and progress known as the Enlightenment, eighteenth-century Britain stood as a beacon of political virtue and a model for the rest of Europe.[30]

What was (and is) known as the British constitution was not, in fact, a written document but rather the accumulation of laws and customs that, among other things, collectively defined and protected liberty in Britain. The first formal, written constitution, with explicit safeguards for individual liberties, was produced in 1787 by the leaders of the thirteen British colonies that had banded together to declare themselves the independent United States.

The new American republic was the political offspring of Great Britain. The colonies had British-style legislatures and cherished British political values, above all liberty.[31] Indeed, they rebelled against the mother country precisely because they believed that the government in London had wrongly infringed upon their own freedoms. The American Revolution was made to secure "the rights of Englishmen" in America.

The creation of the American Constitution was a landmark in the history of the rule of law, and for that reason also a landmark in the history of liberty, which it was designed to protect by limiting the powers of government. It did this by distributing that power among three separate branches of the national government so that they could check and balance each other. It further divided official authority between the national—that is, the federal—government and the governments of the states (the former colonies) that together made up the federal union.[32]

To the main text of the Constitution, which designated which powers would be wielded by which governmental bodies, the framers of the document added ten amendments, known collectively as the Bill of Rights, spelling out the areas of social life in which none of these bodies could intervene. The first of these amendments enumerated political liberties. It enjoined the legislature from making any law "abridging the freedom of speech, or of the press; or the right of the people peaceably to assemble, and to petition the Government for redress of grievances."

The same First Amendment also addressed religious liberty: "Congress shall make no law respecting an establishment of religion, or prohibiting the free exercise thereof." Here, the Americans went beyond the British practice. Whereas in Great Britain, one denomination, the Church of England, enjoyed the status of an established religion, the

Constitution prohibited a favored status for any one version
of religious faith.[33]

The 1787 Constitution did not mention property, but this
was not because its authors did not respect the institution of
private property. To the contrary, property was, on the whole,
as secure as in Britain.[34] Property was enshrined, along with
political freedoms, as a designated liberty in another, similar
document issued in Europe two years after the American
Constitution was written. This document, the Declaration of
the Rights of Man, appeared at an early stage of the French
Revolution.[35]

The French Revolution counts as one of the most important political events in all of human history, perhaps *the* most
important one.[36] It had a powerful impact first on France, then
on Europe, and eventually on the entire world. Its effects
could still be detected two centuries after it had taken place.
Perhaps its broadest and most enduring effect, the one dis-
cernible in the political affairs of the twenty-first century, was
its assertion that all legitimate authority stems from the
people. The third article of the Declaration of the Rights of
Man declares that "The principle of sovereignty resides essen-
tially in the nation. No office and no individual can exercise an
authority not expressly emanating from it."[37] To the question
of who should govern, the French Revolution delivered a clear
answer: the people—all of them.

That answer was, by the standards of the late eighteenth
century, indeed by the standards of virtually all previous history, a revolutionary one. True, ancient Athens had governed
itself through an assembly of all free males (a distinct minority
of the population),[38] non-English monarchs had convened ad-
visory parliaments beginning in the Middle Ages, Italian city-
states had had assemblies of notables with significant powers,

and some post-Reformation Protestant denominations had practiced forms of religious self-government, with issues being decided by majority vote.[39] In none of these cases, however, was the right to rule explicitly said to belong to the public as a whole.

To the contrary, in eighteenth-century France, throughout Europe, and almost everywhere else in the world, sovereignty—the right to rule—resided in a single sovereign, a particular person, whether a king, an emperor, or a chieftain. He (it was almost always a man) held his office by right of birth, with a permanent entitlement to the office often said to have been conferred on the ruler's lineage by the deity.

Moreover, in Europe and elsewhere, hereditary rulers routinely held sway over people who had different racial characteristics, practiced different religions, and spoke different languages than they. It was normal, that is, for the question of who ruled to be decided on the basis of what social scientists call "ascriptive" criteria rather than achieved ones: by who the ruler was (a function of who his parents were) rather than by anything he did. It was normal as well for many, if not most, of the inhabitants of the planet to be ruled by individuals whose defining characteristics were alien to them.

By asserting that the government was ultimately the property of the governed and not the governors, and that monarchies were neither divinely ordained nor uniquely fitted to rule, the French Revolution proposed to overturn these age-old principles of governance and put in their place something that existed nowhere else on the planet. The literal term for this new system of governance is "democracy," from the Greek word *demos*, meaning "the people." Since democracy has come, in the twenty-first century, to include liberty as well, however, a more appropriate term for what the French Revolution brought to the world is "popular sovereignty." It is, with liberty, one of the two constituent parts of the political system that George W. Bush celebrated and vowed to propagate on January 20, 2005, and it is the political system based on the combination of the two that earned the good name that democracy had come to enjoy when Bush made his speech.

The career of popular sovereignty followed a different course from the one that liberty took. Having come later to the world, popular sovereignty spread much farther much more rapidly. It rose to global supremacy on the backs of an all-conquering intellectual current and the most powerful political trend in the modern world, both of which were compatible with rule by the people but not with the rule of hereditary monarchs.

The intellectual current, a major development in the world's political thinking, was the rise of the concept of universal political equality, or rather the decline of the once universal and virtually unchallenged conviction that some people are suited to govern others by virtue of the families into which they are born or the ethnic or racial category to which they belong.[40]

The idea that particular individuals have the inherent right—often considered a divine right—to rule gave way steadily in the wake of the French Revolution. Absolute monarchs in Europe either had to accept restraints on their powers, or lost these powers, or, in sequence, both.[41] World War I largely put an end to this form of government in Europe, where it had flourished for centuries.

The idea that some groups are innately superior to others and thus entitled to rule over them had a longer and more robust life. Indeed, at the end of the nineteenth century, it enjoyed perhaps wider currency than ever before, as European countries brought most of Africa and Asia under their imperial control.[42] In the 1930s and 1940s, this idea formed the basis for the campaigns of conquest, economic exploitation, and mass murder conducted by Nazi Germany and imperial Japan. With their defeat, however, the principle of radical inequality that they had proclaimed and practiced fell into deep disfavor. In the second half of the twentieth century it disappeared more or less completely. To be sure, effective political inequality among different groups within sovereign jurisdictions persisted; but by the end of the century, in few places did dominant groups unabashedly insist on their superiority as a matter of principle.[43]

The demise of the idea of the inevitability and justice of the traditional forms of political hierarchy removed the theoretical and moral basis on which the alternatives to popular sovereignty—monarchy and empire—had rested. At the same time, the world's kings and emperors experienced an assault from a political movement that was compatible with popular sovereignty but not with the perpetuation of their rule. That movement was nationalism, which holds that people with common traits—language, ethnicity, religion, historical experience—share a common destiny that must be realized through the creation of a political unit that the group dominates, the nation-state.[44] Nationalism drew its formidable strength in the nineteenth and twentieth centuries from a variety of sources: the revival and celebration of long-standing communal identities and deliberate efforts at constructing and disseminating such identities; the flow of people into cities, the standardization of the languages they used there and the spread of literacy among them through the establishment of systems of mass education in these languages; and the rise of mass armies in which, especially during wartime, powerful social bonds and political allegiances were formed.[45]

In the century following the French Revolution, nationalism became the most potent political force in the world. The dominance it achieved is evident in a major difference between two postwar peace conferences held a century apart—the Congress of Vienna, which convened in 1815 in the wake of the Napoleonic Wars, and the Paris Peace Conference of 1919–1920, which assembled to work out a political settlement following World War I. On the first occasion, the victors parceled out among themselves the territories that Napoleon had conquered as if they were chips in a game of poker, without any regard to the wishes or the identities of the people who happened to live in them. A century later, the procedures for disposing of the territories that had been governed by the vanquished powers had changed dramatically. At Paris, the victors proceeded, or tried to proceed, according to the principle of nationalism—or, as they called it, national self-determination.[16]

The peacemakers in Paris tried to draw borders not for the purpose of enhancing the power and wealth of the victorious powers, of which they were the leaders (and none of which, in contrast to 1815, was an absolute monarchy) but rather to create coherent nation-states. By 1919, therefore, the principle of popular sovereignty, which the French Revolution had unleashed upon the world, had become the global norm, the only legitimate basis for government.

From the perspective of the twenty-first century, democracy's two component parts, liberty and popular sovereignty, go together as naturally and smoothly as the popular song of the 1950s said love and marriage do. In both cases, however, what may seem to the contemporary eye to be an inevitable, indissoluble partnership was not the rule historically. Just as most marriages in most places at most times before the twentieth century were arranged affairs and thus had little or nothing to do with love, so liberty and popular sovereignty did not, until relatively recently, appear together. Liberty long predated popular sovereignty, and even in its eighteenth-century exemplar, Great Britain, the people as a whole did not rule. The country was governed by a small oligarchy of the landed aristocracy.[47]

Indeed, for most of recorded history, even including much of the history that followed the French Revolution, liberty and popular sovereignty were widely seen not only as separate, but as incompatible. The harmonious partnership that is taken for granted in the twenty-first century was considered, during the nineteenth century and for all the centuries preceding it, to be an impossible combination because one of the partners was deemed a mortal threat to the other. The tidal wave of popular sovereignty, it was widely believed, would uproot and sweep away the fragile blossom of liberty.

THE ODD COUPLE

A frequently reproduced oil painting commemorating an uprising in Paris on July 28, 1830, that hangs in the Louvre Museum in that city is entitled *Liberty Leading the People*. It depicts Marianne, the symbol of France, wielding the French flag, the tricolor, and leading a group of armed citizens forward, over the bodies of fallen comrades, with the smoke of battle all around them. As it happens, the message the painting conveys is the opposite of what most observers of political affairs for most of history took to be the relationship between its two subjects. Rather than rallying to defend and promote liberty, it was generally thought, the people, if empowered, would crush it.

Indeed, for most of recorded history the rule of the people was seen as a horrifying prospect. The risks it posed were considered grave ones. The term commonly used to denote popular rule, "democracy," had almost as low a reputation as "dictatorship" does in the twenty-first century.[48] The rule of the people, it was believed, would lead to corruption, disorder, mob violence, and ultimately tyranny. It would surely stifle liberty.[49] The eighteenth-century champions of liberty in France, Britain, and even the infant United States shared this dim view of popular sovereignty.[50]

Their pessimism about the consequences of government by the people stemmed in part from their understanding of the fate of popular sovereignty in the few places where anything like it had ever been practiced—in ancient Greece, in the Roman Republic, and in some of the Italian city-states. These political systems had usually degenerated into disorder and oppression.[51] Their pessimism stemmed as well from the conviction that the average person lacked the education, the judgment, the temperament, and the commitment to the public good to play a constructive role in public life.[52] Ignorant and unsophisticated, the masses could be easily swayed by the siren appeals of demagogues, who would lead them in dangerous directions, as had occurred in ancient Athens.

The actual introduction of popular sovereignty as the foundation of government provided further evidence for the conviction that liberty would suffer if the people gained political power. The French Revolution, which at its outset embraced the same liberties that the people of Great Britain enjoyed and that the American Constitution enshrined, produced a reign of terror and the dictatorship of a Corsican-born soldier, Napoleon Bonaparte, who proclaimed himself emperor. Later in the nineteenth century Napoleon's nephew, Louis Napoleon, came to power by popular vote—an election in 1848 and a plebiscite in 1851—but then proceeded to impose dictatorial rule, jailing his political opponents and restricting political freedom. The twentieth century, when the end of monarchical rule and the collapse of multinational empires left virtually every government basing its claim to legitimacy on popular sovereignty, provided many examples of countries in which liberty did not flourish. In that century, the "illiberal democracy" became a familiar political species.[53]

In the wake of the French Revolution, as the movement for popular sovereignty gathered momentum, the question of how liberty could be protected loomed as an increasingly urgent one. It was the subject of two major pieces of political writing of the nineteenth century: the French aristocrat Alexis de Tocqueville's *Democracy in America* and the English philosopher and political economist John Stuart Mill's *On Liberty*.[54] Each considered an expanding role for the people in social and political life to be inevitable, and the prospects for the individual liberties that each writer highly valued therefore to be shaky. The rising importance of the public as a whole in civic and political affairs posed, for each man, two distinct, if related, dangers: the tyranny of the majority over the minority, and the enforcement of a dull social and intellectual conformity by the oppressive weight of public opinion. The danger of the second particularly troubled Mill because he believed that human progress depended on giving free rein to the creative impulses of the talented few, which the prejudices of the uninformed masses might well stifle.

Both Tocqueville and Mill hoped that popular sovereignty and liberty could be successfully combined, that certain features of the emerging social and political systems that they observed (or recommended) would provide adequate safeguards for the freedoms they cherished.[55] But neither was certain that this would come to pass.

The widespread reservations about popular sovereignty manifested themselves, where liberty was best established, in a protracted political conflict, stretching well into the twentieth century, over the right to vote. In *Democracy in America*, Tocqueville predicted that, because popular sovereignty would gain ever-increasing weight in political and social affairs, universal suffrage was inevitable.[56] His prediction was borne out, but not until almost a century after he had made it, a century marked by strenuous and, for long periods, successful resistance to permitting every citizen an equal voice in choosing the government.

In the late eighteenth century, the first two governments recognizable as at least partly democratic by twenty-first-century standards, those of Great Britain and the United States, were chosen by elections, but only a small proportion of the adult population was permitted to vote in them. Over the course of the next century and beyond, the franchise was broadened in both places and in other Western countries, but only very gradually and in the face of determined opposition by those who believed that this would inevitably bring political instability and bad governance.

In Great Britain, before the first hard-fought victory for wider voting rights, the Reform Act of 1832, only 1.8 percent of the adult population could vote. After that Act the figure increased to 2.7 percent. The Chartist movement of 1846–1847, the first mass political movement in British history, called for universal suffrage, thereby placing the issue on the country's political agenda. Mill and other partisans of liberty opposed this, however,[57] and the next expansion of the franchise did not come until 1867, as the result of which 6.4 percent of adult Britons could cast ballots in elections for parliament. In 1884, another legislative change brought the total to 12.1 percent.

Universal suffrage, including the right to vote for all adult women, came to Great Britain only in 1930.[58]

In the United States the franchise expanded more rapidly in the first part of the nineteenth century. In the election of 1828, more than 50 percent of white males were eligible to vote.[59] At mid-century, however, the movement to expand the pool of eligible voters encountered effective opposition. Between 1857 and World War I, the dominant trend in American electoral matters was the narrowing rather than the widening of the franchise.[60] Not until 1920 did women get the right to vote, and that right was not fully available to citizens of African descent until the late 1960s.

Universal suffrage did ultimately become firmly established in the countries most committed to liberty. The partisans of liberty relaxed their resistance to it as governments devised methods for protecting, by generating broad support for, the particular liberty that popular participation in public affairs had seemed, even before the French Revolution, most seriously to threaten: private property. In the eighteenth century and for most of the nineteenth in Great Britain, the United States, and other Western countries, only men who owned property could vote.[61]

The property qualification was consistent with, indeed followed logically from, the low estimate of the political competence of the mass of people that many supporters of liberty shared. The possession of property, they believed, gave a person the independence necessary to withstand the sentiments of the mob and the appeals of demagogues: the propertyless, uneducated masses could be herded like sheep by their economic betters or by clever, unscrupulous, eloquent politicians.[62] The possession of property was thought to endow its owner with the judgment and sense of responsibility necessary for constructive participation in public affairs.[63]

It was, moreover, widely believed that those without property would, out of greed and envy, move to seize it from its owners if the wider public took control of the machinery of government. Popular sovereignty would, it was feared, launch a spree of looting in the society unfortunate enough to experience it.[64] The French Revolution supplied evidence for this fear. It led to the confiscation of property on a large scale, especially the property of the Catholic Church. The political message of the Revolution, moreover, if it did not lead directly to the expropriation of property, at least was not at odds with this practice. If sovereignty rested with the public rather than with the monarch—if the country belonged, in a political sense, to the people rather than to the king—it required no great leap of logic to conclude that the country's material assets also belonged to the people as a whole rather than to the fortunate, well-born few.

The confiscations of the French Revolution served as a precedent and a goal for those who took up the revolutionary cause in its wake. One of them, Karl Marx, who inspired the movement that, in the twentieth century, came to control a large part of the world's population, declared in *The Communist Manifesto*, written in 1848 with Friedrich Engels, "The theory of the Communists can be summarized in the single sentence: Abolition of private property."[65]

The impoverished multitudes did indeed resent the political and economic systems that had produced glaring material disparities. Some were moved to take part in efforts to overturn these systems, by means that on occasion included violent insurrection. The wealthy few, for their part, sought to defend their possessions by whatever methods seemed effective, which often included active opposition to both features of democracy—liberty (of the political variety, at least) and popular participation in politics.

In the twentieth century, governmental policies to make the distribution of land more equitable reduced the resistance to democracy. Land reform, which usually involved the breaking up of large estates and giving the resulting parcels of land to individuals who had cultivated but not owned them, helped to clear the way for democratic government in Japan, in South Korea, and in Taiwan. By contrast, in a number of countries in which a few families held a very large proportion of the land, stable democracy did not take hold despite recurrent efforts to establish it. Pakistan and Haiti followed this pattern.[66]

Land was, of course, the principal source of wealth for millennia. But the Industrial Revolution, which began in the latter half of the eighteenth century and gathered momentum in the nineteenth, produced new sources of wealth and new forms of property. To the actual and potential inequalities in industrially generated property, the Western countries developed a response that, like land reform but on a larger scale, helped to make possible the peaceful union of liberty and popular sovereignty and the good name of the political system that this union produced.

The use of machinery running on inanimate sources of power to make an ever-expanding array of products replaced the ownership of land as the principal source of wealth in the world. This transformed the structure of the societies in which the Industrial Revolution took place—and ultimately it reached every part of the world—creating a new class of workers in the mines and factories that became the main industrial workplaces.

Marx constructed a theory of history and launched a political movement on the premise that the industrial system would inevitably lead to the concentration of wealth in the hands of a very few owners of the workplaces—the capitalists. At the same time, and by the same process, the vast majority of the new workers—the proletariat—would be reduced to stark poverty. Had Marx's theory been correct, had industrial societies divided into a handful of plutocrats and a mass of impoverished workers, the prospects for democratic political systems combining liberty and popular sovereignty would surely have been dismal.

Marx turned out, however, to be wrong. The workings of the economic system the Industrial Revolution created did not plunge the majority of people into economic deprivation and misery.[67] To the contrary, it ultimately improved the material conditions of most of those affected by it. The distribution of wealth in most industrial societies ultimately looked less like a pyramid, with most of the assets concentrated in a few hands, and more like a diamond, with some very rich, some very poor, and most somewhere in the middle.

This relatively egalitarian distribution did not emerge simply from the spontaneous operation of the economic system. Governmental initiatives adjusted the distribution of wealth generated by industrial production to make it less unequal. The most important of those initiatives were the policies that created what came to be known as the welfare state.

In the last decades of the nineteenth century and throughout the twentieth, in parallel with the extension of the franchise and the rise to a position of global dominance of the principle of popular sovereignty as the basis of political legitimacy, governments first in the West and then throughout the world established the programs of which the welfare state consists:

unemployment insurance, compensation for injuries sustained in the workplace, old-age pensions, health care, and assistance to families with children. Most of these programs were universal in scope: that is, all citizens of the country could participate in them.

Unlike private property, the benefits that these programs conferred could not ordinarily be transferred to others at the behest of the beneficiary. In two important ways, however, the benefits the welfare state provides do resemble private property. First, they cannot, except under extraordinary circumstances, be revoked. They are benefits to which people are entitled—in the United States they are commonly called "entitlements"—simply by virtue of being citizens.[68] Second, like private property, they give the recipient a source of material well-being, in cash or in services, for which a non-governmental source of income would otherwise be required.

The welfare state in effect made the distribution of property universal, which made the institution of private property more widely acceptable than it would otherwise have been. Beyond broadening the commitment to private property by giving everyone in the society a form of it, the welfare state solidifies support for democracy by helping to prevent the kind of mass immiseration that Marx foresaw. Government programs of social welfare collectively assure a standard of living at a certain level. They form a social safety net below which, in theory, no one is allowed to fall.

The welfare state also served to broaden and deepen public support for another crucial feature of democracy, the rule of law, because its benefits were guaranteed by law. Victor Hugo once wrote sardonically that the majesty of the law resides in the fact that it prohibits rich and poor alike from sleeping under bridges. In the case of government social welfare pro-

grams, however, the law works in favor of all citizens, especially the least affluent of them, not only the wealthy and the
privileged.

In the political parlance of the twentieth and twenty-first
centuries, efforts to expand the welfare state count as "progressive"—that is, they promote political and social change.
The welfare state itself can equally appropriately be seen,
however, as a conservative project, one perpetuating an economic system that is vulnerable to popular resentment and
that therefore might not survive without it. The foundations
of the welfare state in Germany were laid by the conservative
chancellor Otto von Bismarck in the 1880s as a way of competing with the socialist parties for the allegiance of German
workers. The New Deal, the series of social welfare measures
enacted in the United States during the 1930s, helped to miti-
gate the social costs of the Great Depression. Without those
measures in place, principled opposition to the economic system that had produced the Depression, which was confined to
the fringes of American politics, would undoubtedly have been
more widespread. The welfare state may even be seen as taking societies backward, into the distant past, by recreating the
kind of network of social obligations among people in different social categories that had marked feudal Europe.

In principle, a country lacking generous welfare programs
can qualify as a democracy. It is possible, in principle, to have
liberty and popular sovereignty without a well-developed set
of government-provided social benefits. In practice, however,
in the twenty-first century, no Western democracy lacks such a
system.[69]

In the West and elsewhere, the welfare state serves a purpose that resembles the role that insulin plays in the lives of
diabetics. It compensates for a potentially fatal shortcoming—

in the case of sovereign states a degree of insecurity, inequality, and poverty that could threaten the perpetuation of their political and economic systems. Just as the required daily dosage of insulin varies among diabetics, so the extent of the welfare state—the generosity of the benefits and the level of taxation needed to pay for them—varies among countries. Indeed, the question of how generous such benefits should be stands at the center of the politics of the Western democracies. In none of these countries, however, does the return to a world without a social safety net command significant support.

The establishment of generous welfare states made possible what for centuries had been regarded as contrary to the immutable laws of politics. It reduced one of the risks of rule by the people by serving as a kind of dowry for liberty, making it an acceptable marriage partner for popular sovereignty. The marriage of the two parts of modern democracy was the equivalent, for government, of the first successful heart transplant operation. It demonstrated that liberty could survive in a body politic previously considered certain to reject it, one in which the people as a whole exercised the dominant influence.

Although the stable marriage of liberty and popular sovereignty counts as one of the most important innovations in the long history of government, unlike major technological innovations—the railroad, the telephone, the Internet—it did not spread rapidly all over the world. Even when what is now known as democracy was successfully established, even after World War II when the wealthiest countries on the planet had full-fledged versions of this form of government, in most of the world the implementation of popular sovereignty and the protection of liberty proved to be, in different ways, problematic.

THE CAREER OF POPULAR SOVEREIGNTY

In the century after the French Revolution, the principle of popular sovereignty came to dominate the world. By the twentieth century, monarchy and empire had lost their once-powerful claims to being legitimate forms of government.

The triumph of popular sovereignty in principle did not, however, lead to its successful implementation in practice everywhere. To the contrary, this proved difficult because drawing the borders within which the people could rule was not easy to do; and even when this fundamental political task was accomplished, the government that held sway, while not placing ultimate authority in the hands of an hereditary monarch or foreigners, often was not subject to effective public control, either.

In the wake of the French Revolution the demands of justice, it was almost everywhere conceded, required that the people rule. Who, then, are the people? To this question, the world of the twentieth century (and the twenty-first, as well), agreed on an answer: the nation. That answer, however, raised another question: what constitutes a nation? And that second question proved to have no simple, definitive answer.

In the wake of the French Revolution, groups of people felt themselves to belong to a single nation on the basis of a common language, or religion, or ethnicity, or historical experience, or some or all of these. The definition of a nation, that is, turned out to be subjective, which made the number of self-identified nations unstable rather than fixed. Peoples who had once seemed content to live in a political unit dominated by others subsequently changed their minds and asserted their rights, as nations, to their own states.

In the nineteenth century, among the many groups inhabiting the Habsburg Empire, for example, only the Germans and the Poles were considered to be "state-bearing" peoples. In the twentieth century, the Czechs decided that they, too, were a distinct nation deserving of their own state, and after World War I, Czechoslovakia was created. In the 1990s, however, after that country broke free of control from Moscow and its people could decide their own fate, the Slovaks, hitherto the Czechs' junior partners, seceded from Czechoslovakia, which became the Czech Republic, and established their own sovereign state, Slovakia.

The tendency for groups to decide that they constituted a nation made the crucial political task of drawing and maintaining borders a difficult one. New claimants to statehood rejected borders that placed them in jurisdictions that they did not dominate. The triumph of popular sovereignty as the basis for political legitimacy made establishing stable, universally accepted borders, and especially establishing democratic, liberty-protecting governments within those borders, difficult for two additional reasons.

First, when empires collapsed, the new sovereign states that emerged often retained the empire's provincial borders,[70] which frequently encompassed more than one group. The logic of national self-determination prescribed dividing these new jurisdictions along national lines, creating separate states for every nation; in a number of cases, however, one of the groups, having gained control of the new state, refused to allow this, insisting on keeping the other group, or groups, under its control. Some successor states to multinational empires, notably including many countries in the Middle East and Africa in the second half of the twentieth century, became, themselves, "empires in miniature."[71]

The international community as a whole, which was loath to sanction the redrawing of any border for fear that this would trigger other demands for border rectification and ultimately lead to international chaos, almost always supported the dominant group. This was the case with Iraq, which the British assembled after World War I out of three provinces of the former Ottoman Empire. Sunni Muslim Arabs kept control of a country that included Shia Muslims as well as non-Arab Kurds through a decidedly undemocratic—indeed murderously oppressive—style of governance.[72]

Second, while in some places one group refused to permit borders to be drawn to accommodate the national aspirations of another, in other places it was impossible to do so because of a mismatch between demography and geography. The settlement patterns of people of different nationalities were not always such as to make it possible to draw borders that separated them cleanly. Sometimes these patterns resembled not a checkerboard but a tossed salad, with the different nationalities mixed together. Such mixtures could be politically explosive, as the different groups struggled for control of their common state, as occurred in the former Yugoslavia in Bosnia and Kosovo.

The problem of socially mixed jurisdictions was resolved in several places by moving not the borders but rather the people within them. This process could be exceptionally brutal. When Greeks moved from the new Turkish Republic to Greece and Turks left Greece for Turkey after World War I, when Germans were driven westward from eastern Europe and the Baltic region in the wake of World War II, and when Muslims fled northern India for Pakistan, and Hindus and Sikhs made the reverse journey after the partition of the Indian subcontinent in 1947, millions of people died and tens of millions lost their homes. When the process recurred in the 1990s in the Balkans after the collapse of Yugoslavia, it became known as "ethnic cleansing."

These episodes of mass expulsion and large-scale killing may actually have made it easier for democratic government to take hold in the countries affected—albeit at a horrible price—by making them socially more homogeneous. For where more than one nationality inhabits a sovereign state in appreciable numbers, democracy has proven difficult to establish.[73] In a stable democracy, people must be willing to be part of the minority. They will accept minority status if they feel confident that the majority will respect their liberties. In a multinational state, depending on the history of relations between and among the different constituent nations, such confidence is not always present. In the Balkans in the 1990s, the Serbs and Croats did not believe, whether rightly or wrongly, that they would find life to be tolerable in a newly independent, Muslim-dominated Bosnia. In Iraq, after the overthrow of Saddam Hussein in 2003, the previously dominant Sunni Arabs had the same attitude toward the prospect of rule by the numerically superior Shia.

To be sure, stable, peaceful multinational democracies are not unknown. Belgium and Switzerland, for example, fit this description.[74] Democracy's success in these countries rests in part, however, on several features that are not easy to reproduce. Both are small, affluent, and have elaborate constitutional arrangements to safeguard not only individual liberties but group prerogatives as well.[75]

In the course of the twentieth century and into the twenty-first, some of the conflicts arising from the inclusion of more than one self-identified national group within the borders of a single sovereign state were settled: by military victory by one side, or negotiated compromises between or among them, or because warring parties stopped fighting out of sheer exhaustion. Moreover, the majority of the many sovereign states that came into existence in the modern era did not harbor violently dissatisfied minorities. Even in countries without this problem, however, the path to full democracy turned out to be neither smooth nor straight.

While by the second half of the twentieth century virtually all governments claimed to be democratic, the universal use of the term concealed as much as it revealed. In fact, there may be said to be three types of democracy, three different forms of government that claim to embody the will of the people.

In direct democracy, all citizens eligible to vote assemble to decide by ballot the major questions of public policy. Ancient Athens governed itself in this way.[76] New England town meetings offer a more recent example. Democracy of this kind is rare because in most political jurisdictions it is impractical. Citizens are too numerous for all of them to vote on every matter that affects them.

The modern world therefore practices democracy of a second type, representative democracy, in which the people choose representatives who then decide, by vote, issues of public policy. This was the system designed by the founders of the United States, which they called a republic to distinguish it from what they identified as democracy, and which they believed could withstand the damaging effects of popular passions that had led the democracies of the past to ruin.[77] The essence of representative democracy—what makes it democratic by the standards of the twenty-first century—is free, fair, regular elections to choose the people who then decide public policy.

For most of the twentieth century most governments were not chosen in this way. These political systems might be called "nominal" democracies. They were nominal in the sense that they insisted on calling themselves democratic, in the spirit of Lewis Carroll's Humpty Dumpty, who declared, "When I use a word it means what I choose it to mean: no more, no less."[78] By twenty-first-century standards, of course, the more appropriate term for these regimes, the one generally used to describe them in countries that did conduct free elections, was dictatorship—the opposite of democracy. Yet the assertion by such governments that they deserved to be called democratic was not entirely without foundation: they differed from the traditional forms of governance—monarchy and empire—in two ways in which representative democracies also differ from them. The leaders of nominal democracies did not inherit their positions and came from the same groups that they governed: they were neither aristocrats nor foreigners. And they claimed to govern on behalf, and in the interests, of the people, even if the people did not put them in power by voting for them. These political systems without free elections therefore qualified as "nominal" democracies in a second sense: they governed in the name of the people.

The most elaborate claim to be pursuing the genuine interests of the wider public even though the public had not chosen the government came from regimes operating according to the doctrines of the twentieth century's secular version of religion—ideology. The most prominent ideology was Marxism-Leninism, which combined a putatively scientific understanding of the laws of history provided by the writings of Karl Marx with a self-selected, secretive political party, a twentieth-century version of the Jacobins, who wielded power at one stage of the French Revolution. The party governed, again putatively, on the basis of Marx's precepts.

In the twentieth century, Communist parties came to control much of the world: the vast former tsarist empire that became the Soviet Union; Central and Eastern Europe as far west as the middle of Germany; China; Indochina; and a few countries in other parts of the world. Communist governments claimed the mantle of democracy by the names they gave themselves—the People's Republic of China, for example, and the German Democratic Republic—and by conducting regular elections. These elections, however, were neither free nor fair. Only Communist-sponsored candidates were allowed to stand, there was ordinarily only one candidate for each office, and that candidate was invariably officially reported to have received 99 percent or more of the votes cast.

Ruling Communist parties asserted that they enjoyed a particular kind of popular legitimacy based on superior knowledge. Their sweeping program for reshaping the societies they governed served the ultimate interests of the people they governed, or so they said. Because the people affected seldom agreed, the Communist program, particularly the abolition of private property, had to be imposed by force. Communism in practice therefore turned out to bear no resemblance to liberty-protecting representative democracy. Instead, it involved a war waged by the government against the society it governed. In these wars, the worldwide total of casualties, the vast majority of them unarmed civilians who had aroused the suspicions of the Communist authorities or simply found themselves in the wrong place at the wrong time, reached the tens of millions.[79]

The ideological ardor that possessed Communists—some of them, at least—when they first came to power diminished over the decades of Communist rule. Ultimately, Communist authorities almost everywhere maintained their grip on power for its own sake, rather than out of genuine conviction that they could use it to build freer, richer societies than had ever before existed. Communist governments came in this way to resemble the many non-Communist unelected regimes that held power in the name of popular sovereignty in every part of the world during the twentieth century.

As in Communist countries, these garden-variety dictatorships, located throughout Asia, Africa, and Latin America, which also usually styled themselves "democracies,"[80] insisted on monopolizing and retaining political power rather than allowing the government to be chosen by free elections. Their motives for doing so arose not from any theory of history or society, but rather from something much older.

From the beginning of recorded history, and no doubt before that, some individuals and groups have sought to amass and retain as much power over others as possible and to pass it on to their offspring or political allies. Constitutional limits on the exercise of power and the selection of those who wield it by regular, free elections are emphatically the historical exception, not the rule.[81]

In most places at most times, moreover, holding power made possible the accumulation of wealth, which gave its holders a formidable additional reason not to relinquish it. Furthermore, if people who wield the powers of government offend or injure others in its exercise—a not uncommon occurrence—they have yet another reason to cling to it: the fear that, if they give it up, those whom they have wronged will retaliate.

Rulers not only have strong motives for keeping power permanently rather than handing it peacefully to others regardless of the wishes of those they govern, they also have ready opportunities to hold on to it, using the instruments of coercion that are part of the apparatus of government everywhere.

All have police forces for keeping order within their borders. The maintenance of order is, after all, the first duty of government. Almost all have also had armed forces to defend themselves against their neighbors, the need for some means of defense being a condition of safety in a world of other, similarly equipped, similarly wary sovereign states.

Rulers, that is, have always had access to armed men trained in the use of force, whom they have usually controlled and whom they could therefore command to act to keep themselves in power. Not surprisingly, leaders of armed forces have used the troops at their command to seize political power, with Julius Caesar and Napoleon Bonaparte being two well-known examples.[82]

In the twentieth century, undemocratic rule by the military became common. In many of the countries that gained independence from the imperial powers, the military seemed a desirable alternative to weak, feckless, incompetent civilian authorities.[83] Like any other group in the age of popular sovereignty, the military could claim to be governing on behalf of the people.[84] More than most other groups, such a claim, coming from the military, was likely to be taken seriously, not least by the members of the armed forces themselves. Because they were charged with defending the country, the armed forces in many of these countries saw themselves, and were seen by others, as embodying the political community as a whole. As such, the military seemed to be the one institution devoted exclusively to the general interest and therefore better suited to govern than squabbling, narrow-minded civilian politicians.[85]

The existence of standing armed forces poses a general problem for the establishment of stable, enduring democratic government, a problem succinctly expressed in ancient times by the Roman writer Juvenal when he asked, "Who will guard the guardians?"[86] In virtually any society, instruments of coercion are all but indispensable. Even democracies need them to protect and enforce the liberties that democracy guarantees. A person's property is secure, after all, only if others cannot seize it, and the government has the responsibility for preventing this, in order to discharge which it employs a police force.[87]

This means that, as James Madison wrote in one of the Federalist Papers urging the ratification of the American Constitution, "In framing a government which is to be administered by men over men, the great difficulty lies in this: you must first enable the government to control the governed; and in the next place oblige it to control itself."[88] How are both to be accomplished simultaneously, especially given the human predilection for keeping and expanding power?[89]

The answer at which Madison and the other framers of the Constitution arrived was to divide power among different branches and levels of the government to prevent any single one, and thus the government as a whole, from becoming too powerful. Their approach laid the basis for more than two centuries of democracy in America. For most of the twentieth century, however, relatively few other countries reproduced the results that the American Constitution achieved. Most other countries, for most of their histories as independent sovereign states, functioned as nominal, not representative, democracies, with their rulers holding power by coercion rather than by the consent of the governed.

The success of the principle of popular sovereignty in displacing other bases of legitimacy in the wake of the French Revolution therefore brought to most of the world government *of* the people: the rulers generally came from the same ethnic or national groups as those they ruled. It also brought, at least rhetorically, government *for* the people: the government invariably claimed to be acting in their interests. In most places it did not, however, bring government *by* the people, either directly or through elected representatives. To those concerned with protecting liberty both before and in the decades immediately after the great French upheaval, this might have come as good news. Because popular rule posed a threat to the freedoms they valued, the fact that the people as a whole did not wield effective power either directly or indirectly would have seemed to augur favorably for the preservation of religious, economic, and political liberty.

Such a calculation, however, would have been mistaken. The absence of genuine popular sovereignty did not guarantee the presence of religious, economic, and political rights; and the twentieth century did not turn out, until its last decades, to be a golden age for individual freedom.

THE TRIALS OF LIBERTY

The programs of most governments for most of the decades following the French Revolution proved incompatible with the full protection of liberty as well as with the conduct of free, fair, regular elections. Communist regimes, which pursued the thoroughgoing transformation of the societies they ruled, suppressed liberty of all kinds: they denied religious freedom (and tried to prevent all religious practice), outlawed private property, and did not permit free speech or assembly, or indeed independent political activity of any kind.

Undemocratic regimes with less grandiose ambitions, such as the many military dictatorships of Africa, Latin America, and East Asia in the 1950s and 1960s, whose rulers wished simply to perpetuate their own power indefinitely, often permitted religious observance and the possession of private property. They did not, however, protect political liberty, which would have endangered their grip on power by marking out political space for an organized opposition to form and operate. Representative democracy requires political liberty—free, fair elections cannot be held without it—and for that reason political freedom threatens the self-perpetuating nominal democracies that proliferated in the twentieth century.

Liberty suffered, in the last century, for another reason. The capacity of Communist governments to suppress liberty of all kinds, and of more modest dictatorships to prevent the exercise of political freedom, expanded dramatically. The social and technological changes that the Industrial Revolution produced and that, together, created the modern world, almost all enhanced government's capacity to control those it governs and to suppress their liberties if it chose to do so.

When people lived in cities in large numbers they became easier to monitor. The large bureaucracies that the apparatus of government became provided the manpower for this task. These bureaucracies, prominently including police forces, made use of the new techniques of surveillance that advances in communication made possible. All in all, governments intruded more deeply and more frequently into the lives of those they governed in the twentieth century than ever before;[90] and these intrusions often had the effect of circumscribing liberty, or even of eliminating it altogether.

At the same time that the material techniques of control were becoming more powerful, the ideas and customs that had historically restrained the exercise of governmental power were weakening or disappearing. The traditional obligations, responsibilities, beliefs, and prerogatives that had often limited the actions of hereditary rulers did not restrain their successors.[91] Stalin and Mao paid no attention to the centuries-old protocols and doctrines that had affected the conduct of their imperial predecessors. Russian tsars and Chinese emperors had never inflicted on their countries the terror, imprisonment, and mass murder that their Communist successors imposed. The Communists took as their mandate for these punishing and unprecedented initiatives the ideology that they embraced and that in theory guided their policies, an ideology unknown to the traditional world that the French Revolution and the Industrial Revolution destroyed. If liberty is measured by the degree of independence that the citizen enjoys from the government, the twentieth-century inhabitants of the countries where the most intrusive regimes held sway enjoyed less of it than any other people in history.

Yet another feature of the modern world obstructed the practice of liberty, this one rooted in the desire of governments everywhere to remain in power. Because they tend to cling tenaciously to power, removing them has historically been difficult. Because they would not surrender power voluntarily, they typically did surrender it only when compelled to do so by force.

In the twentieth century the term "revolution" was often applied to changes of government. It was usually employed to denote a sweeping social transformation engineered by the new government, of the kind that the French Revolution, and later the Russian and Chinese Revolutions, brought to the societies in which they took place. Sometimes this was what occurred; but even where the self-styled revolutionaries simply unseated the incumbents and proceeded to govern much as their predecessors had—cases in which the appropriate term for the transfer of power was not "revolution" but "coup d'etat"—violence accompanied, indeed made possible, that transfer. Using force to change the government departs sharply from the democratic method for change: elections. Moreover, the violent method of replacing one government with another has seldom yielded a democratic successor regime. In changing governments, undemocratic means have usually produced undemocratic ends.

This has been so because violence is incompatible with the values and the procedures that are fundamental to political systems that combine liberty and the representative form of popular sovereignty.[92] The use of force turns political opponents into enemies to be defeated, as in war, whereas in representative democracy opponents are regarded, and treated, as people with some differing interests with whom compromise is possible and desirable.

The use of force in transferring political power leads to the presumption, which is standard in war, that a decisive encounter between two opposing sides will settle their relationship once and for all. In a democratic political system, by contrast, multiple, indeed regular, peaceful conflicts are assumed—votes by elected representatives on issues of public policy in legislatures, and the elections to choose those representatives—in which no group, faction, party, or individual will win all of the time. The use of force in political transitions therefore makes unlikely the conduct of regular free elections and the vigilant protection of liberty, especially political liberty, by the new regime. Victorious armies do not typically offer those they defeat the opportunity to try to regain power, nor are they solicitous of the liberties of those whom they have fought in the past and might therefore have to fight in the future.

All this leads to a pessimistic conclusion about the prospects for democracy and makes the late-twentieth-century rise of democracy all the more puzzling. Undemocratic regimes governed everywhere for virtually all of human history for reasons that seem rooted in human nature: those who hold power ordinarily do not wish to risk giving it up peacefully and voluntarily by competing in free, fair elections. Because governments will not give up power voluntarily, force is required to remove them. But the use of force prevents the successor regime from functioning according to democratic rules and procedures.

Yet the history of the last three decades of the twentieth century, in which democracy became the dominant form of government all over the world, demonstrates that this conclusion, however logical its premises, is inaccurate. The logic was overcome by a remarkable development, a political innovation as unexpected, because as contrary to previous historical experience, as the fusion of liberty and popular sovereignty to form modern democracy itself.

Beginning in the 1970s, in almost every part of the world, countries divested themselves of undemocratic governments by peaceful means.[12] In southern Europe, Spain, Portugal, and Greece discarded dictatorships with almost no bloodshed and adopted the democratic political system that predominated among their Western European neighbors. In Latin America, where dictatorships—many drawn from the military—had governed most of the countries when the 1970s began, two decades later few undemocratic regimes remained: Cuba, in the Caribbean, was the conspicuous exception, encumbered with the personal Communist dictatorship of Fidel Castro. In Asia, where no stable democracy had existed before 1945, the Philippines, South Korea, and Taiwan shifted from undemocratic to democratic governments, again without mass violence, joining India and Japan as countries that both protected liberties and chose their political leaders by free elections.

Perhaps most significant and certainly most surprising was the collapse of the great Communist empire of Eurasia, inspired by Marx and Lenin and conquered by the Red Army of the Soviet Union in the Russian Civil War of 1917 to 1922 and in the war against Nazi Germany from 1941 to 1945. Its collapse liberated the six Central and Eastern European members of the Soviet-dominated military organization, the Warsaw Pact, in 1989,[94] and put an end to the Soviet Union itself, out of which fifteen independent countries emerged, in 1991.[95] This great geopolitical upheaval, which in the breadth and profundity of its consequences bears comparison with the French Revolution and the two world wars of the twentieth century, occurred with almost no shots being fired.[96]

Historically, most political transitions other than the smooth transfer of power from a monarch to his (or occasionally her) designated heir involved violence because the holders of power resisted relinquishing it. In almost all of the peaceful transitions beginning in the 1970s, by contrast, the sitting regime cooperated in the process by which it was replaced. On some occasions, as in Spain in the 1970s and Taiwan in the 1980s,[97] the regime actually initiated this process. On others, the impetus for change came from outside the government, from the society as a whole and the political opposition that emerged from its ranks. Large, peaceful demonstrations in the Philippines in 1986 and in East Germany in 1989, for example, set in motion chains of events at the end of which new, democratic governments were installed. When the pressure for change came from outside the government, however, the holders of power responded either by engaging in a peaceful political process, the outcome of which was a change of regime, or at least by refraining from mounting armed resistance for the purpose of retaining their power.[98]

Often in these peaceful transitions the government entered into negotiations with opposition figures that led to arrangements for what had previously been prohibited: free and fair elections to choose a new government. This reproduced, although in reverse order, the normal procedure in democracies, in which negotiations about the composition of the government and on issues of public policy ordinarily *follow* the election of the society's designated representatives. Just as the use of force makes the transfer of power from one government to another a form of warfare, with adverse consequences for the prospects for building democracy, so negotiations and elections made the transitions to which they were central examples of democratic politics, which is why the new governments often turned out themselves to be democracies. In these cases, democratic means produced democratic ends.

Not every peaceful replacement of an undemocratic government in the last three decades of the twentieth century led to a stable, democratic government, however. A non-violent transition from dictatorial rule seems to be a necessary condition for the establishment of a modern democracy, but it is not, by itself, a sufficient one.

This is so because democracy is a complicated political system. It requires an overall design, usually embedded in a constitution, that limits the power of the government, safeguards the different forms of liberty, and assures that the offices of state are managed by people who have been freely elected. The historical record suggests that human groups do not spontaneously protect liberty and conduct elections: if anything, they seem disposed not to do either.

A working democracy requires not only a constitution to embody democratic principles but also institutions to put those principles into practice. Democracies need functioning legislatures; governmental bureaucracies; a full-fledged legal system with police, lawyers, prosecutors, and judges; as well as political parties to conduct elections and form effective parliamentary groupings. Even the existence of a constitution, or the relevant institutions, or both, do not, however, by themselves guarantee genuinely democratic politics and government.

Operating the institutions requires skills, some of them, such as in the case of the legal profession, highly specialized. As for constitutions, unless the values underlying them enjoy broad public support, they can become dead letters, documents to which no one pays attention and that have no impact on public life. This was the case for the several constitutions of the Soviet Union, which mandated democratic practices that the regime ignored. Whatever the wording of its constitution or the design of its political system, to practice democracy a country's people must accept the peaceful settlement of political differences through compromise, they must respect the law, and they must agree on the supreme importance of liberty. Just as a legal system requires lawyers, so, more generally, a democratic political system requires democrats.

In this sense, democracy may be appropriately compared to horticulture. A tree, a plant, or a flower will only take root and flourish in appropriate soil and in the proper climate. Similarly, without the appropriate mix of skills and values in a society, a democratic political system is unlikely to be successfully established, even where an undemocratic regime has been peacefully uprooted. The equivalent, for a country, of the climate and the soil for horticulture, the social basis of its political system, is its political culture, which consists of the skills and habits that have accumulated over time and the values that underlie them.

The conditions affecting horticulture remain more or less fixed. While the soil and the climate of particular regions do change, this happens very slowly, over hundreds, indeed thousands, of years. Political culture changes as well, and far more rapidly, but it does not change overnight. The skills and values in which democracy must be anchored cannot be called into existence by fiat any more than it is possible for an individual to master the techniques of basketball or ballet without an extended apprenticeship. The relevant unit of time for creating the social conditions conducive to democracy is the generation. Democracy can take hold when one generation possessed of the attitudes and habits necessary to sustain this form of government replaces, in positions of leadership in a society, the preceding generation that had lacked them.

This raises the question of how a new generation can acquire the social bases of democracy. In the normal course of social life, the major features of a country's political culture are perpetuated over time, with one generation passing them along to the next.[99] An undemocratic government will not deliberately inculcate them. If anything, it will endeavor to stifle them.

Before the last quarter of the twentieth century, democracy was successfully established in several places, but under the political equivalent of hothouse conditions: that is, circumstances that are rare and do not occur in most of the world. Either the social prerequisites evolved over several centuries, as in England, or communities already endowed with the necessary skills and values were transplanted to largely unsettled territories, as in North America and the Antipodes, or one people brought the features of democratic political culture to another by governing them for a long time, as the British did in India. Those methods, effective though they were, could not be, and were not, universally applied. Yet democracy appeared in many places where they were not employed.

How did this happen? How, despite the formidable difficulties involved in establishing it—the human impulse to hold on to political power and the complicated governmental machinery required to operate it—did democracy become what, on January 20, 2005, George W. Bush rightly said it was: the world's most common form of government? How, in particular, did non-violent methods come to supplant the historically normal use of force in overthrowing undemocratic governments, thereby making it possible to establish democracies in their place? And how did the skills and values, the habits and attitudes necessary for a democratic political system appear in countries where they were never deliberately cultivated and were often actively discouraged?

What is remarkable, in historical perspective, is not that an appreciable number of countries remained undemocratic at the outset of the twenty-first century, but rather that so many had embraced liberty and the representative form of popular sovereignty despite the formidable obstacles to their doing so. Those obstacles make the rise of democracy an unlikely, and therefore remarkable, event. How can it be explained? Each individual country has its own particular history, of course, but democracy's remarkable rise stems in large part from two major developments in the modern era that affected all of them. Both developments created pressures and opportunities for the establishment of democratic government that had not previously existed. One of these developments is the widespread, indeed by the twenty-first century almost universal, presence of the free-market system of economic organization. The other is the rise to a position of power and wealth surpassing those of all other countries of the two oldest democracies on the planet—in the nineteenth century Great Britain, in the twentieth century the United States.

DEMOCRACY FROM WITHOUT: THE COURSE OF MODERN HISTORY

"Nothing succeeds like success."

—FRENCH PROVERB QUOTED BY ALEXANDRE
DUMAS THE ELDER, 1854

THE LEADING BRAND

At the outset of the twenty-first century, democracy had become the most widely practiced form of government on the planet. As such, it may be compared to the leading brand of a consumer product, a brand being a particular make or variety of the product that is denoted by a title—the brand name—and often a symbol.[1] Among the various forms available, democracy had become the one most frequently adopted by the equivalent of consumers, sovereign states.[2] A country's form of government, like the consumer products individuals and families purchase, is a matter of choice in the sense that, while for most of history political arrangements were generally considered fixed and immutable (and even divinely ordained), in the decades since the French Revolution changes of government and of systems of government have become a familiar feature of political life everywhere. On this score, the comparison between brands and consumer products, on the one hand, and democracy, on the other, is particularly appropriate because, of all forms of government, democracy places the greatest emphasis on free choice. Consent lies at the heart of democratic government.

To be sure, coercion has played a major role in democracy's remarkable rise. It has prospered when, and because, democratic countries have won major wars. Even in peacetime, democracies have mustered formidable armies to defend themselves against undemocratic adversaries. In some countries, moreover, elements of democratic governance were first introduced by conquest. Yet democracy remains, ultimately, voluntary.

This is so because a genuinely democratic country, that is, a representative rather than a nominal democracy, selects its leaders through a voluntary process: free and fair elections. Furthermore, while some features of democracy were imposed by force in some parts of the world, the imposer—the imperial power—ultimately withdrew in almost all cases. To the extent that democratic forms persisted, as in India, this was because the country in question chose to retain them. (Indeed, given that choice, many rejected democratic practices.) In most places where democracy had taken root at the beginning of the twenty-first century, it had never been imposed at all. It was voluntarily adopted, just as consumers voluntarily purchase particular brands of the products they want or need.

Democracy's status in the last decades of the twentieth century and the beginning of the twenty-first as the leading brand of political system was the principal reason that, in this period, so many countries adopted it. Democracy's good name, that is, was both a cause and a consequence of its spread around the world.

Its dominant global status had a particularly powerful impact because, by the last third of the twentieth century, the ongoing technological improvements in transportation and communication had brought the different parts of the world closer together than ever before.[3] Many more people were aware of democracy's standing than they had been before the age of the jet aircraft and the international broadcast of television images. The world was filled with knowledgeable political consumers, and they gravitated to the most successful brand.

Democracy's widely recognized status weakened support for undemocratic governments even as it strengthened the appeal of liberty and popular sovereignty. That status also helps to account for the remarkably peaceful way in which many undemocratic governments gave way to democracy. Just as winning a war depends in part on the morale of the soldiers waging it, so keeping a grip on political power depends on the morale—the confidence, the belief in themselves and in the system over which they preside, and the determination to maintain control—of the rulers. The dominant status of democracy undercut the morale, and the will to power, of undemocratic leaders. Many, such as the Communist rulers of Eastern Europe in 1989, refrained from using the military and police forces at their command to keep themselves in power at least in part because they had lost faith in the political system over which they presided.

Democracy's dominant position in the world of the late twentieth and early twenty-first centuries made possible its spread by a snowballing, or "bandwagon" effect: more countries became democratic because so many other countries were already democratic. It became increasingly popular because it was already popular. This, however, begs the important question, how did democracy attain its initial popularity? Here the comparison with popular consumer brands is instructive.

Leading brands achieve dominance in their particular markets in two closely related ways: by effective performance and by a good reputation. Democracy rose to a position of global dominance by the same methods.

Consumer products perform effectively when they fulfill the requirements for which they are produced. Often, more than one purpose is involved, and the relevant purposes can change over time. Some car owners value automobiles for their price, for example, others for their appearance, still others for the power of their engines. And in the last three decades of the twentieth century more and more motorists came to evaluate cars on the basis of how many miles they could be driven for each gallon of gasoline they used. Similarly, democracy's signal achievement, the tasks it performed effectively and the basis of its appeal, has varied over the course of modern history. In the twentieth century, the great global conflicts— World Wars I and II and the Cold War—imposed stiff military, political, and economic tests on all forms of government. Democracy passed these tests, emerging strengthened from each conflict. Other, rival forms of government did not. The cumulative effect of the three conflicts was to help to elevate democratic government to the dominant position it held at the outset of the twenty-first century.

By their performances, consumer products earn reputations, and the companies that make them seek to publicize and enhance these reputations by having well-known and highly regarded persons testify, in paid advertisements, to their merits. Democracy's reputation rose steadily because the most powerful, affluent, and generally successful countries of the modern era, Great Britain in the nineteenth century and the United States in the twentieth, were also the two countries with the oldest and most deeply rooted traditions of democratic governance. British and American history served as an advertising campaign for democracy. It was as if the President of the United States, the Queen of England, the Pope, and all Nobel laureates endorsed the same brand of automobile.

Products also become popular when they have reputations that are relevant to potential customers, reputations that often come not from paid advertising but from observation, informal encounters, and private conversations, known collectively as "word of mouth." A car will be attractive to a would-be purchaser if his or her neighbor, or relative, or co-worker, or someone whose driving habits are similar or who has roughly the same income, drives it with satisfaction.

Students of American voting behavior have discovered that people's political choices are influenced by the preferences of those they know. This is called the "friends and neighbors" effect. Sovereign states are subject to a similar influence. They are disposed to adopt democracy at least in part to the extent that neighboring and culturally similar political communities have already done so.[4] Because they seem relevant, the experiences, examples, and reputations of friends and neighbors have particularly powerful effects.

A fool learns from experience, the saying goes, while a wise person learns from other people's experience. Both kinds of experience contributed to democracy's remarkable rise. Undemocratic political systems performed badly, turning the people living under their rule against them; and what helped to make them unacceptable was the superior performance of democratic governments that they observed, which also made democracy attractive. Democracy attained its dominant status, therefore, principally through the example of effective performance. It spread by what is sometimes called the "demonstration effect," with the success of the democracies demonstrating their political system's virtues to others.

By the beginning of the twenty-first century, many countries, in all parts of the world, governed themselves in democratic fashion. Their number helped to make the democratic example an impressive one, and the variety of democracies meant that almost every country could find an example of democracy relevant to its own circumstances. Before there were many democracies, however, there were just a few. Before there were few, there were none. Then there was one.

The initial stage in democracy's ascent, the appearance of the first democratic government, was the hardest. Innovation is far more difficult than imitation. The first example of anything by definition lacks a model to copy. Indeed, before the first example of anything appears there is no guarantee that it can actually be produced and perhaps no demand for it. Innovations occur, therefore, as much by accident as by design.

By the twenty-first century, the spread of democracy had come to resemble a landslide, which gains momentum as it goes along and at the peak of its power sweeps everything before it. Landslides often begin with the displacement of a single rock. For the spread of democracy, the equivalent of the initial rock can be identified. What had become, by the twenty-first century, the world's most popular form of government began on a medium-sized island off the northwest coast of the Eurasian landmass.

ENGLISH EXCEPTIONALISM

The acorn from which grew what became the mighty oak of democracy was planted, and first sprouted, in England. If the democratic form of government could be registered as intellectual property, Britain would own the patent and would be collecting royalties from 118 countries.

The English did not set out to produce a new kind of political system. When the newly independent Americans designed their constitution in 1787, they were deliberately imitating—and, as they saw it, improving upon—the form of government practiced in Great Britain, and this has been broadly true of all subsequent adoptions of democracy. The system the Americans and their successors attempted to reproduce had not, however, been deliberately designed. It had instead evolved over several centuries, during which the practices and institutions that make up the core of democracy—liberty—had come into existence in England and nowhere else.

The pattern of English political development differed significantly from those of the countries of the European continent, not to mention the patterns found in other parts of the world. It is common in historical writing about the United States to emphasize the dissimilarities between the American experience and the political, social, and economic development of the older countries of Europe. The theme of American exceptionalism is a staple of modern historiography. Under the eyes of eternity, however, English exceptionalism is more consequential.[5] All countries have their own particular histories, of course, and each country's history has some effect on the histories of others, but the impact of what is singular about England's past is unmatched. What England and, after the union with Scotland in 1707, Great Britain became in the eighteenth and nineteenth centuries, and what that country did, set democracy on the path to becoming the world's dominant form of government in the twenty-first century. Of all the countries in the world, Britain is the one most responsible for the rise of democracy because it was responsible for the appearance of democracy in the first place. The British people's contribution to democracy's rise, moreover, went beyond playing host to its initial appearance. They spread its elements far beyond their island, to the distant corners of the planet.

Besides the first appearance of liberty, two other developments of world-historical importance originated in the British Isles and contributed to democracy's twenty-first-century status. The Industrial Revolution, the harnessing of inanimate power to produce an ever-greater variety of goods on an ever-increasing scale, began there. As the cradle of the Industrial Revolution, the country became an even more attractive model than its pioneering role in the establishment of liberty had made it. Moreover, through conquest the British assembled the largest empire the world had ever seen, which served, albeit not always deliberately, as a vehicle for disseminating democratic ideas and practices.

In the 1954 film *Beat the Devil*, Humphrey Bogart and Gina Lollabrigida tell a story about Americans who ask an English gardener how his country has produced such splendid lawns and are told that the secret is to "get some good grass and roll it every day for six hundred years." English liberty has a history of comparable length. From the Magna Carta of 1215, an agreement between the king and the nobles, comes the tradition of limits on executive power. Recognizable forms of private property also appeared as early as the thirteenth century.[6] Other elements of liberty—religious and political freedom—came later to England than the high medieval period but earlier than to other countries.

In natural evolution, the origins of new features of species are obscure, usually the consequence of genetic accidents, but the reason they persist, when they do, is well known: they are "adaptive" to the environment in which the species lives and so are "selected" for reproduction. The ways in which the features of different species are adaptive is one of the principal subjects of evolutionary studies. Similarly, the origins of English exceptionalism are not altogether clear, but the survival and flourishing of liberty once it appeared can be explained. Liberty prospered, first in England and then in Great Britain, because Britain is an island. From the last decades of the eleventh century onward, the English Channel served as a barrier to invasion from the European continent. No foreign power was able to conquer the English, occupy their land, and extinguish their liberties. Nor did foreign powers present a threat urgent enough for English and British monarchs to suppress the freedoms of their subjects as part of their preparations to resist it. Because it was an island, England did not need as powerful an army as did the states of the European continent. Powerful armies have historically jeopardized liberty: they require financial support on a scale that leads to the temptation to confiscate property to provide it, and they have sometimes seized control of the government themselves, at the expense of the public's freedom.[7]

The liberty that the British people enjoyed helped make possible the second great historic development in the British Isles, which in turn contributed to the rise of democracy in the modern world. The Industrial Revolution is responsible for the rise of democracy throughout the world in the very broad sense that it, more than any other development, created the modern world, the world that, in the twenty-first century, every government, democratic and undemocratic, had to inhabit. The great transformation of economic life that began in England in the eighteenth century cleared the way for democracy's rise in another, narrower sense: it swept away the socially, economically, and politically static traditional world, which was hospitable to undemocratic governance. Hereditary monarchies that assigned power to a particular family in perpetuity fit easily into a world in which little else ever changed. Since its beginning, the Industrial Revolution has passed through a number of stages, and the latest of them, into which much of the world entered in the last decades of the twentieth century, proved singularly compatible with the type of economic system that turned out to be itself compatible with a democratic political system.[8]

Why the Industrial Revolution began in Britain, and indeed why and how it began at all, are questions that have inspired a large and growing body of scholarship that has not, however, yielded a consensus on the answer.[9] Among the causes frequently cited, however, is Britain's pronounced and, in the eighteenth century, virtually unique commitment to the protection of liberty of various kinds. Students of economic history have singled out private property, in particular, and the possibility of securing patents on inventions and so deriving financial gain from them, as necessary conditions for the new machines and new techniques that produced, for the first time in human history, sustained economic growth.[10]

The limits on the power of government in Great Britain protected the private economy from the potentially rapacious appetite of the country's rulers. If left unchecked, as was the case elsewhere, the political authorities might have imposed excessive taxation and even seized control of the new sources of wealth, which could in turn have stifled the process of economic expansion. And the general climate of political and economic freedom that prevailed in the British Isles gave encouragement to the inventors and entrepreneurs whose initia-

tives launched and sustained the economic expansion that began there.[11]

The Industrial Revolution made Great Britain wealthier, in
the second half of the eighteenth century and the first half of
the nineteenth, than any other country, and in so doing gave
the others another reason besides its flourishing liberty to ad-
mire and seek to emulate the British. Economic growth also
made Britain more powerful than other countries, and therefore better able to spread its political values and institutions beyond its own borders. The most important vehicle for doing
this was the third great development with its origins in the
British Isles that shaped the modern world: the British Empire.

Empire—the control of territories beyond a country's own
borders—is a very old political form, dating back at least to the
ancient world. Of all of history's many empires, the one that
Great Britain assembled from the sixteenth through the nineteenth centuries was the largest. In the first decade of the
twentieth century, it included 400 million people, of whom
only 41.5 million lived in the British Isles (294 million inhabited the Indian subcontinent), and stretched across 12 million
square miles, almost one-fourth of the Earth's land surface.[12] It
covered so much of the globe, reaching far beyond the British
Isles to the Americas, Asia, and Africa, that it was said to be the
empire "upon which the sun never set."[13]

The British Empire grew so large because, unlike most of
the great imperial agglomerations of the modern age—the
Austrian Habsburg Empire, for example, or the Russian Romanov or Turkish Ottoman Empires—it was composed of territories far beyond its metropolitan center. It was an overseas
rather than a continental empire. Many more people lived beyond Europe than inhabited the lands between the Atlantic

Ocean and the Ural Mountains, and gaining control of them met less resistance from the indigenous societies and rival empires than did attempts at conquest within Europe.

The English and then British success in acquiring a vast overseas domain, like the flowering of liberty in the British Isles, had its roots in geography. As an island, the country cultivated the skills of seamanship and emphasized the development of a navy. Its location off the northwest coast of Eurasia, as with Spain and Portugal, both situated on the Atlantic coast, gave Britain a westward orientation, and it benefited from the commercial as well as imperial opportunities available on the farther shores of that ocean. Sending their ships venturing outward on the Atlantic far beyond their own home waters, all three countries acquired overseas territories, but the British surpassed the other two, and ultimately all other imperial powers, because of their mastery of the planet's oceans.[14] Britain was able to acquire the largest empire in the world because it became the foremost maritime power in the world.

The Industrial Revolution enhanced, but did not create, Britain's maritime supremacy, which the British achieved when ocean-going ships were powered by sail rather than steam. As with the Industrial Revolution, however, Great Britain's democratic features had something to do with its naval mastery and the empire that its naval power undergirded.

The principal method by which Britain achieved and retained maritime supremacy and collected and protected its vast empire was war. From the seventeenth century through the early years of the nineteenth, the country fought and won many. Waging war was expensive: warring powers had to raise money to do so, primarily through taxation and borrowing. Here Britain did better than all other countries, and it was the liberties at the heart of its political system that made this possible.

Because property was secure there, and because the parliament checked the monarchy in fiscal as well as in other matters, it was easier to collect taxes from the citizenry, which regarded the demands for revenue as more legitimate than did peoples subject to undemocratic rule. For the same reasons, the British government inspired confidence among would-be lenders that their loans would be reliably repaid. Britain was therefore consistently able to borrow more money more cheaply than its European rivals.[15] Access to money translated into the military power on which the country's network of overseas possessions rested. Those possessions were of two different types.

Like the ancient Greeks, the British established colonies beyond their borders composed of individuals and families who emigrated from the British Isles and founded new communities. As with the Roman Empire, the British also governed territories largely populated by indigenous, non-British peoples whom a thin stratum of British officials controlled. Great Britain transmitted elements of democracy to both types of possessions, although in different ways.

Britain spread democracy to North America, to Australia, and to New Zealand by sending democrats to settle there.[16] In these places, it succeeded in establishing new, self-sustaining communities of expatriates that grew steadily in the seventeenth, eighteenth, and nineteenth centuries because the indigenous peoples were neither numerous nor powerful and were thus relatively easy to displace. The attachment of the European settlers to democratic values, institutions, and procedures was, in one sense, surprising because they had reason to resent and reject the norms of the place they had left. Many of the early immigrants to North America were escaping religious persecution in the Old World, including in England,

and the first British settlers in Australia were convicts, sent to the other side of the world in lieu of serving prison sentences in Britain. Yet along with their religious beliefs and whatever stigmas they bore for past misdeeds, they also brought democracy to their new homes. Private property, limited government, and religious tolerance took hold in the colonies. The new settlements governed themselves, as did the people of Great Britain, through representative assemblies.[17]

As part of a London-based empire, these settlements did not initially enjoy the other distinguishing feature of modern democracy, self-government. At the end of the eighteenth century, however, the thirteen colonies on the eastern seaboard of North America overthrew British rule and formed the United States as an independent republic; and in the course of the nineteenth century, Canada, Australia, New Zealand, and ultimately the British settlements in South Africa achieved effective self-rule, while retaining an affiliation with the mother country.[18] At the beginning of the twentieth century, fully half the members of the world's still-small community of modern representative democracies consisted of former British colonies.[19] By that time, however, Britain had acquired other, larger imperial possessions, to which it had a different kind of political relationship.

In Asia, Africa, and the Caribbean, Britain conquered and governed non-European peoples in large numbers, but British settlers did not displace the indigenous peoples, who were too numerous and culturally cohesive for this to be possible. Britain's governance of these possessions, which made up by far the largest part of its empire, did not qualify as democratic.[20] The peoples of those territories were deprived of one of democracy's two principal components: they did not govern themselves, nor had they ever given their consent to British rule over them.

For their part, the British did not assemble their empire for the purpose of spreading the blessings of liberty and popular sovereignty to its inhabitants.[21] The adventurers who first planted the British flag in distant places were generally seeking economic gain. Where the British government assumed control of foreign territories, this was often for strategic reasons, to prevent other imperial powers from acquiring them or to take control of locations useful for overseas military bases.[22]

Some imperial administrators did consider themselves obligated, by virtue of their positions and the power inherent in them, to work for the betterment of those they governed,[23] but that sense of responsibility did not necessarily lead to the view that the people of the empire should govern themselves. Just as often, it reinforced the conviction that Great Britain had to retain power over them until the distant (indeed sometimes unforeseeable) day when they would, thanks to imperial tutelage, finally be competent to handle their own affairs properly.[24]

Yet even where a handful of British officials governed large non-European populations, Britain did implant some of the elements of democracy. It did so indirectly by destroying (sometimes unintentionally) the preindustrial, traditional, and almost always undemocratic political structures that came under imperial rule, which cleared the way for new and different political forms. In much of the empire, moreover, the British introduced, directly and deliberately, the institution of private property, and the imperial government protected the property that it recognized.

To much of the Empire, as well, the British brought honest, effective administration that enforced the rule of law, which often replaced administration according to the personal whim of the ruler.[25] British imperial rule also created a cadre of local people who acquired Western educations and Western skills and, along with them, sometimes, Western political values, including a commitment to democracy. Such people often played major roles in their countries after imperial rule ended.

Toward the end of their rule in Asia, Africa, and the Caribbean—although usually not until the very last minute, when it had become clear that the imperial era had run its course—the British did try to establish formal democratic institutions, including free elections, political parties, and working legislatures with real power.[26] In some places where the British had governed—India is the outstanding example[27]—democracy took root and survived their departure. In other places, in virtually all former British possessions in Africa, for example, this did not happen. Instead, democracy withered or was overthrown after independence. Even where democratic practices did not long survive the British departure, however, a residue, an historical memory, a body of experience in operating democratic institutions remained, which sometimes served as the basis for subsequent attempts to revive liberty and representative government.[28]

While the British Empire made substantial contributions to its establishment, the case of India illustrates another feature of the career of democracy: the role of individuals. The great historical upheavals and the broad, impersonal, social and economic trends of the modern era—the singular history and accomplishments of Great Britain and of the French and Industrial Revolutions—had a great deal to do with democracy's rise to its twenty-first-century position of global dominance. History, including the history of democracy, is made by the interaction of such great events and broad forces with human choices.

Sometimes the choices and actions of particular individuals have powerful effects, and so it was with the rise of democracy.

George Washington's modesty, his sense of propriety, and his refusal to exercise the powers of a monarch ensured that the newly established American republic, whose independence he had helped to secure as the leader of its army and then served as its first president, adopted and sustained democratic institutions and procedures.[29] In May 1940, Prime Minister Winston Churchill's personal determination, combined with his political skills, ensured that Britain continued to resist, rather than come to terms with, Nazi Germany. British resistance made possible the ultimate defeat of the German threat to democracy, after the Soviet Union and the United States had joined the fight against Adolf Hitler.[30] The last leader of the Soviet Union, Mikhail Gorbachev, did more than anyone else to bring communism in Europe to a peaceful end by initiating reforms that made the societies governed by Communist parties freer and, contrary to his intentions, the Communist political systems weaker, and then by declining to sanction the use of force to keep communism in power across Eurasia.[31]

Were there an equivalent of Mount Rushmore for individuals who have made major contributions to the rise of democracy around the world, Washington, Churchill, and Gorbachev would each have a strong claim to a place there. So, too, would independent India's first prime minister, Jawaharlal Nehru.[32]

Nehru dominated Indian public life during his years as prime minister, from independence in 1947 to his death in 1963. To him belongs major credit for establishing durable democratic institutions and procedures in circumstances that were not particularly favorable to them. India had no pre-imperial experience of liberty or popular sovereignty, and unlike the settler colonies of North America and the Antipodes, it did not exercise the powers of effective self-government before independence. Indeed, prior to British rule, the Indian subcontinent had never been a single political unit, and the population of independent India was marked by the kinds of religious and linguistic differences that have often obstructed the formation of stable democratic government.

Moreover, it would have been relatively easy for Nehru to assume dictatorial powers. He enjoyed enormous prestige for having been at the forefront of the struggle for independence, and the one leader of the movement for Indian independence whose standing equaled, perhaps even surpassed, his own, Mohandas Gandhi, was assassinated shortly after the end of British rule. While Nehru faced parliamentary opposition throughout his term as head of the Indian government, because his Congress Party had led the independence movement no rival party had anything approaching its standing in the country. Other, similar countries at mid-century did forsake or eschew democracy. Nehru played a prominent part in the Nonaligned Movement, a loose association of countries, most of them newly released from imperial rule, that sought to emphasize their independence from both of the two opposing camps of the Cold War. The Nonaligned Movement's other major figures— Nasser of Egypt, Sukarno of Indonesia, Tito of Yugoslavia— were dictators, as were the leaders of most of its members. India's neighbor, Pakistan, which was also carved out of the British Empire in South Asia and therefore shared, so to speak, India's political DNA, began its independent existence as a democracy but soon thereafter, and for much of its subsequent history, came under military rule. Indeed, Nehru's own daughter, Indira Gandhi, who became prime minister in 1965, suspended parliamentary government and inaugurated a period of undemocratic rule known as "the Emergency" in 1974, thereby demonstrating India's vulnerability to authoritarian impulses in its leaders. Eighteen months later, however, in 1976, Mrs. Gandhi decided to hold free elections, was defeated, and peacefully left office, thereby demonstrating the resilience of the political system her father had done so much to establish.

Nehru's commitment to liberty and representative democracy never wavered, perhaps because he had acquired that commitment early in his life. He had received his secondary and university education in England.[33] Like George Washington, he held fast to British political values even as he fought to change Britain's relationship to his own country.

In 1835, while serving as an imperial administrator in India, the historian and parliamentarian Thomas Babington Macaulay wrote a report on education in which he advocated the creation of "a class who may be interpreters between us and the millions whom we govern; a class of persons, Indian in blood and colour, but English in taste, in opinions, in morals, and in intellect."[34] Nehru embodied Macaulay's vision, and as a result, India became, in the second half of the twentieth century, a democracy.

The period in which Great Britain established, consolidated, and expanded its rule in India—the eighteenth and nineteenth centuries—was the era of British primacy in world affairs. It was the era, as well, in which Britain became the exemplar of liberty to the rest of the world. In the eighteenth century, two armed conflicts of global scope took place: the Seven Years' War, in which Britain opposed France from 1756 to 1763, and the long series of wars between France and the other European powers that began in 1792, three years after the Revolution, and ended with the final defeat of Napoleon in 1815. Great Britain was on the winning side in both, and both victories enhanced British power and prestige and therefore the power and prestige of its political system.[35] The hundred years from 1815 to the outbreak of World War I in 1914 was a more peaceful period, which also worked to Britain's advantage. The country extended its empire and reaped the benefits of the Industrial Revolution.

In the twentieth century large-scale conflict returned. Once again the British were on the winning side in each of the three great global conflicts—the two world wars and the Cold War—but that century's wars weakened rather than strengthened Britain, precipitating the loss of its empire and putting an end to the era when it acted as the world's foremost champion of democracy. While the three great wars of the twentieth century led to the decline of Great Britain, however, they also contributed to the rise of democracy around the world.

THE TWO WORLD WARS

In the first half of the twentieth century, two world wars determined which countries would be democracies, and much else besides. Both wars, in different ways, helped to strengthen democracy's international standing, but each also left in its wake obstacles to the spread of democracy, obstacles that were subsequently overcome at considerable cost. Indeed, the twentieth century as a whole may be seen as a kind of violence-filled geopolitical tournament, with three rounds—the two world wars and the Cold War that followed. The tournament decided which form of government would dominate the international system. After each of the first two rounds the winning coalition split, and the former allies opposed each other in the next round. At the end of the third round, the Cold War, democracy emerged as the tournament's winner, the possessor of the best—indeed the only good—name, the most popular and powerful form of government on the planet.

In World War I, traditional political institutions and practices suffered a definitive defeat at the hands of modern forms, including democracy. Hereditary monarchies and, to a lesser extent, far-reaching multinational empires had come under pressure and had been in political retreat since the French Revolution had introduced the idea of popular sovereignty as the basis of political organization. They might well have survived longer and in more places than they did, however, if World War I had never taken place.[36]

The war destroyed the great continental empires governed by hereditary rulers possessed of absolute, or at least formidable, power: the German Hohenzollern, the Austrian Habsburg, the Russian Romanov, and the Turkish Ottoman emperors lost their thrones, and the domains that they had ruled fragmented. Some parts of these empires became independent countries. Others were taken over by the countries that had won the war, but only for a limited period of time since the victors' empires dissolved in the wake of World War II. (Lenin's Bolshevik Party reconquered the Russian Empire, and the Communist empire that it built lasted until the end of the Cold War.)

World War I not only destroyed several formidable continental empires but it also weakened the very idea of empire and of hereditary monarchy. Although several of each survived the war, never again would either enjoy the presumption of legitimacy that had supported them for so many centuries: the reprieve that victory in the war provided to the French and British Empires proved temporary.[37] The war, and the peace conference in Paris that followed it, gave rise to three other important democracy-promoting developments.

In the last stages of the conflict and at the peace conference the United States emerged, for the first time, as a global power.[38] American troops were dispatched to the continent in 1917 and helped to turn the tide of battle against Germany and its allies. The American president, Woodrow Wilson, took part in the peace conference, the first American chief executive to visit Europe while in office. In the second half of the twentieth century the United States was to succeed Britain as the world's greatest commercial and military power, with momentous consequences for the future of democracy.[39]

It was the United States that introduced a novel war aim for the conflict: democracy itself. His country had entered the war, Wilson said, not for the traditional purpose of gaining territory or even because the opposing side threatened the United States or its vital interests, but for a loftier, more disinterested reason: to make the world safe for democracy. Spreading democracy, Wilson believed—and the belief gained adherents during the course of the twentieth century—was the key to making the world peaceful and so avoiding cataclysms such as the one through which the world had just passed.[40] The principal coalition partners of the United States, Great Britain and France, although themselves democracies, had not gone to war for this purpose and their leaders pursued other, more concrete goals at Paris.[41]

The work of the conference did not achieve Wilson's declared aim. If anything, the world became more dangerous for, and less hospitable to, liberty and free elections in the two decades following the end of World War I. It certainly did not become wholly democratic, as Wilson and his followers, including his successor in the presidency eight decades later, George W. Bush, anticipated.[42] Still, Wilson placed the spread of democracy squarely at the top of the world's political agenda for the first time, and it remained on that agenda, although not necessarily at the top, in the ensuing decades.

Finally, and of greatest importance for democracy's global prospects, the Paris Peace Conference, led by Woodrow Wilson, embraced the principle of national self-determination to replace the discredited concepts of hereditary rule and empire. At the peace conference and in the ensuing decades, the principle proved difficult to apply: not all the world's sovereign political communities in 1919 and thereafter were (or are) nation-states, and not every self-proclaimed nation managed to acquire its own state.

After 1919, however, the reigning presumption in the international system held that nations were entitled to their own states and, less emphatically, that states should, wherever possible, be composed of single nations. The principle that the French Revolution had unleashed became the global norm. World War I, especially the peace conference that followed it, stands, in retrospect, as the historical moment when one of democracy's two defining features, popular sovereignty, gained acceptance as the global standard to which all governments ought to conform.

Although the three major victorious powers were democracies, the triumph of modern over traditional political forms in World War I did not bestow a global monopoly of that form of government. Instead, two modern, but undemocratic, political systems appeared: communism and fascism. Both were modern in that they rejected the selection of political leaders by heredity, were committed to promoting economic growth, and claimed to hold power in the name, and on behalf, of the people.

While differing in important ways, moreover, communism and fascism did share some significant features: both exalted the role of the political leader, both aspired to extensive—in the case of communism virtually total—governmental control of the economy, and both deemed war to be a central and necessary part of relations with other sovereign states. These similarities and the common aspiration of the principal Fascist and Communist powers—Nazi Germany, imperial Japan, and the Soviet Union—to expand the territories they controlled might seem to have made them natural allies, and indeed, Germany and the Soviet Union did form an alliance in August 1939, using the occasion to conquer and occupy the countries—Poland and the Baltic countries—that had the misfortune to be located between them. In December 1941, however, Hitler's armies invaded the Soviet Union, thereby creating an opposing coalition composed of that Communist country, on the one hand, and, on the other, the two major democracies, Great Britain, which was already at war with Germany, and the United States, which entered the conflict six months later. This was the alliance that won World War II, and in so doing furthered the worldwide cause of democracy in two ways.

The war demonstrated that democracies could defend themselves. The capacity for effective self-defense is the ultimate test for any country or form of government, and the events leading up to the conflict and its early months called into question the resilience and the toughness of the democracies. Between 1922 and 1942, a number of countries lost or abandoned democratic political systems under the pressure of the Great Depression and the power and appetites for conquest of the Fascist and Communist states.[43] In the 1930s, rather than resisting Hitler's progressive dismantling of the post–World War I political settlement in Europe, the British and French governments, under the influence of the war-averse publics to which they were accountable, acceded to it for most of that decade before finally taking a stand against him in 1939. Throughout that decade, the United States steered clear of direct involvement in the political affairs of Europe.

Both Germany and Japan based their geopolitical strategies in part on the assumption that the democracies lacked the will to wage effective war. In May 1940, when Britain stood alone against Germany, the British government came close to negotiations for ending the conflict.[44] Even after both the Soviet Union and the United States had entered the war, Germany and Japan very nearly achieved their goals of dominating Europe and Asia, respectively. For much of 1942, it appeared that they would succeed in doing so.

In the end, however, the determination of the British and American publics and the extraordinary productive capacity of the American economy, in combination with the monumental sacrifices of the people of the Soviet Union, prevailed over German and Japanese armed forces, which fought fiercely to the bitter end. Victory required smashing their militaries, bombing their major cities, and occupying their countries.

World War II also strengthened democracy by discrediting a principle antithetical to it. Although modern in every way, fascism borrowed from traditional political practice an emphasis on inequality. Germany and Japan considered the people they conquered to be inferior and treated them brutally, exploiting, enslaving, and even exterminating Jews and Slavs in the first case and Chinese in the second. The Fascist powers deprived the people they ruled of both liberty and popular sovereignty: their defeat removed a mortal threat to both of democracy's principal components and removed, as well, any remaining justification for the British and French to maintain empires that deprived their inhabitants of both.

The Cold War followed the pattern of the two world wars: the winning coalition divided, with the democracies opposing the Soviet Union and its Communist allies and satellites. From this third great conflict of the twentieth century, democracy emerged as the world's dominant political system. The Cold War differed in significant ways from the two global conflicts that preceded it, however, and those differences proved crucial to its outcome.

The Contest of Systems

World War I lasted four years and ended with the victory of modern over traditional political systems. World War II lasted six years and ended with the decisive defeat of one undemocratic form of modern politics, fascism. The Cold War, in which the democratic West prevailed over the Communist East, went on for far longer, playing out over four and one-half decades. Its duration gave rise to two features that distinguished it from the previous global conflicts of the twentieth century and that made major contributions to the triumph of democracy: the political transformation of democracy's two World War II adversaries, Germany and Japan; and the fact that the Cold War turned out to be not only, and, at the end, not even mainly a military contest.

In the decade after the end of World War II, Germany and Japan abandoned the doctrines, practices, and institutions—the celebration of war, the concentration of power in the hands of unaccountable leaders—that had governed them in the 1930s and 1940s, and both became democracies. Following the war, both countries assiduously protected the political and economic liberties of their citizens. In both, parliaments chosen in free, fair, regular elections enacted the laws, and

competent bureaucracies and courts administered them. Each
country respected the right of other peoples to govern themselves, as they emphatically had not under Fascist rule, and
each maintained, in sharp contrast to the Fascist period,
peaceful relations with its neighbors. In both cases, that is, the
villainous Mr. Hyde became, in a remarkably short period of
time, the virtuous Dr. Jekyll.

In the wake of World War II democracy was introduced to
Germany and Japan, as it had been to India, at gunpoint. Having conquered and occupied its two wartime adversaries, the
United States—in Germany in conjunction with Britain and
France—sought to construct democratic political systems
within their borders. To be sure, promoting democracy was a
more deliberate and urgent goal for the victorious allies after
World War II than it had been for the British in India. The
Americans, especially, were convinced, as Woodrow Wilson
had been after World War I, that implanting liberty and representative government would inoculate their former adversaries
against a recurrence of the aggressive policies that had led to
war.[45]

As in the case of India, the occupations of Germany and Japan ended and the people of those countries assumed control
over their own internal affairs; and when they did, they kept
the political systems that had originally been imposed upon
them. Although they had initially accepted elements of democratic government because they had been forced to do so by
their conquerors, Germany and Japan retained them because
they chose to do so.

The ongoing Cold War helped to seal the two countries'
adoption of democracy. Europe and Asia divided into two opposing camps, generating pressure to join either the American
or the Soviet one and install its patron's political system. Some

countries resisted aligning themselves with either camp, and others joined one of them without adopting its political system, but circumstances pushed Germany and Japan to align themselves with the United States and establish democratic governments. Each was territorially divided between the two camps: the eastern third of Germany became the Communist German Democratic Republic, and the Soviet Union occupied the four northern islands of the Kurile chain that had belonged to Japan until 1945. Partly for that reason, the German Federal Republic and Japan felt directly threatened by the Soviet Union. They therefore sought shelter in an alliance with the United States, whose troops remained stationed within their borders, but with a mission that changed from occupation to protection.

As the political creed and political system of their protector, democracy came to have a particular attraction for Germany and Japan.[46] At the same time, its military presence gave the United States a degree of influence over German and Japanese internal affairs in that the people of these countries would have been reluctant to carry out policies and build institutions radically unacceptable to the power on which they depended for their safety.[47]

The post-1945 experiences of Germany and Japan made major contributions to democracy's good name. After their conversions, they served as powerful exemplars of democracy for other countries. Their examples impressed others because both were important countries that had, in recent memory, held sway over much of Europe and Asia, and because they had transformed themselves into democracies rapidly and thoroughly. Indeed, with the conversion to democracy of its major World War II enemies, and with the declining likelihood of a massive, destructive, global conflagration like the two world wars of the first half of the twentieth century, the power of example rather than the use of force became the chief external impulse for democracy around the world. It was the example of the growing community of democracies rather than any military victories that made democracy the world's most popular political brand by the dawn of the twenty-first century.

Germany's and Japan's democratic transformations promoted the spread of democracy as well because each one brought something new to the world; and the two innovations that those transformations represented extended democracy to the European continent, where it was weakly established, and to East Asia, where it was nonexistent.

Democratic Germany formed part of the core of the most important institutional innovation in international politics in the second half of the twentieth century, the European Union (EU). The series of agreements that ultimately produced the EU began with the Schumann Plan of 1950, in which Germany and France pooled their coal and steel industries not only for the sake of economic efficiency but also to create a measure of economic interdependence that would help prevent further wars between the two countries, which between 1870 and 1945, had fought each other three times. In 1957, Germany and France, along with Italy, the Netherlands, Belgium, and Luxembourg, signed the Treaty of Rome, which created the European Economic Community (EEC). By 2007, the EEC had become the EU, had expanded its membership to include twenty-seven countries, and deepened the economic cooperation among them to the point that thirteen of them shared a common currency.

The EU furnished to the world an example of democracy as impressive and attractive, in its way, as the one that Great Britain had offered at the height of its power. All of its members had democratic political systems, which became a condition of membership. The formation and expansion of the EU demonstrated that democracy could thrive beyond the confines of the Anglo-American world in which it had first appeared. This, combined with the stable, peaceful, free societies that made up the EU's membership, inspired in European non-members the desire to join it.

Joining required exchanging undemocratic governments for democratic ones, and this is what happened beyond the EU's original borders over the last three decades of the twentieth century. From its Western European base, the EU expanded to the south in the 1980s and to the east in the first decade of the twenty-first century.

To be sure, the impulse to discard undemocratic political systems in favor of democracy did not arise exclusively from the existence of the EU. Spain, Portugal, and Greece, which threw off authoritarian rule and joined the EU in the 1970s, had long had close ties with Western Europe. In the post–World War II era, all belonged to the Western military alliance, the North Atlantic Treaty Organization (NATO), before they joined the EU. The powerful attraction of the EU did help to undermine the dictatorships that governed them, of which the one in Greece had come to power only in 1967. After dictatorial rule ended, their many connections with their neighbors to the north made them logical candidates for EU membership.[48]

Unlike countries in the southern part of Europe, those of Central Europe—Poland, Hungary, the Czech Republic, and Slovakia—as well as the three Baltic countries, Estonia, Latvia, and Lithuania, had found themselves cut off from Western Europe after 1945 and governed by Soviet-imposed Communist regimes, with the Baltic countries incorporated into the

Soviet Union itself. The Communist governments never gained full acceptance from the people they ruled, as uprisings against them in East Germany in 1953, Hungary in 1956, Czechoslovakia in 1968, and Poland in 1980—the first two occurring before the formation of the EEC—demonstrated. The regimes' fundamental illegitimacy in the eyes of those they governed was the principal cause of the remarkable events of 1989. Between June and December of that year six Communist governments fell from power almost entirely peacefully. By providing a plausible and attractive alternative to it the EU and its predecessors rendered Communist rule even less legitimate in Central and Eastern Europe than its origins had made it. Having emerged from Communist rule, the countries of these regions all aspired to EU membership.

For the countries of Southern, Central, and Eastern Europe, the EU offered not only a model of democracy and an incentive to become democratic, because membership required it, but also a blueprint for doing so.[49] To join the EU a country had to bring its laws and institutions into conformity with those of the existing members, which made the accession process an exercise in, among other things, strengthening democratic institutions and practices.[50] As well as by example, therefore, the EU, with a transformed Germany at its heart, spread democracy directly.

Before Germany's post-1945 conversion, democracy in Europe, while rare, was scarcely unknown. Before Japan's similar transformation following its defeat in World War II, by contrast, no genuine democracy had existed in East Asia. In the nineteenth century, Japan had become the first non-Western society to master the Industrial Revolution and thereby make itself powerful enough to compete with the Western powers in economic and especially military terms, a competition that led ultimately to the war in the Pacific between 1941 and 1945. The Japanese experience after that war demonstrated that a democratic political system could take root outside Europe, far from the societies in which the political and intellectual precursors of democracy—the Reformation and the Enlightenment—had taken place. Like the formation of the EU, therefore, democracy in Japan counts as a major development in world affairs and as an important milestone in democracy's remarkable rise.

Unlike in Europe, no pan-Asian economic association came into being in the second half of the twentieth century. Japan therefore lacked the organizational basis for conveying to its neighbors the example of liberty and popular sovereignty and encouraging the adoption of democratic institutions and practices that the EU provided. Nor, in part because of the absence of an organizational focus for cooperation such as the EU or Europe's principal security organization, NATO, did its neighbors and World War II victims become as rapidly and fully reconciled with Japan in the postwar period as did Germany with the European countries it had conquered, occupied, and severely mistreated. Still, Japan established economic ties with the other countries of the region and its example did exert some influence on them, at least indirectly contributing to the installation, in the 1980s and 1990s, of democratic governments in the Philippines, Thailand, South Korea, and Taiwan.

In addition to demonstrating that democratic political systems could thrive on the European continent and in East Asia, the German and Japanese examples helped to foster democracy in another, less direct but equally important way. Each exemplified economic success, which had a powerful impact on neighboring countries and even on countries far from their borders because the third great world-shaping conflict of the twentieth century turned out, in the end, to be in no small part an economic contest.

From its outset, the protagonists had understood the Cold War as a conflict not simply between two armed forces but between rival and alternative political and economic systems. In 1947, as his country's relationship with the Soviet Union changed from wartime ally to postwar adversary, the American president Harry Truman said that "at the present moment in world history nearly every nation must choose between alternative ways of life."[51] As for the Soviet Union, the Bolshevik Party established it as a new kind of state, a rival to the capitalist system of the West that was designed, by making people and machines more productive (and, although this was not part of the founding doctrine, by building more powerful armed forces), to be its superior and so ultimately replace it. The goal of the Soviet Union, in which its founder, Lenin, certainly believed and to which his successors, until the last one, Mikhail Gorbachev, at least paid lip service, was the global triumph of the Communist system.

After 1945, the division of several countries into Communist and non-Communist parts provided a dramatic focus for the global contest of systems. West Germany, South Korea, and Taiwan became part of the Western camp and built free-market economies and, early in the Cold War in the case of Germany, later on the Korean peninsula and the island of Taiwan, democratic political systems. East Germany, North Korea, and mainland China, by contrast, all governed by Communist parties, installed economic systems operated by the Communist method of central planning, from which market principles were excluded.

The economic aspect of the Cold War grew in importance because it became increasingly clear that, while both sides had armed themselves heavily, the conflict was not going to be decided on the battlefield. The possession of nuclear weapons in large numbers by both sides made a shooting war, the traditional method of conducting tests of strength between and among sovereign states, potentially far too destructive to employ.

At the same time, a country's economic performance became an increasingly important measure of its government's competence. The achievement of an impressive expansion of economic output over long periods of time, first in the West and Japan and then in other parts of Asia, demonstrated that, like democracy, sustained economic growth was not only possible, it was possible everywhere.

Economic growth came to be even more widely regarded as desirable than democratic government. Virtually every government of the many countries outside Europe that gained independence from imperial rule in the middle years of the twentieth century proclaimed its major aim to be "economic development"—that is, economic growth sufficient to make the country powerful and its inhabitants, if not rich, at least less poor than they had always been. So important and so widespread did the goal of economic development become in the second half of the twentieth century that it came to supplement, if not altogether supplant, the capacity to defend the country's borders and the embodiment of popular sovereignty in some form as a test of the political legitimacy of all governments.

The military part of the Cold War ended in a standoff, but in the economic competition, the West scored a clear victory. In the early years of the conflict such an outcome had seemed unlikely. The Communist countries—starting, to be sure, from a much lower economic level—achieved higher growth rates than their capitalist competitors. The success of the Bolsheviks in making the former Russian Empire an industrial and military power that withstood the German assault in World War II made a favorable impression on the leaders of other countries. Among them was India's Nehru, who endorsed a similar, although less extensive and intrusive, form of the economic planning practiced in the Communist world for his own country.[52]

By the latter decades of the twentieth century, however, the countries with market economies, although not free of economic difficulties, were decisively outperforming those with central planning. West Germany was much richer than the Communist German Democratic Republic; South Korea grew far more rapidly than North Korea; and Taiwan became a more modern, prosperous place than the Communist-governed Chinese mainland. Countries such as India, with milder or partial versions of the Communist system of economic organization, gravitated toward greater reliance on market institutions. During the 1980s, so did China itself, which was rewarded with two decades of extraordinarily rapid economic growth.

The Cold War victory of the market system of economic organization was a victory for political democracy as well, for three reasons. First, their economic shortcomings played an important role in the collapse of Communist regimes from the center of Germany to the western border of China in 1989 and 1991, and the collapse of its great ideological rival bears considerable responsibility for the rise of democracy because it eliminated what had, for almost fifty years, been the main political alternative to it.

Second, the democratic features of the market system—the same features, as it happens, that made the Industrial Revolution in Great Britain possible in the first place—contributed to its triumph over central planning. Specifically, the institution of private property provided the incentives for innovation and improvement that were and are crucial for intensive growth,[53] which requires, as well, a political environment conducive to economic experimentation and change. Democracies supply both; communism provided neither. Finally, the triumph of the market assisted the rise of democracy because the market system proved not only to be compatible with, but an important basis for, democratic politics.[54]

The political transformation of Germany and Japan, along with their economic performances and the political and economic examples they set for their neighbors, had a crucial impact on the outcome of the contest of competing examples that the Cold War became, above all on the economic competition at its heart. The country that made the largest contribution to democracy's good name in the twentieth century, however, was neither of those two. It was the United States of America.

THE AMERICAN ERA[55]

The United States succeeded Great Britain as the most powerful country in the world. In some ways American power exceeded Britain's strength and influence at the height of its international standing. In the immediate aftermath of World War II, in which, unlike the other warring powers, its economy had not been battered, the United States accounted for fully 40 percent of the world's total output.[56] Nearly half a century later, after a period of high economic growth worldwide, the American economy still supplied close to 30 percent of the global product and, unlike after World War II or in the case of nineteenth-century Britain, the United States had no serious military rival.

Like Britain in the nineteenth century, and for the same reasons, the United States in the twentieth century set a political example for the rest of the world. In May 1989, to take one instance among many that could be cited, when students occupied Tiananmen Square in Beijing to protest the policies of China's Communist government, they constructed a replica of the American Statue of Liberty.

In the spreading of democracy America exercised less direct influence than had Britain, never directly governing several hundred million people in dozens of societies. The United States bought considerable indirect influence to bear on the rise of democracy, however, both because of its power and the impression its power made on the rest of the world and because, more than Great Britain, indeed more than any other country, it was committed to assisting in the spread of democratic governance.

The commitment arose from its origins. The United States was founded not on the basis of an ethnic or religious identity, or a centuries-long identification with a particular piece of territory, as were most other sovereign states, but rather on a set of political principles. Foremost among those principles was liberty, a concept of which virtually every twenty-first-century American is reminded every day because the word is stamped on the coins they use. The principles of democracy form the basis of American identity. In the nineteenth and twentieth centuries, millions of immigrants came to the United States from other parts of the world and became Americans by embracing the founding principles. It was those principles that held the country together.

From the beginning of their republic, Americans had expected that their form of government would be taken up by others. For the first hundred years of American history, when the United States was weak in comparison with the older powers of Europe, its preferred method of propagating democracy was through the force of its democratic example.[57]

In the twentieth century, an increasingly powerful United States sought to make the world democratic more directly,[58] in three related but distinct ways: by protecting existing democracies, by assisting in the transition from undemocratic to democratic political systems, and by seeking to foster democracy where it did not exist.

The protection of democracy was a central theme in twentieth-century American foreign policy. In each of the three global conflicts of that century the United States belonged to the winning coalition, which included other democracies. In each conflict, American leaders made the protection of liberty and popular sovereignty, as well as the protection of the countries that practiced them, an important goal.

In World War I, the United States, if not its coalition partners, fought, in Woodrow Wilson's words, to make the world safe for democracy. Two decades later, in August 1941, American President Franklin Roosevelt joined British Prime Minister Winston Churchill in issuing an eight-point declaration, which included an endorsement of sovereign rights and self-government for all people, that became known as the Atlantic Charter and served as a statement of common aims when the United States entered World War II in December of that year. If anything, the United States waged the Cold War even more explicitly than it had the two world wars in defense of democratic principles and of the countries that practiced them, which the military power and undemocratic ideology of the Communist countries threatened.

During the Cold War, American military power not only protected the democracies of Western Europe and Japan from the Soviet Union, it also provided a secure environment for one democracy-promoting institution as well as for another set of institutions and practices that did a great deal to foster democracy around the world. The first was the EU, the safety of whose core countries was assured by the American security guarantee they received because they also belonged to NATO. These guarantees also helped to make the EU possible by eliminating what had historically kept the countries of Western Europe at odds with one another: the political and military rivalries among them. Franco-German reconciliation took place under the umbrella of American military power.

The set of institutions and practices was the international economic order, featuring the relatively free flow of goods and capital across sovereign borders. The United States led the way in constructing it in the wake of World War II and in sustaining it thereafter, in part by providing the military forces that insured against the interruption of international commerce.[59] As in the case of the EU, countries had substantial economic incentives to participate in the global economic order, and, as with the EU, the policies and institutions required to do so were compatible with, and encouraged the promotion and consolidation of, democratic political systems.[60]

The American alliances with other sovereign states differed from alliances of the past in ways that reinforced democracy in those countries. Historically, alliances were temporary marriages of convenience between and among countries that often had little in common except, for the moment, a common adversary: the World War II partnership between the United States and the Soviet Union fit this description. America's Cold War alliances lasted longer and were accompanied by, and nurtured, extensive political and economic connections among the allies. With a common military purpose as their foundation, they grew into broader communities of interest and served as vehicles for transmitting and reinforcing the elements of democracy.

As well as with fellow democracies, the United States consummated military alliances with countries that were not governed democratically. In some of these countries, during the second half of the Cold War, the United States used its influence to encourage and ease the removal of an undemocratic government and its replacement by a democratic one. In Greece in 1974, in the Dominican Republic in 1978, in the Philippines and Haiti in 1986, and in Chile and South Korea in 1988, when an undemocratic regime's grip on power began to weaken, the American government made clear its strong preference for a peaceful transition to democracy and by so doing helped to bring about such a transition.[61] American diplomatic initiatives also helped to forestall anti-democratic coups, primarily in small Caribbean and Central American countries but also in larger and more distant places such as the Philippines.[62]

The United States did not initiate the political crises that challenged authoritarian rule, which were triggered by internal events: a rigged election, defeat in war, the death of a leader. After the crises were under way, however, the United States could affect the outcome of events because of its military power, its economic influence, and its political standing. Precisely because the American government had maintained friendly relations with the dictator of the Philippines and the generals who ruled South Korea, its advice to them to step aside peacefully carried weight. This American role as facilitator of transitions to democracy also helps to account for their generally peaceful character.

Mikhail Gorbachev played a similar role in the peaceful end of Communist governments in Central and Eastern Europe in 1989. Those governments depended on the Soviet Union for their very existence in a way that few undemocratic regimes in the Western camp relied on the United States. Because the Communist governments had been put in power and kept there by Soviet military forces, when the Soviet leader declined to offer them robust support in the face of peaceful protests against Communist rule, let alone to dispatch troops to quell the protesters as his predecessors had done, the Communists concluded that they had no basis for retaining their offices and so gave them up.[63]

While the United States took advantage of opportunities that arose spontaneously to press for the spread of democracy, it also, on occasion, adopted a more deliberate, systematic approach to propagating its own political principles and institutions. Twice in the twentieth century American presidents initiated policies of active democracy-promotion.

The first of them was Woodrow Wilson. More inclined by temperament and intellect than most American politicians to regard politics and diplomacy as crusades on behalf of lofty principles, Wilson got the chance to promote democracy at the Paris Peace Conference in 1919, when the victorious powers undertook the task of remaking the political arrangements that World War I had shattered.[64] He took the lead in redrawing the map of Europe in a way that, he hoped, would create stable democracies on the ruins of the multinational empires the war had destroyed.

Six decades later, in the 1980s, Ronald Reagan, the fortieth president, also made the active encouragement of democracy a central tenet of his foreign policy. Convinced that the democratic world was stronger and the Communist systems more fragile than was generally recognized, Reagan's speeches placed greater emphasis than had those of his Cold War predecessors on the universal validity of democracy and the transient character of its ideological adversary.

Reagan's efforts to promote democracy went beyond rhetoric. His administration gave military assistance to anti-Communist insurgents in Central America, Africa, Southeast Asia, and Afghanistan, a series of programs that came to be known, collectively, as the Reagan Doctrine.[65] In 1982, following a Reagan speech extolling the common Anglo-American democratic heritage at the Palace of Westminster in London, the seat of the world's oldest parliament, the United States established the National Endowment for Democracy, a government-funded organization to assist democrats all over the world.[66]

Reagan's presidency coincided with the period in which the spread of democracy gathered momentum, reaching a crescendo shortly after he left office with the collapse of Communist governments and their replacement, in many cases, with democratic ones all across Eurasia. Although their effect is impossible to gauge with any precision, Reagan's efforts to promote democracy surely contributed to these developments. Their impact on events was limited, however. What the United States did on behalf of democracy was not the principal factor in determining when and where it took root, both because the American government did not always stress democracy-promotion in its relations with other countries and because, even when it did, its capacity to create a democracy where none had existed was modest.

At no point during the second half of the twentieth century, even during the Reagan years, did the promotion of democracy take priority over all other goals in the conduct of American foreign policy.[67] In fact, during that period, the United States often affirmatively supported undemocratic regimes. The frequent deviations from the long-standing commitment to the spread of democracy stemmed from the logic of international conflict.

From 1941 to 1991, the United States was almost continuously at war. Especially when the highest stakes are involved, as they were in those years, war imposes a rule that the belligerent parties invariably feel compelled to follow: my enemy's enemy is my friend. Churchill gave pithy expression to this rule when he declared, after the Nazi invasion of the Soviet Union had made Stalin's bloody tyranny a British ally, that "If Hitler invaded Hell I would make at least a favorable reference to the Devil in the House of Commons."[68]

Many of the world's governments that rejected Communist ideology and opposed the geopolitical designs of the Soviet Union nonetheless did not embrace democratic norms. Indeed, in the early decades of the Cold War, outside Western Europe and Japan—in Asia, Africa, and Latin America—most of the countries allied with the United States were not democracies. All other things being equal, the United States would have preferred that the governments with which it made common cause be democratic; but the American government seldom geared its policies to that preference because all other things were not equal.

Undemocratic allies posed what came to be called the "friendly tyrant" dilemma:[69] the danger that exerting pressure on an anti-Communist dictatorship to become more democratic, while it might succeed, to the advantage of the United States, might also, instead, have the perverse effect of weakening the regime to the point that it would fall from power and be replaced by rulers no more committed to democracy but, unlike their predecessors, actively hostile to the United States.[70] In the 1970s dictators friendly to the United States in Nicaragua and Iran were replaced by governments equally undemocratic, if not more so—the pro-Communist Sandinistas in the first case, the fundamentalist mullahs of the Islamic Republic in the second—that proceeded to conduct virulently anti-American foreign policies.

Even where the United States brought the full weight of its power to bear in favor of democracy abroad, however, even where, in the post–Cold War period, the United States occupied other countries and tried to build working democracies within them, it did not succeed. In none of these countries—Somalia, Haiti, Bosnia, Kosovo, Afghanistan, or Iraq—did the American efforts produce an independent government able to exercise power without outside military assistance that respected civil, political, and economic liberties and regularly submitted itself to the judgment of the people it governed in free elections.

The reason for this blanket failure is that for any country the process of democratization has two stages and forces external to the country, even the determined efforts of a country as powerful as the United States, exert major influence only on the first stage. That first stage involves a country's *intention* to become a democracy. Here, events beyond its borders can have a considerable impact. The course of modern history—the outcome of the two world wars and the Cold War, the rise to a position of great global power first of Great Britain and then of the United States—created a favorable impression of, interest in, and ultimately a demand for democracy the world over.

The second stage entails the country's *capacity* for democratic government. This can, in certain circumstances, be imported from without, as was the case in Britain's settler colonies and, to a lesser extent, in the British Empire. In most countries, however, the capacity for democracy must be homegrown. Most countries will not be occupied by another, or, if they are, the other will not try to establish democracy; or, if it does, it is unlikely to succeed. This should not be surprising. Children, after all, do not invariably comply with the wishes and directives of their parents, and governments within sovereign states do not always manage to shape the conduct of the people they govern in accordance with their preferences. The government of one country ordinarily has less power and influence over the people of another than parents and indigenous governments do over their charges. A government's capacity to design and implant political institutions outside its own borders is therefore bound to be limited. Even a society trying to install a working modern, democratic political system, *even in the absence of external coercion or internal resistance*, will not find the task an easy one. For success requires the cultural resources necessary to build and sustain democracy.[71]

A country's transition to democracy therefore resembles the process by which individuals become physicians. To become a doctor requires both the inspiration and the desire to pursue a medical career, which comes to a person from what he or she observes of life, and the knowledge and skills needed to practice medicine, which must be acquired in a medical school. The knowledge and skills needed to practice democracy, the equivalent of attending medical school, came, for many countries, from the experience of operating a particular kind of economic system, one that achieved worldwide popularity and came into almost universal use by the end of the twentieth century because of its success in generating the wealth that all societies sought. The school for democracy was the free-market economy.

3

Democracy from Within:
The Magic of the Market

"The commerce that has enriched the citizens of England has helped to make them free."

—Voltaire, *Lettres Philosophiques*, 1730[1]

The Constant Companion

Free markets, the evidence of modern history strongly suggests, make for free men and women. In the twenty-first century, every country that practiced political democracy, without exception, conducted its economic affairs according to some version of free-market principles.[2] To be sure, not every country with free markets protected liberty and chose its government by free elections. Some market economies continued to function, as they always had, under the auspices of undemocratic governments. But in every sovereign state that did embrace democracy's two constituent parts, the economy operated according to free-market principles: the institutions of private property flourished, producers competed with one

another for customers, and the basic economic decisions—
what and how much to produce—were largely made according
to the criterion of profitability, which was calculated through
the price mechanism, with the balance between supply and demand as its driving force.

The relationship between democracy and free markets did
not have a formal, contractual status. The constitutions of the
democracies did not, for the most part, mandate private property, competition, or free prices. Still, liberty and representative government were always found in the company of private
property and economic competition. If not legally joined together, free politics and free markets can certainly be said to
be constant companions.

Why should this be so? One reason is purely negative.
Whatever the affinities between the free market and democratic politics, non-market economies coexist uneasily, and in
some cases cannot coexist at all, with genuine democracy.

The twentieth-century antithesis of, and alternative to,
free-market economics, socialism, which arose in response to
the Industrial Revolution and its effects, came in three different varieties distinguished by differing degrees of government
involvement in economic life. Social democracy accepted basic
market principles but redirected, through taxation and social
programs, some of what the market system produced in order
to compensate for the hardships, such as the loss of jobs, that a
working market invariably creates. By the twenty-first century,
every Western democracy provided its citizens with some version of a social safety net—old-age pensions, unemployment
insurance, and health care benefits. All of them therefore qualified as social democracies. In socialist economic systems,
many of them established during the second half of the twentieth century in poor countries, the government not only un-

dertook to redistribute some of what the society produced, but also involved itself extensively in determining what should be produced—exerting influence on investment decisions—and owned and operated farms and factories.[3] In the third, extreme case, the countries ruled by Marxist-Leninist political parties in Eastern Europe, the former Russian Empire, China, and elsewhere, the government controlled all aspects of economic life: it made all decisions about investment and production, set all prices, and owned all major property.

The more socialist the economy of a country is, the greater the power of its government. Because a cardinal feature of democracy is limits on the power of government, the more socialist a country is, the greater the difficulty it will have in establishing a functioning democracy. While social democracies find it entirely possible both to create a social safety net and to safeguard liberty and conduct free elections, and while more extensively socialist countries could and sometimes did practice democratic politics, in orthodox communist countries democracy was impossible. In such countries, all power belonged to the government, which the ruling Communist Party completely controlled. The all-encompassing and unchallengeable authority of the Communist Party was the central tenet of communist political practice, and left no room at all for individual liberty or free, fair, regular elections.

The free market is therefore associated with democracy, in the first instance, by default. The rival form of economic organization, socialism, is in varying degrees incompatible—and one version of socialism, communism, is entirely incompatible—with a political system that respects liberty and in which the people choose the government. While democracy may not be possible in its absence, however, the public does not generally associate the free market with democratic governance. For one thing, the dominant market institution, the private company, does not itself operate according to democratic principles. Large firms (and most small ones) are governed hierarchically—that is, autocratically—not democratically. Managers give orders, workers follow them. The workers do not control the company. Moreover, the owners and proprietors of private firms have not always supported the cause of democracy or opposed undemocratic rule.[4]

Furthermore, if liberty and popular sovereignty seemed an odd, if not impossible, couple until well into the nineteenth century, democracy and the market can appear ill-matched even in the twenty-first. The two have contrasting reputations. While democracy enjoys the best of good names and is honored and valued almost everywhere, the free market is often distrusted and sometimes vilified.[5] Democracy carries with it the same kind of aura that surrounds medicine: it is seen as a high human achievement that improves the lives of those fortunate enough to come into contact with it. The free market occupies, in the minds of many, a status closer to that of the diseases that medicine attempts to combat.

This is because the workings of the market do have unwelcome side effects. Even as they perform their main task, producing wealth, markets also cause disruption and dislocation. In the modern era, the free market, harnessed to the Industrial Revolution, has battered jobs, communities, and centuries-old ways of life, sometimes sweeping them away altogether. The welfare benefits that all democracies have come to provide for their citizens are designed to protect them from, and compensate them for, the injuries that free markets inevitably inflict.

As it happens, the absence of working markets also causes injury. Where private ownership, private investment, and a high level of private commercial activity are lacking, hundreds of millions of human beings live in stagnant, hopeless, rural poverty or in crime- and disease-ridden urban slums all over the world.[6] While markets are blamed for the hardships they do produce, their absence is far less widely understood as the principal cause of the global poverty that is so regularly deplored.

Even when it works well—indeed, especially when it works well—the free market has another side effect that tarnishes its reputation. While the market makes many if not most people whom it affects richer, it enriches some more than others. It creates inequality, which frequently inspires resentment in those less favored.[7]

A common alternative to market-created inequality is equality of poverty, which is not a formula for widespread happiness. This was the normal state of affairs in traditional society, but is not unknown in the modern world. When Mao Zedong imposed communist orthodoxy on China, the gap between the richest and poorest citizens of that country was considerably narrower than it had become by the end of the twentieth century; but few Chinese would wish to exchange the country that Mao ruled in the 1950s and 1960s for the China of the twenty-first century.

The market's reputation has also suffered from attacks from two directions: by champions of the ostensible values of the social and economic system that the market, in concert with the Industrial Revolution, replaced; and by the partisans of the system that aspired, but failed, to supplant the free market. The free-market system, that is, is often criticized by those nostalgic for the traditional world on the grounds that it promotes selfishness,[8] which was happily missing from that world, and also by socialists because it produces inequality.

While the market rewards the pursuit of self-interest, the dominant class of the traditional world, the aristocracy, gave priority (at least in theory) to selflessness, a sense of obligation to others (including the less well-born), and personal conduct according to a code of honor. The age of chivalry and noblesse oblige is long gone, but the values that theoretically predominated in that distant era have retained their appeal, especially among those, such as artists and intellectuals, for whom considerations of profit and loss have less importance than do other social norms.[9] The market does not promote these traditional aristocratic values. Indeed, it actively subverts them. As Adam Smith noted, it is selfishness that makes the market work.[10] The one traditional institution that has survived into the modern world with some of its authority intact is organized religion, and religions tend to take a dim view of activities geared exclusively toward profit.[11] Markets have flourished in Christian countries but Christian teaching holds that it is easier for a camel to pass through the eye of a needle than for a rich man to enter the kingdom of heaven.

The world in which selflessness and social solidarity are thought to have flourished was one in which few of the citizens of the twenty-first century would wish to live, marked as it was by poverty, disease, short life expectancies, and sharp and immutable social and political inequality; but those who bemoan the market's elevation of self-seeking seldom if ever take this into account.

Similarly, the nineteenth- and twentieth-century partisans of socialism presented it as a system in which both the inherited inequality of traditional life and the market-created inequalities of the modern world would disappear. The vision of equality that socialism offered gave it a moral and aesthetic appeal comparable, in some ways, to what religion has long furnished, an appeal that sustained its popularity well into the twentieth century, even as the socialist distribution, if not of wealth then certainly of political power, proved to be even more unequal than it was in other economic and political systems.[12] Its failure to fulfill the promise of equality, and especially the even more conspicuous failure of its promise of affluence surpassing what market-based economies could achieve, discredited socialism; but its decline did surprisingly little to burnish the public reputation of the free market.

Unloved at best, vilified at worst, the free market therefore seems an unlikely partner for a political system, democracy, that has inspired enthusiastic support, sometimes bordering on reverence. The invariable association of political democracy with market economies would seem, given their contrasting reputations, an odd coincidence, certainly as unlikely as the fairy-tale match between Beauty and the Beast. In fact, the two have worked in concert. The democratic example has persuaded people living under different political systems of the desirability of liberty and representative government. From without, the visible successes of Great Britain, the United States, and an increasing number of other democratic countries have created the demand for democracy. Within the societies in which democracy has taken root, the workings of the free market have instilled the values, habits, and attitudes and have helped create the institutions that democratic governance requires.

The market is to democracy something like what a grain of sand is to the pearl that an oyster contains: the core around which it forms. Despite its unhappy side effects, and independently of the intentions of the people who take part in it and the government that presides over it, the free market complements the powerful example that contemporary democracies have set by creating, in effect, the supply of democracy. Woodrow Wilson observed that "Democracy, like every other form of government, depended for its success upon qualities and conditions which it did not itself create, but only obeyed."[13] The free market does more than anything else to create those conditions.

Both the working of the market—its processes—and the results of market activity—its products—contribute to the growth of democratic political institutions and practices. The market's most important product, the one that those who engage in commerce according to free-market rules actively seek to promote, is wealth, and wealth helps to foster democracy.

THE WEALTH EFFECT

Wealth promotes democracy by making democratic countries that are wealthy attractive models for others.[14] The free world is also the rich world, and for the citizens of countries that are neither, the prospect of affluence holds an appeal just as powerful as, if not more powerful than, the promise of liberty.

In addition to stimulating the demand for democracy, wealth increases the capacity for democratic governance. Democracy comes with affluence. With the conspicuous exception of states made rich by oil,[15] the higher a country's per capita output, the more likely it is to protect liberty and choose its government by free, fair elections.[16] Many studies conducted over five decades have found evidence for such a link.[17] Moreover, the rapid spread of democracy over the last three decades of the twentieth century occurred, for the most part, in countries that, in previous decades, had raised their economic outputs.[18] By some accounts, the level of per capita income at which sovereign states become highly, perhaps even irresistibly, susceptible to democracy can be established with some precision. At a mean income of between $4,000 and

$5,000 annually, a country enters a transition zone. When it reaches $7,000 per year, democratic governance, once established, seems to become all but irreversible.[19]

Why should this be so? The reason is that the wealth that successful market economies generate reinforces both parts of democracy. It bolsters liberty and supports the practice of popular sovereignty through representative government.

Market-created wealth enhances liberty because one of the defining features of a free-market economic system, private property, is itself a form of liberty. Property rights are individual rights that concern things that can be bought and sold. In affluent countries, the institution of private property is widespread and well protected, which means that liberty, or at least one important form of it, is firmly established.

The protection of private property brings with it another important element of liberty: the rule of law. It is law, clearly spelled out and reliably and fairly enforced, that protects property. Such protection is crucial to give buyers and sellers the confidence that transactions will be completed and the terms of contracts fulfilled in markets that extend broadly in time and space. And only by participating in extensive markets, as distinct from purely local exchange, can societies become rich. The connection between property and law is almost as strong as the association between free markets and democracy.[20] Where, as in affluent societies, private property is widespread and secure, the rule of law tends to be well established.[21]

Wealth also encourages, indeed it subsidizes, the kind of political participation required by representative government. Democracies differ from undemocratic governments in that the people rule; but in modern democracies they do not rule directly. Representative democracy avoids, for most citizens, the problem that Oscar Wilde identified with socialism—that it takes too many evenings.

In modern democracy, most people do not engage in politics and government on a full-time basis. Instead, they periodically choose, through free elections, representatives who, working through the large and complicated bureaucratic structures that governments have become, enact and administer the laws by which their societies operate. This means that democratic government involves three different levels of political participation; and market-generated affluence makes an important contribution to each one.

Most citizens of democracies take part in the political process only occasionally, when they vote in the elections that choose their government. The propensity to vote rises with the level of an individual's income. Rich people take part in elections more faithfully than do poor people. On the whole, moreover, rich societies are more likely to provide regular opportunities to vote—rich countries tend to be democratic— because their citizens follow, and expect to have a say in, how they are governed. The foundation of that interest and expectation is literacy; and the rate of literacy in a society rises with the level of wealth.[22]

A smaller fraction of the population of democracies goes beyond casting an occasional ballot to take part in public affairs more often, although not full-time. Such people not only follow issues of public policy far more closely than most of their fellow citizens, but they also volunteer their time and contribute money to political causes and candidates. Those engaged at this second level of political participation require time away from their regular work—leisure time—for these activities. It is the affluent who have it, and who can therefore afford to devote some of their time and money to these pursuits.

Finally, an even smaller proportion of the population of democracies makes the business of government its full-time occupation. An affluent society is far better able than a poor one to support these elected officials and professional administrators, and especially to support them in sufficient comfort that they are not powerfully tempted to use their positions to enrich themselves illegally—through bribes. Affluence also contributes to democracy by making available comfortable berths in the private sector for retired officials, thus reducing the undemocratic temptation to remain in power indefinitely and to prevent free elections in order to ensure such permanence. In affluent democracies, elected officials can, and often do, improve their economic fortunes after relinquishing political power.[23]

To summarize: the effective working of free markets produces wealth, and wealth supports the two principal features of democracy: liberty and representative government. The correlation between wealth and democracy, however, while substantial, is not perfect. Not all rich countries are democracies, and not all democratic countries are rich.

This is so because it is not only what they produce but also the processes by which free markets operate that promote democratic politics. The fact of a functioning market is as important for democracy as the wealth it generates. The processes of buying and selling, saving and investing, producing and distributing under market rules contribute to the growth of liberty and representative government. These processes require, and therefore create, a particular set of institutions, institutions that are independent of the government and the existence of which makes modern democracy possible. The term that has come to denote this group of institutions is "civil society."

CIVIL SOCIETY

Democracy defines the relationship between two entities: the government and the people it governs. Democracy's rules specify both what the people can do to the government (replace it) and what the government cannot do to the people (violate their liberties). In practice, however, modern democracy rests on three pillars, not two.

Civil society is the third essential element of a twenty-first-century democratic political system. It occupies an intermediate position between the public and those who hold power. It serves both as a link and a buffer between them, connecting the people to their government while at the same time protecting them from it. The constitutions of democratic countries do not formally enshrine civil society as part of the political system they establish, but twenty-first-century democracy would not be possible without it. Contemporary civil society, in turn, would not be possible without a market economy.

Civil society consists of all of a society's non-governmental associations in which membership is voluntary:[24] fraternal organizations, religious congregations, professional guilds, trade unions, and clubs of stamp collectors, gun enthusiasts, and the like. People can, and ordinarily do, belong to more than one. Collectively, these associations play a crucial part in safeguarding democratic liberties by providing protection for the individual against the state. They also play a crucial part in supporting representative government by furnishing mechanisms by which the people can control those who hold power.

Almost all such associations in democracies owe their existence, directly or indirectly, to the free market.[25] The eighteenth-century British writer and statesman Edmund Burke referred to the secondary associations in his country as "little platoons," but in the contemporary world some of them are not little at all; and many of the largest, most powerful non-governmental bodies are the private firms that engage in the basic activities of the market, producing and selling what individual consumers and other firms buy and use. General Motors, Microsoft, and Exxon form part of civil society, as do local shoe repair shops and corner grocery stores.

Not all non-governmental associations have as their purpose the earning of a profit. The free market is indirectly responsible for the existence of non-profit organizations as well because it subsidizes them. They subsist largely on the contributions of their members, who make these contributions out of the income they earn from participating, as workers or investors or both, in the free market.

The citizens of ancient Greece and the residents of New England towns during the colonial era managed to govern themselves in democratic fashion without the panoply of independent associations that make up modern civil society. Two features of the modern world that those societies lacked, however—more powerful and intrusive governments than traditional societies experienced or even imagined and far larger populations within particular political jurisdictions—make the protection of liberty and the conduct of representative government all but impossible without the rich variety of voluntary organizations found in twenty-first-century democracies.

Contemporary governments have far more power than did their premodern predecessors. Themselves large organizations, governments have at their disposal the personnel and technology to assert themselves in every corner of what are often geographically vast domains and to monitor virtually every aspect of social life. Twenty-first-century government's reach is longer, its eyes are sharper, and its grip is stronger by very wide margins than were those of the monarchies and empires of old. Today's governments can intrude in, and monitor, the daily lives of those they govern to a far greater extent. Liberty is the capacity to act independently of government, and preserving it in the face of the enormous power of modern government requires some form of protection for it. Civil society supplies that protection, in two ways.

Private associations offer places of refuge from the state, social settings in which individuals can pursue their interests largely free from the control of government. In this sense, civil society provides in modern democracies (and some countries that are undemocratically governed) something like what forbidding geographic terrain—high mountains, for example—furnished in traditional societies: places to escape the long arm and the heavy hand of the authorities.

Civil society also helps to preserve liberty by serving, collectively, as a counterweight to the increasingly powerful machinery of government.[26] In traditional societies, liberty flourished where the aristocracy was formidable enough to secure a measure of independence from the monarchy.[27] In the modern world, civil society has replaced the aristocracy as the social formation that counterbalances executive power and thereby secures the social space in which individuals can act independently of governmental authority; and the mainstay of civil society is the series of organizations and associations, large and small, that arise directly or indirectly from the workings of the free market.

Popular sovereignty, the other half of modern democratic government, also depends on elements of civil society that the free market makes possible. While in ancient Athens and colonial New England, citizens themselves decided issues of public policy in assemblies that included all of them, modern societies have grown far too large for direct democracy of this kind. Instead, the people choose, in free elections, representatives to conduct the public business. The two major channels through which they make their choices and otherwise convey their wishes to those in power—political parties and interest groups—have their roots in the free market.

The principal mechanism through which the public selects officials is the political party. Parties aggregate and organize individual preferences and channel them into the selection of candidates who run for office on behalf of those preferences and, if they win, seek, as office-holders, to enact them into law.[28] Parties are the instruments through which individual citizens can, in the large political units of the twenty-first century, exert a measure of democratic control over their governments.

What became modern political parties first appeared in Great Britain in the eighteenth century as groups of personal friends who banded together to enhance their political weight in Parliament.[29] By the end of the nineteenth century, parties had become permanent features of democratic politics in North America and Europe. In the twentieth century, with universal suffrage, they became mass organizations and were usually formed on the basis of economic, and therefore market-created, interests.

In most modern democracies, one or more parties represent the interests of workers, others those of owners. While the interests of labor and of capital are important in all market economies, they are not the only economic bases for democratic political parties. Some parties champion the economic interests of the particular regions of the country in which they operate. Others serve the needs of particular sectors of the economy, such as agriculture, or industries dependent for their profits on exports. In all of these, however, the free market created the basis for translating the wishes of millions of individuals into a manageable number of agents who could carry out the tasks of governance.

Political parties also have non-economic bases. They are often assembled, for example, to promote the interests of people subscribing to particular forms of identity—race, religion, nationality, ethnicity, and language. Market-based considerations have, however, often become part of the programs of identity-based parties, which have pressed for economic benefits, as well as language rights and political privileges, for the groups they represent.

In addition to serving the interests of those belonging to specific categories of identity, political parties have come into existence to promote particular ideas, sometimes even collections of ideas coherent enough to qualify as ideologies. Some of these ideas, however, have included prescriptions for the proper organization and management of economic life. Here again, therefore, it is the market that, at least in part, gives rise to the party.

Political parties operate chiefly during and through the periodic elections that modern democracies hold. Between elections, citizens can bring influence to bear on their governments though another market-based institution: the interest group. Many of these are created to lobby the government on behalf of a particular economic agenda. While parties bring together many different interests in a broad coalition, especially in countries in which two of them dominate the political system, interest groups (also known as pressure groups) that lobby the government between elections characteristically have a narrower focus. They promote the interests of sugar growers rather than the entire agricultural sector, for example, or of automobile makers but not all manufacturers.

While political parties have a broader scope than interest groups and gear their activities to the rhythm of the electoral cycle rather than the legislative calendar, both arise from the functioning of the free market. Moreover, while the two are not perfect vehicles of the public will—parties do not always respond to the wishes of those they purport to represent and interest groups promote only a narrow range of causes—both make modern democracy possible by providing channels through which the population can exercise sovereignty.

Voluntary organizations and associations independent of the control of the government existed well before the twenty-first century. Civil society first appeared in something approaching its modern form in Europe in the eighteenth century.[30] Montesquieu, writing in the eighteenth century, and Tocqueville, observing the United States in the early decades of the nineteenth, noted the significance of intermediate bodies between the executive and the public.[31] It was, however, the twentieth-century rise, and then fall, of orthodox communism that highlighted the importance of these institutions for democratic politics.

Communist parties in power paid perverse tribute to civil society by seeking to erase every trace of it. They recognized that free, voluntary, non-governmental groups were incompatible with the total social control they aspired to exercise. No independent organizations enjoyed official tolerance in Communist countries, which therefore lacked the counterweight to government power, the seawall protecting individuals against the engulfing tide of the state, that safeguards zones of liberty in democracy.[32] When communism collapsed, the

absence of civil society complicated and frustrated the efforts
to establish functioning democracies in its place.

Not only does the operation of the free market call into existence the institutions of civil society, it also makes democracy
possible by its effect on individual citizens. The market creates
democrats. In market economies, that is, individuals learn the
skills and habits and adopt the values and attitudes that, in the
realm of politics, make for a working democracy.

The School for Democracy

The practices in which entrepreneurs, patrons, and consumers
engage as participants in a market economy do a great deal to
establish the practices in which individuals engage as citizens
of a democracy for two reasons: some of the economic and political practices are very similar, even identical; and the agents
of the market economy and the citizens of a political democracy are the same people.

Just as democracy spreads by the power of example, when
inhabitants of undemocratically governed countries adopt the
different political practices they have observed in similar, often
neighboring countries, so it also spreads through the workings
of the market when the same people apply the habits and procedures they are already carrying out in one sphere of social
life—the economy—to another one—the political arena. In
both cases, democracy spreads by crossing permeable borders:
in the first, the political borders between and among sovereign
states; in the second, the less formal social border within sovereign states that divides economics from politics.

If democracy is a consumer product—something people
willingly choose—the democratic example of other countries
serves as a kind of advertisement for it, which generates the de-

sire to live in a democratic political system, while the experience of functioning in a market economy is the equivalent of an
instructional manual that shows how to assemble and operate a
democracy. The market, to employ a different metaphor, is the
major school for democracy. Those involved in it acquire what
turn out to be three prerequisites for democratic politics: a
particular kind of collective identity, nationalism, that under-
pins many democratic political systems; the experience and expectation of sovereignty, one of the two core features of
democracy; and two related political habits that are indispensable for the proper functioning of democratic government—
trust and compromise.

Nationalism is the conviction that political borders should
correspond to national ones, with national characteristics generally defined in cultural terms, most frequently language.[33] Its
partisans often claim that nationalist sentiment is a fundamental and enduring feature of human communities, one that,
while suppressed for long periods in many of them, is present
from their very beginnings. The claim is inaccurate. Nationalism is a modern phenomenon, dating, in almost all cases, from
the nineteenth and twentieth centuries; and the free market
did more than any other social institution to create it.[34]

With the coming of the Industrial Revolution, both literacy
and the standardization of the written language became far
more widespread. Industrial production and the operation of
large organizations, unlike agricultural labor, required both,
and the expansion of the scope of markets that the dramatic
advances in transportation made possible put a premium on a
common medium of communication.[35] Governments began to
foster a standard language within their borders through laws
and especially through the systems of mass public education
that they established beginning in the nineteenth century. The

most important borders became linguistic ones because they defined the territory within which those who had mastered a particular language could feel socially comfortable and could readily qualify for employment.[36] As a consequence, according to a prominent scholar of nationalism, "political units had to adjust themselves to cultural boundaries."[37] The conditions of economic life in the modern world, which conspicuously include free markets, have made the nation-state, usually (although not always) defined by a common language, the normal political unit throughout the world.[38]

Nationalism can be the enemy of democracy. It furnishes a focus of political allegiance other than the principles of liberty and representative government. Undemocratic regimes have regularly relied on nationalist sentiment to mobilize political support for themselves—and against democracy. Hitler's popular appeal stemmed in large part from his adamant opposition to the post–World War I political settlement on the grounds that it had unfairly excluded many Germans from Germany proper. He began World War II, among other reasons, for the simplest of nationalist motives: to gather all Germans within a single political jurisdiction. The Communist government of China, to take a contemporary example, relies on a similar tactic for such political legitimacy as it enjoys. Beijing insists that the offshore island of Taiwan rightly belongs to China, a nationalist claim supported by many Chinese otherwise unsympathetic to Communist rule. Since the Taiwanese do not agree, and Beijing asserts the right to enforce its claim by military means, Chinese nationalism looms as a potential cause of war in the twenty-first century.[39] Nationalist sentiment has triggered wars within countries, as well as between and among them: for example, in the Balkans in the 1990s among different national groups that had been part of Yugoslavia.

In all these cases, and in similar ones, nationalism inhibited the practice of democratic politics; but in other places at other times nationalism has also helped to make democracy possible in two ways. First, it undermined the most prominent traditional form of undemocratic government. In the twentieth century, the multinational empires that dominated the planet disintegrated under the pressure of the nationalist demands of their subject peoples and were replaced by nation-states in which political boundaries more closely corresponded to cultural ones. Nation-states, unlike empires, enshrine one of the two defining principles of modern democracy—popular sovereignty.

Second, states organized along national lines lend themselves to democratic governance because their homogeneity eliminates one of the commonest forms of democracy-destroying civil strife.[40] In a stable democracy, people are willing to be outvoted. They peacefully accept the defeat of their preferred candidates for office and become, temporarily they hope, part of the political minority. They are willing to do this if, and only if, they believe that they will be fairly treated by the majority. They are more likely to anticipate fair treatment if they feel a fundamental kinship with their political adversaries. People are more willing to yield power peacefully to, and be governed by, those who resemble them in ways they consider important than by those who do not. Nationality is a potent indicator of likeness and thus can serve as a bulwark of democracy.

Participation in a free-market economy also cultivates the exercise, and the expectation of exercising, sovereignty, both of them central to democratic politics. As citizens of democracies have control over their political system, so owners of property exercise control—on a different scale and more directly, to be sure—over what they own. Citizens acquire the habit of sovereignty not only as property owners but in their capacities as consumers as well. It is the consumer who, through his or her purchases, has the ultimate say over the major economic decisions in a market economy. Indeed, just as democracy is a political system of popular sovereignty, so the free market is governed, to use a term from the vocabulary of economics, by consumer sovereignty.

The consumer does not, of course, make every decision in a market economy any more than citizens directly decide matters of public policy in representative democracies. In both cases, the decisions are delegated: legislators vote on laws; managers and owners decide what to produce, in what quantities, and at what prices to sell what is produced. Still, the broader public—citizens and consumers—in both instances exercises ultimate authority because it can, in effect, hire and fire the people who do make these decisions. In democratic political systems, the public exerts control through elections. In market economies, consumers decide, through their purchases, which products will continue to be produced and which firms remain in business. When the volume of purchases is great enough, the firm makes a profit, thus ensuring its viability. When this is not the case, the firm ceases its operations.[41] Consumers "vote" for firms with their purchases, making a market economy a kind of ongoing plebiscite, just as citizens vote for their representatives. An insufficient vote total turns a representative out of office. Insufficient demand for a product imposes on its makers the commercial equivalent of electoral defeat: bankruptcy.

As with the institution of private property, the experience of consumer sovereignty forms the habit, and the expectation, of exercising, through individual choice, a measure of control over the larger economic system in which the individual participates. It is natural for them to carry over into the larger political system in which participants in the market also reside; and this habit, and this expectation, encourage the practice, essential to democracy, of popular sovereignty.

In addition to sovereignty, the experience of participating in a successful market economy fosters two other habits that are indispensable for democratic governance: trust and compromise. For government to operate peacefully, citizens must trust it not to act against their most important interests and, above all, to respect their political and economic rights. For governments to be regularly chosen in free elections, the losers must trust the winners not to abuse the power they have won. In the absence of trust, governments rule by coercion, and coercion—except in the enforcement of democratically enacted laws—is incompatible with modern democracy.

Trust in others does not come naturally. To the contrary, in modern political systems that suppress and punish political dissent, personal safety can require distrust. Someone who places sufficient trust in the forbearance of the regime to proclaim dissenting political views, or merely trusts fellow citizens enough to express these views privately, can pay for his or her candor with imprisonment, or worse.

Since most democracies were governed in undemocratic fashion before establishing liberty and representative government, and since in undemocratic political systems trust does not flourish, people must acquire it elsewhere. In most societies, the most accessible and influential school for trust is the free market.

Trust is required for markets that extend beyond direct local exchange. When a seller personally delivers a product to a buyer and receives payment directly in return, as was the case in the economies of traditional, largely agricultural countries, the transaction is easy to monitor. When the product is shipped over great distances, however, and payment for it comes in installments that extend over time, as is common in modern market systems and is necessary to sustain the level of prosperity that the wealthiest countries enjoy,[42] buyers and sellers must trust in each other's good faith and reliability. Reliability is all the more important because economic success requires repeated transactions with many parties. A person may get away with the failure to deliver or pay what is promised on one occasion, but whoever suffers the consequent loss will not do business with the defaulter again. This is the reason that, in business, honesty really is the best policy.[43] A modern market economy operates on credit, and the word "credit" comes from the Latin verb *credere*, "to believe." To believe that another will repay a debt is to trust that person.

To be sure, in a well-functioning market economy the government stands by to enforce contracts that have been breached. But in a well-functioning market economy of a prosperous country, so many transactions take place that the government can intervene in only a tiny fraction of them. Market activity rests more on trust in others to fulfill their commitments than on reliance on the government to punish them if they fail to do so.[44]

Similarly, the habit of compromise inhibits democracy-threatening violence in political life. Different preferences on issues of public policy, often deeply felt, are inevitable in any political system. What distinguishes democracy from other forms of government is the peaceful resolution of the conflicts to which these differences give rise. Usually this occurs when each party gets some, but not all, of what it wants.

In undemocratic regimes, those in power impose their preferences on others. Democracies do things differently. They partly satisfy most of the people most of the time by incorporating some of their views into most laws and policies. In dictatorships, the minority gets what it wants. In democracy, the majority gets what it can tolerate and avoids what it cannot, under any circumstances, accept, and on this basis is willing to forgo violence in the pursuit of its goals.

Enacting laws in a democracy is typically an untidy exercise that often produces jerry-built statutes that are not entirely logical or internally consistent. This is the reason for Bismarck's often-quoted remark that the public should never be exposed to the making of either sausages or legislation. Its aesthetically unappealing features are, however, part of the price of democracy. The messiness of the process and the awkwardness of the results stem from the centrality of compromise to both; and it is compromise that makes peaceful politics, and therefore democratic politics, possible.

Compromise is also essential to the operation of a market economy. In every transaction, after all, the buyer would like to pay less, and the seller would like to receive more, than the price on which they ultimately agree. They agree to accept a lower or a higher price than is, from their different perspectives, optimal because the alternative is to have no transaction at all. Participants in a free market learn that the best can be the enemy of the good, and acting on that principle in the political arena is essential for democratic government.

The role of the free market in cultivating the individual attitudes, skills, and habits on which democracies depend for their proper functioning helps to account for three features of the remarkable rise of global democracy that are otherwise difficult to explain. The first is the appearance of democratic political systems in countries with no recent experience of operating one. While some countries have had some democratic institutions and practices imposed upon them by occupying foreign powers—India by Great Britain, the Philippines by the United States, for example—many have not. The undemocratic regimes that governed most twenty-first-century democracies prior to their embrace of liberty and representative government did not generally permit democratic institutions or practices within their borders, often actively suppressing them.

The appearance of democratic government where it did not previously exist therefore has the quality of a magic trick, a rabbit being pulled out of a hat. It raises the same question that such a trick is designed to induce in a dazzled, but mystified, audience: where did *that* come from? The answer is that while the inspiration for adopting democracy generally comes from outside the borders of an undemocratically governed country— from the attractive example of working democracies elsewhere—the experience necessary for making the system work is acquired within the country itself, through market activities.

The role of the market in fostering democracy also helps to account for a second noteworthy feature of the great global wave of democracy-creation in the last three decades of the twentieth century and the early years of the twenty-first: the peaceful form that most transitions from authoritarian to democratic rule have taken.

While the pattern of changing a country's form of government that attracted the most attention in the nineteenth and twentieth centuries was revolution—the forcible overturning of one regime and replacing it with another—the rise of democracy around the world more closely resembled the natural process of metamorphosis. Within the outer cocoon of authoritarian rule, the habits of liberty and self-government grew, and this occurred as people transferred the habits, values, and expectations they acquired by participating in economic life to the realm of politics. Ultimately, this process resulted in the country in question shedding its undemocratic trappings and emerging, like a butterfly from within a chrysalis, as a full-fledged democratic political system.

The way the free market fosters the elements of democracy explains yet a third otherwise puzzling feature of democracy's rise: the fact that it has occurred in so many different countries with different historical and cultural backgrounds around the world. Democracy could appear almost anywhere because, in the second half of the twentieth century, free markets could be found almost everywhere. The market came to be seen as the economic system best designed to deliver material well-being to a society by achieving economic growth. In the final decades of the century, it decisively surpassed the principal alternative form of economic organization, socialism in its various guises, on this count.

Market-produced affluence proved universally alluring. As the market generated more wealth in more countries, the demand to duplicate the pattern in countries in which it was not occurring became increasingly insistent.[45] This in turn made the market more and more popular, even with regimes—the Communist government of China is an outstanding example—that wanted no part of democratic politics. The free market acts as a kind of Trojan horse, welcomed by those whose interests it ultimately subverts.

The market holds two distinct appeals to dictators. It can enhance their power by making the countries they rule richer and thus placing more resources at their disposal. Maximizing their own capacities to bully and bribe tends to appeal to un-democratic rulers, even if expanding the welfare of those they govern does not. Increasingly, however, the standard of living of the countries they govern does matter to unelected leaders because if it is not rising, public dissatisfaction with them tends to grow. Market-created prosperity therefore not only enhances, it also helps to secure, in the short run, the power of governments that have no interest in the democratic by-product of this wealth-creating mechanism.

It follows that undemocratic regimes come under pressure to give way to democracy however the economy performs. If it does poorly, whatever popular support they enjoy declines.[46] If it does well, people acquire the habits and attitudes that foster democracy.

The powerful and widespread link between market eco-nomics and democratic politics has something in common with a nineteenth-century doctrine that had great influence in the twentieth, the theory of history advanced by Karl Marx. He believed that the economic trends at work in the world would have specific political consequences. They would lead, inexorably, through the impoverishment of the vast majority of people and the deep opposition to the system that this would provoke, to the overthrow of the existing political order in Europe and the advent, in its place, of the happy, if vaguely defined, political conditions that Marx called communism. The march to communism, he believed, had the absolute and invariable property of a law of history.

As it turned out, Marx was mistaken. Contrary to his ex-pectations, the functioning of the free market in the major countries of Europe did not make the vast majority of people poorer. Instead it had, with the assistance of the politically inspired social programs that constitute the welfare state, the opposite effect: it made them steadily richer. Because it made them richer, the market became increasingly popular, and its popularity and widespread adoption had the side effect, a century after Marx's death in 1883, of lifting democracy from minority to majority status in the world.

Yet the establishment of democracy everywhere is not, as Marx wrongly expected the triumph of communism to be, inevitable. There is no law of history according to which every country must one day have a government that protects its citizens' rights and is chosen through free, fair, and regular elections. Nor does the presence of a working market economy guarantee that democratic governance will follow. In promoting democracy, the free market, while powerful, is not all-powerful.

MARKET FAILURES

Two distinct streams—the example of successful democratic countries and the democratizing effects of the operation of a free market—combined in the last quarter of the twentieth century to form a powerful global current pushing all the sovereign states of the planet toward democratic governance. None of the countries still governed, at the outset of the twenty-first century, in undemocratic fashion was immune to the tug of this global current, but not all were necessarily destined to become democracies. Against this current stood three obstacles, one or more of which was present in many places where liberty and free elections were absent.

First, resistance to the installation of freely elected, rights-protecting governments comes from the rulers of undemocratic regimes who stand to lose their power, and the advantages that it brings, if democracy triumphs. Second, while the workings of the free market generate, over time,

pressures to practice democratic politics, in some countries at
the outset of the twenty-first century, especially where it had
only recently been installed, as in the countries that had once
been republics of the Soviet Union, the market worked badly,
weakening its democratizing effects. Moreover, these effects
were nonexistent where, as in parts of sub-Saharan Africa, because of the absence of effective government machinery, the
market barely functioned at all. Third, a market system in a
country whose principal economic activity is the extraction
and sale of natural resources, especially oil, does not produce
the habits, attitudes, skills, and values that underpin democratic government.

It is not surprising that those who hold power in undemocratic political systems usually resist giving it up. They have
frequently gone to some trouble to obtain it. The longer they
have held it, moreover, the more important it seems to them
to retain it and the more severe the disadvantages they fear if
they lose it. In the long history of human political organization, autocracy has been far more common than democracy.

Whether, and for how long, undemocratic regimes manage
to hold out against the pro-democracy current at large in the
world depends heavily on the force and guile with which the
world's remaining dictators work to stay in power, which are in
turn the products of local and often idiosyncratic circumstances that cannot be predicted with any accuracy. The opposite experiences of two major countries at almost the same
time—Russia, where a ruling Communist government collapsed, and China, where, by contrast, a Communist government crushed a challenge to its authority and retained its
monopoly of political power—illustrate the enormous importance of one particularly idiosyncratic and unpredictable cir-
cumstance: the personalities of individual political leaders.

The lion's share of the responsibility for the end of communism in Russia, and in Europe, belongs to one man: Mikhail Sergeyevich Gorbachev, the last leader of the Soviet Union. The Soviet political system vested enormous political power in his hands, which he used to implement political and economic changes that made the people of the Soviet Union freer than they had ever been, but that also had the ultimate and surely unintended effect of destroying the communist system and the Soviet Union itself, which disintegrated in 1991 into fifteen separate sovereign states.

Gorbachev pressed ahead with his reforms, even when they began to undermine the foundations of the political system over which he presided, out of a combination, peculiar to him, of three personal traits: ignorance—he did not understand how little active allegiance the communist system actually commanded, especially in Central and Eastern Europe, where it had been imposed by Soviet troops; arrogance—he was certain that he possessed the wisdom and political skill to regenerate communism by transforming it; and decency—every time he confronted a choice between using force to stop the political processes he had set in motion and allowing them to proceed and thus endanger his own authority and ultimately communism itself, he chose not to do what all his predecessors as the supreme Soviet leader had routinely done: unleash the formidable military power at his disposal and crush the opposition.

If Mikhail Gorbachev's singular personality led to the fall of communism, a singular series of events put him in the position in which his decisions could have such far-reaching effects. He was elevated to supreme power after his three immediate predecessors died within the space of three years. One of them, Yuri Andropov, the onetime head of the KGB, the Soviet secret police, was a formidable individual who would surely not have initiated the radical changes that Gorbachev introduced. Andropov was expected to hold power much longer than he did, but he succumbed to kidney disease, leading to the only partly facetious historical verdict, which emphasizes the contingent nature of any particular country's transition to democracy, that communism fell because Andropov had weak kidneys.[47]

In the People's Republic of China, also a highly centralized communist political system, the regime resisted a challenge to its authority in 1989. It forcibly suppressed a series of demonstrations around the country, the most prominent of which took place in Tiananmen Square, in the heart of Beijing, the Chinese capital. At least hundreds, perhaps thousands, of peaceful protestors were killed, many others were imprisoned or harassed by the government, and organized public opposition to the country's undemocratic government disappeared.

As with Mikhail Gorbachev in the Soviet Union, one person had a decisive influence on events in China: Deng Xiaoping, a longtime communist leader. As in the Soviet Union, his central role came about through a series of developments that could not have been predicted and, with minor alterations, could easily have led to the opposite outcome. Deng had retired from active leadership, but a secret protocol adopted by the Chinese Communist Party decreed that, in the event of a stalemate in the active leadership on an important matter, he and a small group of other retired officials, a group that he dominated, would have the right to decide the government's course of action.[48] That rule was unusual even for a communist country, and it was also remarkable that Deng was alive in 1989 to take advantage of it. By that time, he was an historical and actuarial anomaly. Born in 1904 and a heavy smoker, he had survived the vicissitudes of twentieth-century Chinese history—the Communist battles with the rival Kuomintang and invading Japanese and the recurrent purges of the Communist Party—that had eliminated most of his contemporaries.

Within the inner circle of the Chinese government, moreover, opinion on how to respond to the protests was closely divided. Had only one or two more people opposed calling in the army, this might not have occurred.[49] In addition, one of the leading proponents of a violent crackdown, the prime minister, Li Peng, exercised considerable influence over Deng by providing a distorted account of what was occurring around the country.[50]

Had circumstances been only slightly different, therefore, Deng might never have had the opportunity to decide what to do, or he might have decided differently. Or, if he himself had not been on the scene, someone else in his position might have made a different decision. If so, the history of the world's most populous country could easily have taken a radically different course from the one that it followed after 1989,[51] just as the history of one of the world's two nuclear "superpowers" of the Cold War era, and therefore world history itself, might have proceeded along very different lines if Yuri Andropov had enjoyed good health. If Andropov had lived longer and Deng had died earlier, in the twenty-first century China might well be a more formally democratic country than Russia, rather than the other way around.

The strength and determination that dictators have to muster in order to resist the pressure to replace them with democratic governments depends, of course, on how powerful that pressure is in any particular country. Its power in turn depends in part on the breadth and depth of the democratic inclinations that the working of the free market, in combination with the power of the democratic example, has produced in the populace. In some countries, in the first decade of the twenty-first century, the market had done little or nothing to foster democratic habits and expectations.

This was particularly so where a free market had been only recently installed. A complicated, effective market system takes time to develop. One of its indispensable elements, for example, a financial system, consists of a series of institutions and a collection of skills that can only be built and acquired over a span of years.[52] Similarly, the social infrastructure of democracy that a free market creates does not appear all at once, full-blown. It accumulates gradually, as the life experiences of individuals teach them to exercise a measure of sovereign control over the larger economic and political systems they inhabit and inculcate the habits of trust and cooperation. The relevant unit of time is the generation. The internal pressure for democracy grows slowly, as people who have been educated in its ways in the school of the free market replace, in the workforce and ultimately in positions of responsibility in the society, their elders who either did not attend this school or never finished it.

Democracy came to East Asia and Latin America in the last three decades of the twentieth century after the countries of these regions had had at least a generation's worth of experience, sometimes more, in operating a full-fledged market economy. In these countries, dynamic industrial and commercial sectors supplemented, and sometimes supplanted, the agricultural production that had traditionally dominated economic life. The countries of formerly communist Eurasia, by contrast, adopted free-market systems only after ruling Communist parties had collapsed, in 1989 and 1991. In building markets, most of them were starting from scratch. Their Communist-era, centrally planned economic systems lacked, indeed suppressed, the features of a free market, above all private property, that lead to democracy. It is not surprising that, in the early post-communist period, the market systems of these countries had shallow social roots, and functioned poorly. The market-inspired foundations for democratic government were consequently fragile, and the majority of post-communist countries did not become modern democracies.

What is surprising is that the post-communist countries of Central Europe—Poland, Hungary, and the Czech Republic—as well as the three Baltic states of Estonia, Latvia, and Lithuania, did manage to install in short order political systems in which the government was chosen in free, fair, regular elections and in which liberty was secure. These countries differed, however, from the other post-communist states, many of which became independent only in 1991, in ways that made the adoption of market institutions and democracy easier. The most important of these differences was the impact of the political and economic example of their neighbors to the west.

The Central Europeans had belonged to the West before 1945, as independent countries after World War I and before that as parts of the Habsburg Empire, with its capital in Vienna. The dominant faiths in Central Europe and the Baltic had historically been the Western forms of Christianity—Catholicism and Protestantism—not the Eastern ones. Beyond religious tradition, the countries of these regions had enjoyed close political, economic, and cultural ties with the countries where free markets had flourished as early as the nineteenth century and where, after 1945, political democracy became firmly established. They themselves had organized their economic lives, before 1945, along free-market lines.

As a consequence, during the Communist period in the decades following World War II, they thought of themselves as

Western countries temporarily held captive in the East—the victims, in effect, of a kidnapping—which had had alien political customs and economic practices forced upon them. As soon as they were released, a powerful consensus formed in each country in favor of resuming their rightful places in the world, which meant embracing, as soon and as fully as possible, free markets and democracy.[53]

Market-created pressure for democracy cannot, of course, exist at all without a market; and even in the twenty-first century, some places lacked any significant market activity beyond small-scale local exchange. In these "failed states," such as Somalia in Africa and Haiti in the Caribbean, where government was too weak to enforce the law, the insecurity and violence that pervaded daily life stunted the economic institutions and stifled the economic activity that instill democratic habits and practices. Stability—that is, civic order—is for markets what oxygen is for humans; and in the twenty-first century some tragic places in the world were too disorderly for free markets, let alone democracy, to operate.

To the rule that wealth is a sign of well-functioning markets, which tend to produce both wealth and democracy, there is a conspicuous exception. Countries that become wealthy through the extraction and sale of natural resources within their territories, especially the "petro-states" that derive their riches from oil, rarely conform to the political standards of modern democracy. Ordinarily, the creation of wealth requires social institutions and individual skills that, transferred to the realm of politics, promote democracy.

A country possessing substantial deposits of petroleum, however, does not need these institutions and skills to become rich. All that is required is to extract and sell its oil, and a small number of people can do this. They do not even have to be citizens of the country itself, and in many oil-rich countries, they are not.[54] A handful of foreigners—along, of course, with the crucial role of oil in modern economies and the enormous global demand for it to which this gives rise—can confer great wealth on a society without its cultivating a sense of common identity, a taste for self-government, or the habits of cooperation and trust that a wealth-generating economy produces in other countries and that move such countries toward democracy.

Petro-states, that is, can become wealthy by doing nothing. Riches from oil come as a windfall. Like individuals who inherit great wealth, the favored societies need not, and therefore usually do not, acquire the skills and attitudes that those who must earn their way in the world develop in order to survive and prosper. Because they do not have to participate in a complicated market economy, the citizens of petro-states do not matriculate at the school for democracy that others, out of economic necessity, are forced to attend.[55]

Not only does the possession of oil enable its possessors to do without the social and political conditions of democracy, it also actively promotes obstacles to democratic government. Because the governments of petro-states own the oil fields and collect the revenues from the sale of what these fields produce, they tend to be large and powerful. The private economies of these countries, which elsewhere counterbalance state power, tend to be small and weak, with many firms depending on government patronage rather than on consumer approval for their business.[56] What constitutes the heart of civil society, which protects liberty and promotes representative government in other societies, is generally underdeveloped in petro-states and so poorly positioned to play those roles.

Moreover, the undemocratic governments of petro-states, particularly those such as the monarchies of the Persian Gulf, where oil is especially plentiful and the populations are relatively small, can use the wealth at their disposal to resist pressures for more democratic governance. They can, and do, offer citizens a bargain: a high level of national well-being, which oil revenues subsidize, in exchange for political passivity. They provide benefits for which citizens need do nothing in return, including paying taxes, except to keep quiet.[57] The hereditary rulers of Saudi Arabia, Kuwait, and their small neighbors in effect bribe the people they rule to forgo political liberty and the right to decide who governs them.

Finally, because the government controls the oil, in a petrostate the incentives to control the government are unusually great, as, therefore, are the disincentives to relinquish power, something that democracy of course requires rulers to be prepared to do.[58] Wealth in petro-states comes from political power and, because their economies, beyond their oil sectors, tend to be small and weak, it has almost no other source. This makes holding and keeping power all the more important and the idea of yielding it peacefully to individuals and groups that have received more votes in a fairly contested election all the less acceptable. In petro-states, wealth tends to be highly concentrated,[59] and gross disparities in wealth routinely produce an anti-democratic political dynamic even in societies without oil, for example in countries such as Pakistan with large agrarian sectors in which a few families hold most of the arable land. Democracy threatens the material well-being of the wealthy because a government representing the population as a whole would take steps to make the distribution of wealth more equal. The rich therefore actively oppose democracy.[60]

In fact, in most societies throughout most of history, seizing and holding political power was the path to wealth. Governments used their monopoly of effective force to prey on the societies over which they presided, like lions sustaining themselves by killing and eating gazelles. This practice was one of the main reasons that, until the second half of the eighteenth century, the sustained economic growth that the Industrial Revolution introduced and that has transformed the world had never appeared anywhere on the planet.[61]

People in the traditional world had little capacity to increase their output by investing such surpluses as they produced because their governments confiscated them. They had, as well, little incentive to increase production because they would not be able to make use of the increase themselves: the government would take it.

It was the separation of wealth from power, the political autonomy of the free market with secure property rights as the basis for the economy's independence from the political authorities, that made possible economic growth and thus the affluence that so many fortunate citizens of the twenty-first century have come to enjoy. Economic growth occurs when it is possible to become wealthy without acquiring political power.

In one sense, therefore, the petro-states' fusion of politics and economics continues what had been all but universal before the modern era. In another way, however, these countries differ from all others by combining, as their oil wealth allows them to do, predatory behavior with affluence. In other wealthy countries, the government does not control economic life. Political power is not a license to commandeer what the economy produces. Power is not the route to wealth. If anything, the reverse is true: in well-established democracies, although every person's vote counts equally, those with money to spend in politics as candidates, campaign contributors, or sponsors of lobbyists can exert more influence than their fellow citizens without such resources.

On the other hand, twenty-first-century countries in which the government plays the traditional role of economic predator do not become rich. To the contrary, the most rapacious governments are often to be found in the poorest countries, and this is not a coincidence: predatory regimes stifle economic activity. The worst of them, Zaire under the rule of Joseph Mobutu, offers a vivid example: steal the resources and the output of the societies in which they hold power until these societies are destitute because there is nothing left to loot.[62]

To be sure, even in the best-managed and most successful market democracies, where the independence of the economy from state control is most firmly established, the separation between politics and economics is not absolute. A market economy cannot operate without a secure legal framework, which only government can supply.[63] Moreover, no society is entirely free of predatory behavior. In its most common form, it is called corruption and involves the use of political power or governmental position to obtain a payment that the recipient could not earn in the marketplace and to which he or she is not entitled by law.

Bribes of government officials to secure favored treatment—to gain a license or a permit or desired legislation—are paid everywhere. In its most benign form, which is the form it takes in wealthy democracies, corruption does not prevent the effective working of the free market. It acts as a kind of tax on economic activity, and although it is nowhere officially encouraged or legally sanctioned, as long as it is modest in scope it does not crush that activity.[64] Where corruption is pervasive, however, as it is in all too many places outside Europe and North America, it has the same effect as did the predatory impositions of governments in the traditional era. As in the fable of the man who killed the goose that laid the golden eggs, it crushes economic activity and so makes and keeps people poor.[65]

Africa in particular has suffered from debilitating levels of corruption. Throughout the continent, government has been an exercise in predation.[66] Accordingly, by the end of the 1980s, per capita income in sub-Saharan Africa was lower than it had been in the 1970s.[67] Even Nigeria, a country with large enough reserves of oil to have earned an estimated $280 billion from it, had become by the 1990s, thanks to rampant corruption, the thirteenth poorest country in the world.[68] Not surprisingly, democracy has not flourished on the African continent.[69]

The average inhabitant of a country with a rapaciously predatory government suffers a wretched existence; but the residents of petro-states, even those wealthy enough to finance generous employment and welfare programs, do not lead entirely enviable lives. For one thing, they enjoy no political freedom, nor do they exercise any control over those who govern them. For another, their standard of living is hostage to the price of oil. When it falls, the regime has difficulty supporting them in the style to which they become accustomed when it is high because there are no other sources of income. Petro-states typically fail to develop centers of economic growth outside their oil sectors.[70]

In addition, the inhabitants of petro-states are more likely to become victims of violence than the citizens of democracy, and not only because their undemocratic governments make far wider use of the techniques of political repression than do democratic authorities. Petro-states also have a greater propensity than democracies to become involved in wars. The causes of war are various, and each conflict has its own particular set of precipitating events. But one feature common to virtually all countries in which the extraction of natural resources dominated economic life came to be seen, in the twenty-first century, as particularly salient in provoking armed conflict: the absence of democratic governance.

The rise of democracy around the world in the last part of the twentieth century was accompanied by the growing conviction, first in academic circles and then in the ranks of public officeholders, that this development, which powerfully affected political life within many sovereign states, had important consequences for relations between and among them as well. The history of the twentieth century provides evidence for the proposition, which gained ever wider currency, that a country's internal political configuration affects its behavior beyond its borders and, more specifically, that democracies do not go to war with one another.

As it gained acceptance, this "democratic peace" theory made the status of democracy in the world an important issue of foreign policy. Most countries have an interest in peace, after all, so if any particular country's choice of a political system determines how peacefully it is likely to conduct itself abroad, that choice becomes a matter of concern to others. The presumed link between democracy and peace, and its implications for foreign policy, burnished democracy's good name and lay behind George W. Bush's second inaugural address.

Given a connection between democracy and the absence of war, a policy of promoting democracy becomes more than an exercise in charity, a mechanism for a fortunate society to extend one of its blessings to those less fortunate. It becomes, as well, an act of self-interest on the part of the promoter, a way of reducing threats to its own security. The spread of democracy, by this account, not only made the countries to which it spread freer, it also made those countries' neighborhoods, and the world itself, safer places. The rise of democracy around the world therefore raises the question of whether this account is true. Are democracies peaceful? And will the spread of democracy have the effect of making the world a markedly more peaceful place?

4

DEMOCRACY AND PEACE

"Freedom and democracy are the best guarantors of peace. History has shown that democratic nations do not start wars."

—RONALD REAGAN, 1985[1]

MODERNITY AND PEACE

If democracy is almost invariably found in the company of free markets, the relationship between democracy and peace, according to some observers of international relations, is just as close, if not closer. The many studies of this relationship converge on a single conclusion: countries governed democratically tend to act peacefully.[2] Democracies have particular features, these studies suggest, that dispose them to deal with other countries in a peaceful fashion. When two democracies interact, these features reinforce one another. For this reason, democracies have very seldom, by some reckonings, and never, by others, fought each other. This "democratic peace" theory is said to come "as close as anything we have to an empirical law in international relations."[3]

From this theory it follows that democracy's rise has had, and will continue to have, major consequences for the international order, as well as, of course, for political life within countries where democracy takes root. Since peace is ordinarily preferable to war, those international consequences are highly desirable. The democratic peace theory leads to the prediction that the more democratic the world becomes, the more peaceful it will be, which provides a good reason to try to hasten and broaden the spread of democracy. Because of its implications for relations between and among countries, what Oscar Wilde is said to have remarked about the Bible is true of the democratic peace theory: interesting if true. But is it true?

The twentieth century can lay claim to being both the bloodiest and the most peaceful of all such 100-year periods. In its first half, two world wars, the most destructive conflicts in human history, took place. The second half of the last century, by contrast, and particularly its final decade, was unusually peaceful. In the years since the end of World War II, no war involving the most powerful members of the international system has been fought—the longest such period in the last 500 years.[4] In the twentieth century's final decade, the number of conflicts involving less powerful countries, including civil wars, dropped sharply.[5]

By some accounts, moreover, much of the violence that did persist into the twenty-first century did not qualify as war at all. Rather than organized exercises in the use of force by formally constituted governments for the purpose of achieving political goals, the recent episodes have more closely resembled the decentralized, episodic, opportunistic acts of violence carried out for personal gain (or other individual motives) that typify criminal conduct.[6]

Something about the most recent period of history has narrowed the scope, reduced the frequency, and decreased the destructiveness of the age-old practice of warfare. While the decline of war coincides with the rise of democracy, lending credibility to the democratic peace theory, the spread of popular sovereignty and liberty is not the only feature of the late twentieth century with a plausible connection to this decline.

Political changes in the second half of the century, for example, removed some major causes of war. Colonial rule came to an end, and with it the bloody twentieth-century struggles by peoples living under such rule to free themselves.[7] In the century's last decade the Cold War also came to an end, and so, too, therefore, did the conflicts between the countries of the American-led Western camp and those of the Communist bloc.[8]

Beyond these major political events, another feature of twentieth-century life had—or was often thought to have had—a pacifying effect on relations among sovereign states: the pattern of economic activity. Beginning in the eighteenth century in Britain, the Industrial Revolution transformed the economic, social, and political life of the planet. It did not create, but it vastly expanded in scale and increased in velocity, one particular kind of economic activity: trade across borders between and among peoples in different political jurisdictions. Well before the democratic peace theory gained broad currency, trade was credited with encouraging peaceful relations among sovereign states. In the mid-nineteenth century, partisans of free trade argued that it would assure non-belligerent relations among the countries that practiced it. Indeed, the champions of this doctrine (most of whom were to be found in the political arena rather than in universities) asserted that free trade was the key to peace.[9]

The best-known nineteenth-century advocate of this proposition was the English parliamentarian Richard Cobden, who was active in public affairs from the 1840s through the 1860s.[10] John Stuart Mill, the influential writer on politics and economics who was Cobden's contemporary and is best known for his defense of liberty, also subscribed to the idea that trade between sovereign states would make their political relations more peaceful.[11]

The reasoning that underlay the faith that Cobden, Mill, and others had in the tendency of trade to discourage war was straightforward: trade makes the countries engaged in it wealthier, as the influential British economic thinkers Adam Smith and David Ricardo had demonstrated in theory, and as the economic success of Great Britain, the country most committed to unfettered cross-border exchange, had shown in practice. War interrupts trade and thus makes trading countries that wage it poorer, or at least curtails their opportunities to become richer. Since no country will choose to make itself poorer than it would otherwise be, none will cut off a major source of wealth by going to war if it can possibly avoid doing so.[12]

By the eve of World War I, the idea of a connection between trade and peace had gained wide currency. A book by the English author Norman Angell entitled *The Great Illusion*, which made the case for that connection and implied that a major European war would bring economic disaster, and that the European powers would therefore be committing an act of folly by waging one, became a best seller.[13] Europe did, of course, go to war in 1914, and the conflict bore out Angell's point: it proved economically ruinous for the warring powers.[14] World War II, which began twenty years after the end of World War I, reinforced the point, destroying lives and property on an even larger scale.

In the wake of World War II, Europe began a process of economic cooperation and integration that led, in 1957, to the formation of the six-country European Economic Community, which by 2007 had grown into the twenty-seven-member European Union (EU). Virtually uninhibited trade took place among the EU's members, thirteen of which used a single common currency, the euro. The idea that animated the European movement toward ever-closer economic relations was the same one that Cobden and Angell had promoted: the way to avoid yet another round of conflict, above all between France and Germany, which had fought each other three times between 1870 and 1945, was to bind the different countries of Western Europe together economically.

The EU had its origins in the conviction that, although trade among the European powers had not prevented the two world wars, the freest possible trade—and in general the closest possible economic links among them—offered the best hope for averting a third. In the decades after 1945, trade expanded rapidly in Western Europe, and at the same time peaceful relations among the countries of the region took hold. By the dawn of the twenty-first century, most of Europe had become a free trade zone, and conflict among the major countries of the continent, including France and Germany, was all but unimaginable.

The world beyond the European continent, however, was neither as closely integrated economically nor as resolutely peaceful as were the countries of Europe. Still, the expansion of worldwide economic interdependence because of the increasingly powerful forces of economic integration known collectively as globalization did seem to add an element of caution to the foreign policies of countries involved in political disputes serious enough to make war possible.[15] The foreign affairs columnist of *The New York Times*, Thomas L. Friedman, proposed a version of Cobden's theory updated for the age of globalization, which he called the "supply-chain theory of conflict prevention."[16] It held that two countries that are part of the same supply chain—the network of producers all of the members of which contribute to the making of a finished product, such as a computer, or the provision of a particular service, such as the worldwide delivery of packages—would not fight each other because the costs of war, due to the income lost from the interruption of the supply chain, would exceed any gain that war might bring.

Friedman found anecdotal evidence that his theory applied to China and India. The world's two most populous countries have been drawn into many supply chains by the process of globalization, which made their governments even more hesitant than they would otherwise have been to contemplate war over the offshore island of Taiwan that China claimed as its own, or, in the Indian case, over its neighbor Pakistan's efforts to loosen India's grip on its Muslim-majority province Kashmir—and this despite Beijing's declared intention to fight to control Taiwan, and New Delhi's history of skirmishes with Pakistan over Kashmir.[17] The expansion of trade therefore counts as one consequence of the Industrial Revolution that seems to have made the world more peaceful all apart from the rise of democracy. There are two more.

The Industrial Revolution made the world a more peaceful place by creating a new form of wealth that war proved not to be useful in acquiring. For all previous human history, riches came principally from land. It therefore made economic sense to fight to gain territory.[18] In the industrial age, it became more profitable for each country to specialize in producing the things it was most efficient in making, and then trading with

its neighbors, than to devote its resources to conquering and
governing them. Voluntary exchange of goods and services became a surer (not to mention safer) path to riches than conquest and plunder.[19] Adam Smith made this point as early as
1776 in his economic treatise *The Wealth of Nations*, but for the
better part of the next 200 years it had little apparent effect on
the foreign policies of the major powers of the international
system, which continued to wage wars of conquest.[20]

In the wake of World War II, however, the foreign policies
of two of those powers underwent a remarkable transformation. Germany and Japan, both of which had sought, in brutal
fashion, to conquer vast territorial empires for themselves,
abandoned that goal completely. They pursued peaceful foreign policies and equipped themselves with very modest
armed forces that they were extraordinarily reluctant to use
and, in fact, in the six decades following 1945, did not use.
Their principal international activity, the one into which they
poured their national energies, that made them far more prosperous than they had been during their imperial eras and that
came to define their common international role, shifted from
war to trade. They transformed themselves from traditional
great powers, with large appetites for war and conquest, to
"trading states" that enriched themselves by non-military
means.[21]

The Industrial Revolution made the world a more peaceful
place in yet another way, by vastly increasing the cost of war.
Industrial war, waged with machines such as tanks and air-
planes, brought about death and destruction on a far larger
scale than ever before.[22] World War I killed ten million people
and devastated large tracts of Europe. World War II left many
more dead—an estimated fifty million, many of them, unlike
in World War I, civilians—all across Europe and in East,

Southeast, and South Asia as well.[23] The toll taken by the fighting between 1939 and 1945 was sufficiently high, and the experience of those who lived through World War II sufficiently ghastly, to make the prospect of yet another major conflict unattractive in the extreme.[24]

Major war became all the more unattractive—to the point of qualifying as virtually unthinkable—with the appearance, at the very end of World War II, of the most powerful weapons ever created, which drew their explosive force from liberating the energy locked in the heart—the nucleus—of matter. A single nuclear weapon can destroy an entire city; two atomic bombs did destroy the Japanese cities of Hiroshima and Nagasaki, respectively, on August 6 and 9, 1945. In the years thereafter the leading nuclear weapon powers, the United States and the Soviet Union, came to possess tens of thousands of them.[25] A full-scale nuclear exchange would therefore destroy those who waged it, a certainty that, not surprisingly, reduced to the vanishing point the willingness to engage in one and so helped to make the world a more peaceful place.

The heightened destructiveness of armed conflict that the Industrial Revolution made possible contributed to yet another development in the second half of the twentieth century that helped to diminish the role of war in human affairs: the emergence of a new social norm against war that came to be widely held in the wealthiest sectors of the planet. For most of recorded history, organized armed conflict was a normal feature of the political life of the human species. It was regrettable, perhaps, but inevitable. Like winter, war might be delayed and it might be mild, but eventually it would come. By the nineteenth century war began to be considered something that should be, and, what was more novel, could be, avoided.[26]

In the second half of the twentieth century the citizens of the countries of Western Europe, Japan, and to a lesser extent the United States increasingly regarded the ancient practice of warfare as unacceptable—indeed repulsive, an abomination, the sort of thing that civilized people should not do. A social and moral stigma became attached to war, making it the subject of a taboo, like once widely employed but by the twenty-first century widely rejected social practices such as slavery.[27] As a consequence, it ceased to be considered an acceptable way of pursuing a country's interest.[28] War became, where this attitude took hold, not only prohibitively expensive but widely regarded as morally wrong. That, too, has helped to make the world a more peaceful place.

To be sure, while the age-old institution of war was, at the outset of the twenty-first century, in steep decline, it had not entirely disappeared and is unlikely ever to do so. Its deepest underlying causes persisted. War is, at some level, the product of human nature, which cannot have changed fundamentally over the course of a half-century—in evolutionary terms the mere blink of an eye. By the well-known definition of the Prussian military writer Carl von Clausewitz, war is the continuation of politics by other means; and politics, and the conflicts that arise from it, show no signs of ending. By the lights of many observers of international politics, finally, beginning with Thucydides, the ancient Greek historian of the fourth century B.C. Peloponnesian Wars, war has its ultimate basis in the anarchic structure of the world—the absence of a supreme global authority that can prevent armed conflict—and the insecurity that this creates for all sovereign states. This condition, too, remains in place.

What is distinctive about recent decades is the emergence of countervailing forces to those that, from time immemorial, have pushed humankind toward war. These new, war-opposing social forces involve more than the late-twentieth-century rise of democracy. Economic considerations, advances in the technologies of destruction, and the development of a social norm against it have all contributed to the decline in the scope and frequency of war; and these factors reinforce one another.

To war's decline, the rise of democracy has not, however, been irrelevant. For one thing, the social and psychological taboo against war has a stronger presence in democracies than in undemocratically governed countries. For another, democracies are more powerfully associated with peace than nondemocracies: in one reading of history, democracies have never fought each other, something that could scarcely have occurred by chance.[29] Finally, democracy has a double-barreled connection to peace in that both parts of democratic government— popular sovereignty and the protection of individual liberty—can be seen to have pacifying effects on the external relations of the countries where they are established.

Popular Sovereignty and Peace

The first fully articulated version of the democratic peace theory appeared at the end of the eighteenth century. This version argued that the spread of popular sovereignty would put an end to war between and among sovereign states. Its author was Immanuel Kant, a scholar in the Prussian city of Konigsberg (now the Russian city of Kaliningrad) whose writings on ethics and metaphysics are landmarks in the history of philosophy.

Like other Europeans of his generation, Kant was profoundly impressed by the French Revolution. He envisioned its central achievement, the fall of the monarchy and its replacement by a system of government in which the people ruled, spreading across the European continent and ultimately all around the world—which is more or less what took place over the succeeding two centuries. When countries acquired such political systems they would, Kant wrote in his 1795 essay "Perpetual Peace," eschew war on the basis of the same kind of cost-benefit calculation that was later to underpin Cobden's confidence in the pacifying effects of free trade.

Wars, as Kant saw it, brought benefits to the monarchical rulers who presided over them, whose power and wealth was increased by conquest, but not to the people they ruled, who had to pay for these wars with their taxes and even their lives but who gained nothing even from successful military campaigns.[30] Once the people had the power to control a country's foreign policies by choosing its government, they would act according to their own interests by insisting on peaceful relations with the rest of the world.

As with Cobden's proposition that free trade would assure peace, history did not, at first, treat Kant's theory kindly. World War I was waged by countries some of which had democratic governments. True, the full-fledged democracies were all on one side of the conflict, so the war did not disprove the axiom that democracies do not fight each other. The political system of their chief adversary, imperial Germany, however, did have democratic features, and the deputies in the German parliament from the party most committed to genuine democracy and who most faithfully represented the interests of working people, the Social Democrats, voted in favor of financing the war. They did so despite their prewar vows to oppose armed conflict on the grounds that it would not serve the interests of those they represented.[31]

After World War II, however, some evidence supporting Kant's prediction began to appear. The sentiment of warlessness took hold in the most democratic countries on the planet, and it was the citizens of these democracies who developed an aversion to war and pressed their governments to avoid it. In Western societies, antiwar sentiment traveled from the bottom up, not from the top down. In the second half of the twentieth century, the citizens of the Western democracies showed, by their political choices, a pronounced preference for social welfare programs, whose benefits accrued to them, over expenditures for defense, foreign activities in general, and war—just as Kant had predicted. Democracies, that is, consistently preferred butter to guns.

This was the case even in the United States, the Western democracy that maintained, at the outset of the twenty-first century, the most powerful military establishment in the world, and whose citizens were, among all the democracies, the least opposed in principle to using it. The United States fought substantial wars in Korea and Vietnam during the Cold War and, in the wake of that global conflict, intervened militarily in a variety of places around the world: Somalia in Africa, the Balkans in Europe, Haiti in the Caribbean, and Kuwait and Iraq in the Middle East. Americans therefore acquired a reputation for bellicosity that was not, however, entirely warranted. While the United States was more willing (and, not coincidentally, better able) to fight than any other democracy, its government was subject to the same popular reservations about and objections to war—albeit somewhat weaker versions of them—as were those of the countries of Western Europe and Japan.

The three longest and costliest post-1945 American wars, which were fought in Korea, Vietnam, and Iraq, all became unpopular with the American public, and for the same reasons: some Americans objected in principle to them, and others, the larger number, came to believe that the wars had become more expensive in lives and money than they were worth. Where war is concerned, that is, Americans, too, have a tendency, albeit a less powerful one than Europeans and Japanese, to behave as Kant predicted the citizens of democracies would.

The world was not wholly peaceful at the outset of the twenty-first century, of course, but neither was it entirely democratic, and the violence was generally to be found where popular sovereignty and liberty were not well established, which is in keeping with the democratic peace theory. What was not, however, in keeping with that theory was the tendency for steps toward democracy where it had not previously existed—specifically the conduct of elections—to trigger the outbreak of violence. In these circumstances, democracy—or, more properly, democratization—was associated not with peace but with war.

The Balkan wars of the 1990s, for example, broke out after Communist Yugoslavia had collapsed and its constituent parts had, for the first time, elected their own leaders. Nor was the association between voting and violence in the former Yugoslavia an exceptional case. To the contrary, by one careful analysis, when a country embarks on a transition from an undemocratic to a democratic system of government, the likelihood of war actually rises sharply.[32] That is, a country in the process of acquiring a democratic government is more likely to wage war than one whose political life includes neither elections nor liberty, which means that war is a risk that has accompanied the rise of democracy.

In the former Yugoslavia and elsewhere, war stemmed ultimately from what preceded the effort to produce democracy: the collapse of imperial government, which had the effect of opening a political Pandora's box. The end of empire has often triggered efforts to redraw sovereign borders, which in turn has led to bloodshed as some people, who had lived involuntarily but more or less peacefully in multinational states such as Yugoslavia, sought to create independent countries of their own, while others opposed them.[33] In such circumstances, however, the injection of democratic practices—or at least one of them, holding elections—has often served to aggravate rather than resolve post-imperial conflicts.

Elections have proved inflammatory because, with the competition for political power suddenly an exercise in mobilizing broad public support rather than maneuvering within a small elite group to gain it or using force to seize it, would-be leaders have had to find ways to appeal to people in large numbers.[34] One effective way of doing so is to claim to be protecting the collective interests of one group against the purportedly (or actually) malevolent schemes of others, thereby earning the allegiance of the threatened group. Enemies have their uses for ambitious and unscrupulous politicians, and countries in transition from undemocratic to democratic forms of government seem to have no shortage of such people. The appeals that politicians of this kind find useful may not create, but do have the effect of worsening, the political conflicts they seek to exploit, often to the point of helping to tip them over into war.

The tendency for the advent of competitive electoral politics to make war more likely would seem to turn the democratic peace theory upside down. Democracy, by this measure, promotes, rather than suppresses, armed conflict. This tendency would seem, further, to vindicate the traditional conviction, the one held by partisans of liberty down through the ages that lost credibility only at the end of the nineteenth century,[35] that placing power in the hands of the people will lead to disaster. It would seem, that is, to vindicate those for whom democracy had a bad reputation rather than a good name.

In the face of this challenge to it, the rescue of the democratic peace theory comes from reverting to the proper definition of democracy. It has, after all, two constituent parts, without either of which a country cannot truly be said to be democratically governed. One of those two parts, popular sovereignty, can, when first introduced, trigger war. The other, liberty, has, however, the opposite effect. While popular sovereignty can be a cause of war, liberty, when it is firmly established, serves as an antidote to armed conflict; and the pacifying effect of liberty forms the basis for another version, different from the one that Kant proposed, of the democratic peace theory.

LIBERTY AND PEACE

Whereas the principle of popular sovereignty provides a way to decide who holds power, the institutions and practices of liberty determine how those who hold power may and may not use it. The first confers political power upon the people and, according to Kant, the people will use their power to prevent war. The second establishes a pattern of conduct of their leaders, and this pattern, with its habits, procedures, and values, and the institutions that embody them, has, according to a second version of the democratic peace theory, a similar pacifying effect. It is not—or not only—the structure of the political system, according to this version, but also the norms of the political culture that inhibit democracies from fighting.[36]

The pattern of conduct to which liberty gives rise, the habits that leaders of genuine democracies adopt, and the procedures they routinely follow, dispose their countries to pursue peaceful foreign policies. This occurs because democratic leaders are inclined to conduct themselves, in carrying out foreign policies, in the same way that they conduct themselves in the domestic arena. Just as the habits and values that people acquire in taking part in a market economy carry over to the realm of politics, thereby laying the basis for democracy, so, too, the pattern of conduct that liberty impels leaders to follow within democracies carries over to the way they deal with other countries.[37] When extended to foreign policy, the habits and procedures that liberty fosters at home lead to peaceful conduct abroad.

Peaceful relations with other countries, according to this version of the democratic peace theory, are the favored and initial response—the default option—of democratic leaders because the countries they govern are democracies.[38] In dealings between two democratically governed countries, each brings this approach to bear, and they reinforce each other, making their relationship a solidly, unalterably peaceful one.[39]

Three particular features of political life where liberty is firmly established, when they are carried over to relations with other countries, make for peaceful foreign policies: the predilection for peaceful compromise that democracy encourages; the drawn-out procedures for making decisions and acting on them fostered by the commitment to limits on the power of government that is the essence of liberty; and the practice of transparency—openness—in the conduct of government, which is a necessary condition of liberty.

Liberty comes in three varieties: economic, religious, and political. Each of them places limits on what the government can do to the people it governs. Political liberty in particular gives rise to the practice of peaceful compromise that, when carried over from the domestic to the international realm, makes for a peaceful foreign policy. Political liberty includes the right to speak freely about public affairs, to assemble with other citizens and organize them freely, and to petition the government freely for political purposes. Citizens of democracies routinely make use of these rights in order to oppose the government in one way or another. The institutions and practices of liberty ensure that they are able to do so without the government's stopping them, as long as they act lawfully. Liberty, that is, prohibits the common response of undemocratic governments to active opposition: violent suppression.

Since democratic governments can neither destroy nor entirely ignore their opposition, they must deal peacefully with it and, when election results favor their opponents, yield power to them. All this makes peaceful compromise the normal form of transactions between political adversaries in democracies.[40] Conciliation is a democratic reflex.[41] Politicians in democratic countries are as powerfully conditioned to practice peaceful accommodation with their opponents as are guard dogs to bark at unknown intruders.

Their social and political conditioning inclines them to approach foreigners in the same way they do those from their own countries—peacefully.[42] They are disposed to respect the sovereign prerogatives of other countries just as they are disposed to respect the political rights of their fellow citizens. When political leaders from two democracies deal with each other in this fashion, the result, inevitably, is peace.

Relations between the United States and Great Britain for most of the nineteenth century bear out this version of the democratic peace theory. A number of contentious and important issues, the kind over which sovereign states have often gone to war, divided the two countries; indeed, they did fight each other twice, in the American War of Independence in the

1770s and in the War of 1812. Thereafter, however, despite their differences, they remained at peace. War-averse populations did not restrain them; in neither country did all adult citizens have the right to vote until the twentieth century. Their mutual restraint came at least in part from their common respect for liberty, which was well established even when universal suffrage was not, and from liberty's effect on their behavior.[43]

Liberty affects not only what governments can do but how they can do it. The rule of law, often in the form of a constitution, establishes procedures that governments must follow in order to act. These procedures typically require the assent and sometimes the active cooperation of different individuals and groups, and they often take time to fulfill. They therefore make it all but impossible for democracies to do anything quickly or on the basis of the decision of a single person, including going to war. The United States, with its system of checks and balances that divides power among three branches of the federal government, is the democracy that most fully embodies the procedural restraints that liberty imposes. The founders of the country separated power among the executive, legislative, and judicial branches at the national level, and further divided legislative authority between two houses of Congress. They also designed the second house, the Senate, to conduct its affairs in deliberate fashion in order to prevent temporary popular passions from forcing through unwise measures.

Other democracies have less elaborate and complicated governmental machinery, but in all of them, public policy must emerge from certain well-established routines, the bypassing of which is forbidden, or at least illegal. The procedural restraints that democracy imposes do not always prevent democratically governed countries from waging war, of course, as the histori-

cal record attests. The people's representatives must vote in favor of war in democracies, but when they believe their country
is in danger, or its supreme interests require the use of force,
they cast their votes accordingly. Moreover, in the United
States, the President has sometimes been able to send American armed forces into action without formal Congressional
authorization.[44]

Still, democracy by its very nature does erect obstacles to
waging war that undemocratic governments do not face. Dictators can start wars without consulting anyone. Saddam Hussein of Iraq apparently did so twice—against Iran in 1980 and
Kuwait in 1990. The Second World War in Europe began at
the whim, and on the timetable, of Adolf Hitler. Even the
most powerful democratically elected leader cannot do this.
Democracies encounter speed bumps on the road to war,
which engender caution and provide the opportunity to pause
to rethink the wisdom of such a course, and perhaps to turn
back from it. When two democracies stop on their way to a
collision, they do not collide.

Liberty promotes a third feature of democracy that underwrites a peaceful foreign policy. That feature is transparency.
The workings of a democracy, the processes by which policies
are chosen and carried out, are, with a few exceptions, open to
public view. Transparency follows from liberty because liberty
imposes limits on the power of governments, and those limits,
to be effective, must be readily observable. Liberty requires
not only that the government obey the law but also that it *be
seen* to obey it. Popular sovereignty, when it takes the form of
free elections, also requires transparency: the public cannot
pass judgment on the government, which is the purpose of
elections, unless it has a clear picture of what the government
is doing.

Transparency fosters peace among the sovereign states that practice it by creating one of the crucial underpinnings of peace (that is also a feature of democracy): trust—that is, confidence in the peaceful intentions of others.[45] A lack of such confidence poses a special danger in international relations. This is so because the international system, which sovereign states inhabit, is anarchic, with no world government to protect each from the others. In these circumstances, each country must be prepared to defend itself. It is natural, following the maxim that it is better to be safe than sorry, to suspect others of aggressive intentions and act accordingly. What seems the essence of prudence can also, however, be dangerous because of what has been termed "the security dilemma," which stems from the fact that external threats and the preparations to meet them are interrelated in unpredictable ways.[46] Thus, measures that a country undertakes for defensive purposes, such as increasing its military forces, can, despite the motives underlying them, appear threatening to others. The other countries may then respond with what they intend to be defensive measures of their own but that appear to the countries at which these measures are aimed to be a prelude to an attack.

Such an unintended dialectic of escalating mistrust, which can culminate in outright war, is called "the spiral model," and it arises from the combination of the anarchy of world politics and the difficulty of fathoming other countries' intentions. The practice of transparency makes democracies less susceptible than undemocratically governed countries to this syndrome.[47]

The worst fear to which the structure of international politics gives rise is that of a surprise attack. This danger became acute in the nuclear rivalry between the United States and the Soviet Union during the Cold War. The time required for an attack became unprecedentedly short: the intercontinental ballistic missiles of each side could strike the other's homeland thousands of miles away within minutes of being launched. At the same time, the stakes in the rivalry grew to colossal proportions: an all-out nuclear assault by either could have effectively destroyed the other's society, killing tens, even hundreds of millions of people.

The two sides took a number of steps to guard against such an attack, among them the negotiation of treaties placing limits on their respective nuclear arsenals. Having signed them, each side had to find ways to assure itself that the other was complying with the treaties' terms. The reconnaissance satellites that each deployed beginning in the 1960s were indispensable to the United States in monitoring the Soviet Union, whose Communist government kept the country closed to outsiders and conducted its affairs in secret. The Soviet side, by contrast, did not need satellites to satisfy itself about American compliance: the democratic political system of the United States made its nuclear deployments transparent.[48]

In the last years of the Cold War the two rival military blocs agreed to restrict the military maneuvers they conducted, to notify each other in advance of such maneuvers, and to ensure that the other side could fully observe the maneuvers when they took place. These agreements, like the treaties limiting nuclear armaments, were designed to engender mutual confidence that neither side was planning to attack the other. They were therefore termed "confidence-building measures."[49] Because the political procedures of democracies are transparent and thus give other countries confidence in a democracy's benign intentions (when they are benign), democracy itself acts as a confidence-building measure; and the confidence that liberty-induced transparency engenders helps to prevent armed conflict.

Democracy contributes to peace in yet another, related way. The elaborate and transparent procedures that a democracy must follow create confidence that, after it subscribes to agreements, it will keep them. Just as they are not prone to launch surprise attacks, so democracies do not suddenly abrogate commitments they have made, including commitments that form the basis for peaceful relations with others.[50]

A predilection for compromise, protracted procedures of governance, and the practice of transparency in public affairs are all properties of political systems in which liberty is well established. All three incline a country in which they are present to peaceful relations with other countries; and a country cannot be counted a genuine modern democracy unless and until liberty is well established within its borders. So while one of democracy's defining features, popular sovereignty, can make a country more bellicose than it would otherwise be, the other, liberty, has a pacifying effect.

It is better, an old saying goes, to travel hopefully than to arrive. For democracy, the reverse is true: on the road to genuine democracy, a country may veer off onto the path of war. Having arrived in the promised land of popular sovereignty through free, fair, and regular elections along with the institutions and practices associated with liberty, any country, whatever its history, tends to behave peacefully, especially toward other democracies.[51] Countries with some, but not all, of the features of genuine democracy—unconsolidated democracies, as they are sometimes called, or "illiberal" democracies that conduct free elections but lack economic and political rights—may be inclined to war: proper, full-fledged democracy—democracy without adjectives, it might be said—disposes a country to peace.

This does not mean, however, that democracy is always, everywhere, and in every way associated with peace. While the presence of popular sovereignty and liberty in a country does incline that country to peaceful relations with its neighbors, the prospect of democracy in a country with an undemocratic government can produce the opposite effect. An undemocratic regime seeking to resist the forces of democracy and maintain power at home may find the possibility, or even the fact, of war abroad to be an effective tactic for this purpose. Democracy acts as an antidote to war, but war itself is an antidote to democracy. The greater the threat to a dictatorship that it will be replaced by a democracy, the more tempted the dictator will be to resort to warlike behavior to hold on to power. This, too, counts as a risk that the rise of democracy poses. For the more democracies there are, the greater will be the global pressure to adopt democratic institutions and practices and the greater therefore will be the temptation to bellicose behavior to counteract it. This is another way in which the spread of democracy can increase the chances of war.

DEMOCRACY VERSUS PEACE

At the outset of the twenty-first century, a specter haunted dictatorships everywhere: the specter of democracy. In response, a dictator's first impulse was to resist democracy through repression. Dictatorships routinely intimidated, or jailed, or killed those of their citizens who called on them to yield to democratic governance. In most such cases, however, undemocratic regimes sought further and more solid bases for continuing in power. Repression, they calculated, was not enough. They sought to enhance their own legitimacy and to discredit, or at least reduce, the appeal of democracy in the eyes of those they ruled. A conflict with another country or group of countries can serve both purposes.[52]

To be sure, such a conflict, when it spills over into an actual shooting war, can shorten rather than prolong the life of the government that prosecutes it. Mobilizing for war can empower the very people to whom an undemocratic regime wishes to deny effective political authority—not least by arming them.[53] Even more perilous for a dictatorship is the chance of losing a war into which it leads the country it governs.[54] Military defeat does not, to say the least, increase the popularity of the regime that presides over it. To the contrary, losing a war has proven to be one of the most reliable ways for a government, especially an undemocratic government, to forfeit power. The Greek colonels' embarrassment over Cyprus in 1974, for example, and the Argentinian generals' defeat by Great Britain in the Falklands conflict of 1982, led to their respective downfalls.

Thus, while a dictatorship may find a political conflict that has the potential for war to be useful and will sometimes press that conflict to the point of actual hostilities with the adversary, it will also often be wary of allowing the conflict to take the form of a shooting war. Sometimes it is in the nether region between war and peace that dictatorships resisting the global tide of democracy feel safest. In such cases, while averting outright war, the dictatorship will also deliberately avoid resolving the political quarrel that can lead to war. It will work to keep the pot boiling while also trying to keep it from boiling over.

The use of the threat of war by a dictatorship to ward off democracy has a great deal in common with the tendency of countries to go to war when a dictatorial regime falls and an electoral competition for power takes place. In both cases, being seen as standing fast against an enemy serves, or is thought to serve, to increase the popularity and legitimacy of individuals and groups seeking to maintain, in the first case, and to obtain, in the second, political power. Would-be leaders in both cases use external enemies as weapons against their internal adversaries, thereby illustrating, when these conflicts are manufactured or avoidable or both, Samuel Johnson's observation that patriotism is the last refuge of the scoundrel.

Acting (or pretending to act) as the defender of one group against an actual or potential assault by another can be an effective tactic for mobilizing the first group. Would-be leaders employ this tactic both to avoid elections and to win them.

Historically, democracy and war have seemed almost as incompatible as liberty and popular sovereignty were once thought to be.[55] This has been so, in the first place, because war requires armies, armies require generals to lead them, and generals, from Julius Caesar to Napoleon Bonaparte to Francisco Franco to the instigators of the many military coups in Latin America and Africa in the 1950s and the 1960s, have often used the military forces under their command to seize political power. All apart from the political opportunities that war, or the prospect of it, gives to the visible, ambitious military leader—the "man on horseback"[56]—however, it can also help civilian dictators keep their grip on power, and in particular to resist demands for democracy, in three ways.

First, conflict with another country acts as a distraction from domestic matters. It can divert the anger and frustration that undemocratic governments often arouse, and that threaten their hold on power, away from the regime itself and toward the enemy.[57] At the very least, changing the ruling regime usually has a lower priority when war looms than when peace reigns.

Second, when hostility toward others dominates a country's public life, democracy can be made to seem an unaffordable luxury. Democratic politics, after all, revolve around the divisions within a society. Such divisions are inevitable everywhere, and their open expression is the essence of democracy, something that is normal, necessary, and healthy. In times of war, however, the expression of divisions, and competition among different interests and points of view, can cause, or be thought to cause, weakness in the face of the enemy. Normal democratic practices can seem to risk defeat and so must be suspended—to the benefit of those who oppose democracy, above all undemocratic rulers. Moreover, the conduct of war invariably expands the power of the government that is waging it, and so contradicts the central thrust of democracy, which is to limit that power.

Third, if war can discredit democracy, it can also fortify dictatorship by imbuing dictators with a political legitimacy they would not otherwise possess. When the political context changes, the public perception of a political practice can change with it. Thus, a dictator who, in peacetime, is regarded by those he governs as a repressive tyrant, can become in their eyes, in time of war, without changing his pattern of political conduct or yielding any of his power, a necessarily stern and even heroic father figure who is protecting them from foreign aggression. Instead of hoarding power for his personal benefit, a dictator can appear, when war is imminent or has begun, to be wielding it for the benefit of the entire political community.

In these three ways, war can serve the interests of rulers lacking other, and especially democratic, sources of support. Recognizing this, governments have sometimes deliberately courted war, or at least engaged in political conflicts with the potential for leading to war. By one account, World War I had its origins in a concerted effort by the old, hereditary elite that dominated the politics of the mightiest states of Europe to resist yielding their power to the public as a whole. In 1914, by this account, they sought to use quarrels with other countries to arouse nationalist passions, and then to capitalize on those passions to consolidate their rule.[58] War, or at least the possibility of it, became, according to this interpretation, "an instrument of domestic politics." Their domestic struggles made the aristocratic governments of Europe willing "to launch or accept external conflict despite enormous hazards."[59]

The origins of World War I were complicated and involved more than deliberate attempts by the belligerent governments to enhance their legitimacy and divert popular energies from the struggle for wider democracy.[60] Domestic considerations of this sort certainly did have some influence, however, on the policies of the power that started the war: imperial Germany. Germany had a hybrid form of government, with a popularly elected legislature sharing power with a hereditary monarch. The monarch and his officials were wary of the democratic challenge to their authority, which affected the policies on which they decided, including their decision to build a high-seas fleet. This alarmed Great Britain because the British depended on their naval supremacy to safeguard their home islands and to control their overseas empire.[61] The policy of fleet-building, which aggravated the Anglo-German antagonism that burst into war in 1914, stemmed partly from the imperial German government's calculation that it would arouse patriotic emotions in the German populace and rally support for the German monarch.[62]

The First World War triggered the Russian Revolution, and the government that seized power in 1917 and held it for more than seven decades thereafter made use of what it designated as foreign dangers to keep political power concentrated in the hands of the Communist Party. While it had other rationales for the extreme form of dictatorship that it imposed—it claimed to possess a superior insight into the laws of history and society that made it uniquely qualified to rule—the Communist Party of the Soviet Union also consistently portrayed the vast multinational empire that it governed as being locked in a mortal struggle with the non-communist world, a perpetual state of war that justified the suppression of liberty and the denial to the public of the right to choose the government.[63]

Even after communism collapsed and a more open political system took its place, the habit of exploiting war to consolidate power persisted. The first two presidents of post-Soviet Russia, Boris Yeltsin and Vladimir Putin, used the central government's conflict with rebels in the southern, largely Muslim, province of Chechnya for this purpose.[64]

The prospect of armed conflict played a similar role in the politics of the other giant Communist power of the twentieth century, the People's Republic of China. In the 1980s and 1990s, the Chinese government discarded most of the Marxist-Leninist ideology on which the Communist regime's founding leader, Mao Zedong, had based his assertion of its right to rule. In economic terms, in fact, China adopted most of the institutions and practices of communism's great rival, capitalism. Needing another basis for their monopoly of political power, China's leaders increasingly relied on their claim to rule the offshore island of Taiwan, which maintained effective, if not formal, independence, and had not in fact been governed from the mainland since the nineteenth century. Beijing's claim on Taiwan played to the nationalist sentiments of the mainland Chinese public and enjoyed wider popularity than any feature of Communist ideology.[65] The regime therefore made this claim central to its foreign policy, warning of the danger that Taiwan would formally declare independence and making preparations to attack the island in such an event. The effect of its stance on Taiwan was to make the Communist government more popular (or at least less unpopular) than it would otherwise have been.

While the use of the threat of war to suppress democracy remained a part of the politics of Russia and China in the twenty-first century, the place where the tendency of the fact, or the prospect, of armed conflict to suppress pressure for free and fair elections and the protection of liberty was most widely and deliberately exploited, and where it had the greatest impact on the character of the regimes in power, was the Middle East.

In the first decade of the twenty-first century, the Arab countries and Iran all had governments that were, in varying degrees, politically oppressive and economically incompetent.[66] None was freely elected, and none accorded full protection to political, economic, or religious liberty. All claimed, in one way or another, to be protecting the societies they governed from threats from beyond their borders. Upon inspection, however, these claims could be seen as a tactic for diverting public attention from their own failures and preserving their monopolies of power.[67]

The threat that they said was endangering their national sovereignties and local ways of life came from the West in general and the United States and Israel in particular.[68] These two countries, Middle Eastern governments told those they governed, aspired to control the politics, exploit the economic resources, change the cultures, and suppress the dominant religion of the region.[69] Vigilance and unity were therefore required of the Arabs and Iranians in order to foil these insidious dangers.[70]

The governments of the Middle East purveyed these claims through a steady diet of grievance and alarm broadcast on, and printed in, the state-controlled electronic and print media, which permitted no dissenting views on the subject (nor the public advocacy of more democratic politics), and through their dissemination by religious spokesmen who enjoyed official tolerance and often the government's sponsorship and patronage.[71]

The picture of the world that the authoritarian governments of the Middle East were at pains to present did not correspond to reality.[72] It was plain, moreover, that those governments knew full well that this was so and that their relentless propagation of a sense of siege and assault was an exercise in deceit and hypocrisy, undertaken for the familiar purpose of securing their hold on power.[73] For the same governments that allowed, indeed encouraged, the demonization of the United States in the public discourse that they controlled simultaneously accepted billions of dollars in American economic assistance, or American military protection, or both.[74]

Particularly venomous anti-American outpourings regularly emanated from Egypt and Saudi Arabia, for example. Yet the governments of both countries depended heavily on the United States. Egypt received an annual $2 billion stipend from American taxpayers. The American military stood ready to defend Saudi Arabia, and in particular its theocratic regime dominated by a single tribe, against external enemies. The campaign that the United States led to evict Iraqi troops from Kuwait had as one of its principal aims the defense of the Saudi regime.[75]

The Arab and Iranian barrage of abuse aimed at Israel surpassed their hostile portrayals of the United States in poisonous nastiness, and contained a generous dose of religious bigotry.[76] In this case as well, however, behind the political vi-

tuperation and blatant anti-Semitism lay the calculation that
hostility to Israel served the interests of the rulers of these
countries. Here, too, their actual practices diverged from their
rhetoric. The governments of some Arab countries, such as
Egypt, found it advantageous to maintain formal diplomatic
ties with Israel, even while promoting popular hatred of it.[77]
Others, the Saudi regime among them, refused to have such
relations but, despite the vicious rhetoric that they condoned,
some of it calling for the destruction of Israel and the massacre
of its inhabitants, took no steps to put their professed principles into practice through military action.

Occasionally, the rhetoric of the Arab dictatorships indirectly and unintentionally revealed the basis for their hostility
to Israel. To justify its refusal to open the political system to
wider popular participation, the Syrian government asserted
that Syria could not indulge in the luxury of democracy as long
as its confrontation with Israel persisted—a confrontation that,
not coincidentally, it showed no sign of seeking to end.[78]

To be sure, the Arab governments had an official rationale
for their ongoing hostility to Israel. It was in the service, they
said, of their commitment to defend the interests of the
Palestinians—the Arabs who lived between the 1967 borders
of Israel and the Jordan River and in the Gaza Strip, many of
whom had fled from within what became Israel after that
country's 1948 War of Independence, and who had come under Israeli rule after the Six-Day War of 1967. The political
status of the Palestinians did present a genuine problem since
they did not want to be ruled by Israel, and Israelis did not
wish to grant them full citizenship;[79] but the Arab governments' professed concern about it, and for their well-being,
was as cynical and hypocritical as their strenuously proclaimed
opposition to the United States and Israel.

Like that opposition, the Arab regimes' announced devotion to the cause of the Palestinians was better understood as a pretext for sustaining a conflict that they found convenient because it bolstered their own power. It could be seen as a pretext, in the first place, because the Arab governments were themselves responsible for the Palestinians' plight, having initiated the 1948 and 1967 wars that had, on the first occasion, made some of them refugees and, on the second, brought them under Israeli occupation.

The Arab regimes' professed concern for the Palestinians was plainly a pretext for other aims, in the second place, because these regimes had never shown the slightest concern for the well-being of the people on behalf of whom they claimed to be persisting in the conflict with Israel. They had attacked Israel in 1948 for their own reasons, not for the sake of the Arabs living within its borders.[80] For the most part, with the honorable exception of the kingdom of Jordan, they refused to grant citizenship to the Palestinians resident in their own countries. Indeed, in the wake of the 1991 war to evict Iraq from Kuwait, in which the Palestinian movement, led by Yasir Arafat, had supported Saddam Hussein, the Saudi and Kuwaiti governments expelled the Palestinians living in their countries in retaliation. For decades, moreover, the various Arab governments conspired, maneuvered, and competed to control the Palestinian movement and use it for their own purposes.[81]

The professed Arab concern could be seen as a pretext for yet a third reason: when Israel offered, in 2000, to settle the conflict on terms that the international community, with the general assent of the Arab world, had said were fair—the creation of a Palestinian state on almost all of the territory Israel had captured in the Arab-initiated 1967 war—the Arab countries refused to bring pressure on the Palestinians, or even encourage Yasir

Arafat to accept them. Arafat proceeded to reject the terms, to make no counteroffer, and to start a new round of violence aimed principally at Israeli civilians.[82] On that occasion, by what they failed to say and do, the Arab regimes demonstrated that they preferred continuing the Arab-Israeli conflict, with all the costs that this imposed on the Palestinians, to ending it.[83]

For all of their fearsome rhetorical hostility to Israel, the Arab governments took care, after 1973, not to launch direct attacks against it. Because Israel had managed to build formidable armed forces and the Arab states had not, a war against Israel carried a high risk of defeat; and military defeat has not, historically, contributed to the achievement of the goal that the Arab regimes used the conflict with Israel to pursue: the retention of power. Still, the kind of anti-American and anti-Israeli rhetoric with which Arab governments saw to it that their publics were saturated did serve to inspire attacks on the United States and Israel. These took place, however, on a smaller scale than formal interstate conflict. They were carried out by loosely organized groups of individuals rather than government-sponsored armies, and they aimed not to capture territory but to demoralize the societies that were their targets. The attacks, that is, came in the form of terrorism; and as terrorism became a major international problem in the first decade of the twenty-first century, it joined war as a social pathology for which, it was proposed, democracy could serve as an antidote.

DEMOCRACY AND TERRORISM

The attacks on the World Trade Center in New York City and the Pentagon in Washington, D.C., on September 11, 2001, which killed almost three thousand people, put terrorism at the top of the world's political and military agenda. They did so because the targeted country, the United States, was so powerful and important that its preoccupations came to concern other countries as well. They did so as well because they raised the possibility that people willing to commit suicide in launching their terrorist assaults, as the perpetrators of the September 11 attacks had been,[84] would gain possession of weapons of mass destruction and with them kill hundreds of thousands, conceivably even millions of civilians.[85]

In response to the attacks, the American government declared war against terrorism. The declaration denoted the seriousness with which the United States took the problem of suicide terrorism; and American armed forces did wage wars that deposed the radical, dictatorial, and murderous regimes of two countries, Afghanistan and Iraq.

Applied to the problem of terrorism, however, the term "war" left obscure as much as it illuminated. It did not designate the individuals and groups that were the objects of the war. Terrorism is merely a tactic, and proclaiming a war against it, it was noted, was no more helpful in defining the enemy than it would have been to call World War II a war against tanks.[86] Terrorism involves the intermittent use of force against civilians by groups other than the governments of sovereign states. As a form of violence, it falls between war and criminal behavior. It takes place less continuously and on a smaller scale than formal warfare; but unlike crime, terrorism has political goals that go beyond the aims that usually motivates criminal activity.

Terrorists aspire to achieve their political aims by producing three effects on their target populations. One is to gain publicity for their cause: terrorism is "propaganda by deed."[87] A second goal is polarization. Terrorists often seek to provoke governments into taking harsh, repressive measures that will win sympathy for them among people previously hostile or indifferent to their goals. The third terrorist aim is to inflict pain on those who oppose them. This strategy parallels that of the practitioners of guerrilla warfare. Neither terrorists nor guerrillas have the power to defeat their adversaries militarily, but both hope to demoralize them by raising the costs of the policies and positions under attack to the point that the stronger foe decides not to defend them.

The assaults of September 11 had all three aims: to win attention and sympathy throughout the Muslim world; to prompt a reaction by the United States and other governments that would increase support for the terrorists' aims; and to compel the United States to end its military presence in the Arabian peninsula.[88]

Terrorism is not new. It dates at least to the age of the Roman Empire and has appeared in many different places at different periods of history and been employed on behalf of a variety of ideologies and creeds.[89] While perhaps not as old or as common as war itself, terrorism certainly qualifies as a familiar, recurrent feature of political life. Like war, terrorism was believed in some quarters, in the initial decade of the twenty-first century, to be susceptible to abolition through the spread of democracy.

The United States, in fact, launched the twenty-first-century version of its recurrent campaign to promote democracy beyond its borders, in the wake of the September 11 attacks, with the explicit aim of removing, through democratic political change, the conditions that create terrorism.[90] In the words of Natan Sharansky, once a political prisoner in the Soviet Union for his Zionist convictions and after his release a cabinet member in the government of Israel, who became a staunch proponent of the virtues of democracy and whose book on the subject influenced American President George W. Bush, "[T]he breeding ground for terror is tyranny."[91]

Behind the assertion that democracy prevents terrorism lay the same kind of straightforward logic that underpinned Kant's conviction that democracies will be reluctant to fight wars: the absence of democracy, and the repression that this involves, inspires the anger and resentment that fuel terrorism. Under undemocratic rule, attacks on civilians become an attractive way to express opposition to the regime and its policies. Indeed, they are the only way to do so because the government blocks other, peaceful, legal channels of expression. The replacement of dictatorship with democracy opens these channels, thereby eliminating the need for terrorism to publicize and win support for dissenting ideas and programs.[92]

This logic applies to some places in which, and from which, terrorism emerged in the twenty-first century, notably the Arab Middle East, where no free elections were held or political, economic, or religious rights protected. In some parts of the world, moreover, where one group was governed against its will by another, terrorist attacks on the wielders of power could be seen as expressing the demand for popular sovereignty. Terrorism, that is, could be said, in such circumstances, to serve as the vehicle for the ubiquitous and most powerful modern political sentiment: nationalism.[93]

In some circumstances, it therefore follows, the introduction of democracy has the potential to reduce the level of terrorist activity by eliminating terrorism's principal causes. Democracy does not, however, offer a universal and unfailing solution to the problem of terrorism. Indeed, the historical record demonstrates that democracy can make terrorist acts easier to commit than they would otherwise be.

Terrorism emerged in democratic Western Europe in the 1960s and 1970s. The radical Marxist Baader-Meinhof group in West Germany and the Red Brigades in Italy carried out kidnappings and assassinations. Subsequently, in 2005, young Muslim men who had been born, raised, and educated in England set off explosions that killed passengers on buses and in the subway in London. These terrorist groups were incubated in full-fledged democracies. Free and fair elections, moreover, can bring to power groups committed to terrorism. This occurred in 2006 in the Palestinian territories when Hamas, a political organization publicly dedicated to a terrorist campaign against Israel, gained a majority of seats in the Palestinian parliament.

Terrorism is possible in societies that operate according to the rules of democracy because the motives that animate terrorists are at least partly personal in nature: anger rooted in childhood experiences that gets directed at a political target, for instance, or the desire for notoriety, or a suicidal impulse manipulated by someone with a political agenda. Such motives are as likely to be present in democratically as in undemocratically governed countries.[94] Psychopathology exists everywhere.

In fact, living in a democracy has the potential to drive individuals or groups to terrorist acts when, and if, it becomes clear, through the opportunities for free expression and fair political competition, that their political goals command little support. They may then resort to terrorism not because their ideas are suppressed but because they are unpopular. The Western European terrorists knew that they would never achieve their radical aims by democratic means. Their acts of violence were designed to attract far more attention to their goals than they would otherwise have received, and to goad the authorities into acts of political repression that would, they fantasized, enhance public support for those goals.

The Islamist terrorists, including those who attacked New York and Washington, D.C., did in fact attract some sympathy throughout the Muslim world. Where the political principles that they favored, which included compulsory adherence to a strict interpretation of Islamic law, served as the basis for governance, however—in Iran, Afghanistan, and Saudi Arabia— the governments enforcing these principles proved unpopular. Furthermore, the goal that some Islamic terrorists professed, of uniting all Muslims in a single political unit, thereby recreating the caliphate of the faith's early days, hardly commended itself to the governments of the various Muslim-majority countries that would be subsumed in it, and had little evident appeal to the peoples of these countries. It could therefore not be said of the Islamic terrorists, any more than it could be said of the Marxist terrorists of Europe, that they were acting on behalf of the majority to bring about political changes that would have been enacted peacefully had the affected populations had the democratic opportunity to do so.[95]

If democracy does not necessarily eliminate the desire to commit acts of terrorism, finally, it can make the commission of such acts easier than in dictatorships. Terrorists have more space to operate in democracies than in dictatorships because in democracies everyone has more space to operate. Democracy, after all, by definition constrains the power of government, including the power to monitor, control, and incarcerate terrorists.[96] Historically, including in the twenty-first century, terrorism has been more common in open than in closed societies.[97] Preventing terrorism is a problem of policing, which can more effectively be carried out by a police state than by a democracy.

While democracy cannot hope to eliminate terrorism altogether—and insofar as terrorism springs from timeless features of the human psyche, no form of government can reasonably aspire to do so—it can reduce the level of terrorist violence in two important ways. First, democracy requires democrats. A political system featuring a freely elected government in which liberty flourishes cannot function unless experience in manning the necessary institutions and a commitment to its central values are widely shared among the people it governs. Such people will not practice, or even countenance, terrorism. Democrats eschew violence in the conduct of public affairs. The arbitrary murders in which twenty-first-century terrorists specialize, which violate the rights of their victims in as egregious a manner as can be imagined, are particularly repugnant to anyone committed to democratic politics.

Second, precisely because terrorist activity is so sharply at odds with democratic norms, governments chosen democratically, by democrats, to govern in democratic fashion will not support terrorists or terrorism. While democratic governments labor under certain democratically imposed handicaps in fighting terrorism, such governments do not ally themselves with those seeking, for their own political reasons, to inflict gratuitous harm on civilians. Terrorists may operate within the borders of democratic countries, but they do so in opposition to the wishes and efforts of those countries' governments.

Undemocratic governments, by contrast, have actively supported terrorism by recruiting, training, equipping, and sheltering terrorists.[98] The Communist regimes of Eastern Europe and the Soviet Union provided all of these services to terrorist groups. With the collapse of these regimes, the number of states deliberately promoting terrorist activities decreased. In the twenty-first century, however, a number of governments, notably those of Iran and Syria, continued to provide active support for terrorism.[99] The removal of such regimes, and their replacement with genuinely democratic governments, would consequently strike a significant blow against terrorism.

The relationship between democracy and terrorism, in sum, closely resembles the relationship between democracy and terrorism's more destructive sibling: war. On the whole, the spread of democracy reduces, although it probably cannot eliminate, both forms of organized violence.[100] If the world was a more peaceful place at the outset of the twenty-first century than it had been for most of the twentieth, with fewer wars, if not necessarily less terrorism, the rise of democracy counted as one cause—but not the only one.

In the nineteenth and especially the twentieth centuries, the soaring costs of war and the growing economic benefits of commerce uninterrupted by warfare heightened the aversion to armed conflict in the wealthiest and least bellicose countries. Moreover, the adoption of one of democracy's two component parts, popular sovereignty, can make political communities more rather than less warlike. It is only with the addition of democracy's other defining feature, liberty, that this form of government regularly and reliably acts as a force for peace. And while the fact of democracy inclines a country toward peace, the prospect of democracy, which the rulers of undemocratic regimes rightly see as a threat to their power, can encourage belligerent policies as tactics for resisting the introduction of political liberty and free elections.

The replacement of the world's dictatorships with democratic governments therefore does not guarantee the end of all armed conflict, let alone of all terrorism. On balance, however, and with the appropriate caveats, the progress of democracy has made the world a more peaceful place. Its association with peace supplies a reason for democracy's good name in addition to the intrinsic value of popular sovereignty and liberty, and an additional reason to hope for the spread of democracy. It offers, in fact, a reason for peace-loving countries to work actively to foster its spread.

Democracy's twenty-first-century progress therefore counts as a matter of geopolitical significance, and two questions concerning that progress have particular importance: Which countries governed undemocratically at the outset of the new millennium, especially those whose geopolitical weight made their forms of government a matter of direct interest to others, could be expected to convert to democratic governance, and at what pace? And what, if anything, could the friends of democracy, which included all the countries that already had democratic political systems, above all the most powerful of them, the United States, do to hasten and widen that process?

5

THE FUTURE OF DEMOCRACY

"As the twentieth century ended, there were around 120 democracies in the world—and I can assure you more are on the way."

—GEORGE W. BUSH, 2003[1]

DEMOCRACY PROMOTION

The attacks on New York City and Washington, D.C., of September 11, 2001, not only placed terrorism at the top of the global political agenda, they also caused the United States, the world's most powerful and influential country, to launch a campaign to spread democracy, especially to the Arab Middle East. The American government identified terrorism as a major threat to the United States and its international interests, one that arose from social, economic, and political conditions fostered by undemocratic government. Just as the eradication of malaria requires draining the swamps that harbor the mosquitoes that carry the disease, so abolishing or at least controlling terrorism, American officials reasoned, requires ending the conditions that breed terrorists. That meant replacing dictatorships with democracies.

The 2001 attacks also triggered invasions, led by the United States, of two predominantly Muslim countries, Afghanistan and Iraq, whose governments had sponsored anti-American terrorism—in the Afghan case those very attacks. Having deposed the undemocratic governments of each—the radical Islamic Taliban regime in the first instance, the brutal secular dictatorship of Saddam Hussein in the second—the United States and its allies undertook to replace them with democracies. The alternative course—installing, or permitting the assumption of power by, another dictator—seemed undesirable because the new autocrat might prove as hostile to the West as the previous regime, and might even resume the policies that had prompted the invasions in the first place. Replacing one dictator with another, even if friendly to the West, also seemed unnecessary because democracy had spread so far in the last three decades of the twentieth century that it could surely take root, American officials believed, even in two countries with no history of democratic governance.

Moreover, as the cost, in taxpayers' money and soldiers' lives, of pacifying Afghanistan and Iraq increased, the American government had to justify these expenses and sacrifices to the American public. The installation of democracy was a goal that had—or was thought to have—wide enough appeal to sustain public support.

As a sign of the new emphasis in his administration's foreign policy, George W. Bush devoted his second inaugural address to extolling the value of democracy and affirming the American commitment to fostering it around the world. The National Security Strategy issued by the White House in 2006 made the spread of democracy a central aim of American foreign policy.[2] The American government launched a special program for bringing liberty and representative government

to the region from which the September 11 terrorists had
come: the Greater Middle East Initiative.[3]

President Bush followed in the footsteps of Woodrow Wilson and Ronald Reagan in making the cultivation of democracy beyond the nation's borders central to American foreign
policy.[4] Nor were Bush, Wilson, and Reagan the only American chief executives to assert a national commitment to
spreading liberty and popular government beyond North
America. Virtually every president affirmed that commitment
in some form. Democracy, and democracy-promotion, are en-
coded in the country's political genes.

Despite the long-standing and deeply felt commitment of
the United States to promoting democracy, and despite the
country's enormous power, the post-September 11 campaign
was scarcely guaranteed to achieve success. It faced formidable
obstacles in the first decade of the twenty-first century, obstacles that had, as it happened, been present in the twentieth
century as well.

One such obstacle was ambivalence on the part of the
American government. Where some countries were concerned, the promotion of democracy conflicted with other
American goals. This had been the case during the Cold War,
when the American government made common cause with
undemocratic, but anti-communist, "friendly tyrants."[5] While
orthodox communism had disappeared from most of the
planet in the post–Cold War era, the United States continued
to have foreign policy goals the pursuit of which provided
powerful incentives for cooperation with governments that rejected the principles of democracy.

One was the campaign against terrorism, which made good
relations with the undemocratic governments in which terrorist cells were or might be active seem imperative. Pakistan was

perhaps the best example.[6] The large American and global appetite for petroleum ruled out a forceful effort to change the methods of governance in oil-exporting countries. The rulers of Saudi Arabia, the al-Saud tribe, for instance, disdained democratic procedures but had a record of reliability in providing access to the enormous reserves of oil located within their domain. Retaining access to oil had a higher priority for the United States than fostering democracy on the Arabian peninsula.[7] American expressions of unhappiness with the autocratic methods of the Russian and Chinese governments, although not nonexistent, were tempered by the need for assistance from both these governments in keeping nuclear weapons out of the hands of the even less democratic and, in American eyes, internationally more dangerous governments of North Korea and Iran.[8]

Even in the absence of goals that competed with the promotion of democracy, the United States was not going to be able, except in rare cases, to exert maximal pressure on other countries in favor of liberty and representative government. The way for one country to exert maximal pressure for democracy, or anything else, on another is to occupy that country. This is how the British brought elements of democracy to India.

By the twenty-first century, however, the age of empire had ended. Nowhere were people eager, or even willing, to be ruled by foreigners. Nor was the American public favorably disposed to protracted occupations of other countries, especially if the American presence met with active opposition. Even in those few countries where the United States, often in concert with allies, did maintain an occupation and where it sought to install democratic institutions and instill democratic values, countries such as Afghanistan and Iraq, liberty and popular sovereignty did not flourish. In such circumstances, democracy-promotion founders on a contradiction: occupation is incompatible with one of democracy's two principal components, self-government. Moreover, in the post-imperial era, occupation by foreigners, no matter how well-intentioned, arouses resentment of and resistance to whatever the occupier seeks to do, including implanting democracy.

The greatest obstacle to the installation of democracy by one country on the territory of another, however, is not the contradiction inherent in the enterprise or the resistance of those to whom the occupiers are attempting to bring the blessings of liberty. It is the inherent difficulty of the task, even when it meets no resistance at all. This is the central truth of democracy-promotion, even—indeed, especially—in an era in which the tides of global politics run so strongly in favor of this form of government.

The reason is that while democracy involves free elections, which can be readily staged, it also, and just as fundamentally, includes liberty, which cannot be produced in a brief period of time. Popular sovereignty is relatively easy; liberty is difficult. Liberty is difficult to create and sustain because it is embodied in institutions, which operate through habits and skills and are supported by values. All take time to develop,[9] and they must develop independently and domestically; they cannot be imported ready-made. For a country to be a democracy the people of that country must acquire the habit of tolerance, for example, and the skills to manage an effective legal system. They can neither import nor outsource these things.

The countries in which the United States had the greatest success in fostering democracy, Germany and Japan after World War II, demonstrate just how difficult a project this is.[10] The effort to install liberty and popular sovereignty benefited in both cases from favorable conditions that are rare in the democracy-free zones of the twenty-first century.[11] Both Germany and Japan had had some previous experience with elements of democracy. Both had well-established market economies. Both had suffered crushing military defeats that had discredited the undemocratic governments that had led them to war. Both were ethnically homogeneous. Both willingly played host for decades to American armed forces, which served as a check on undemocratic political tendencies. The American presence proved acceptable because its mission changed from occupying the defeated powers to defending them against the Communist countries that threatened them.

Because the circumstances in which democracy came to Germany and Japan were so unusual, the general prospects for promoting liberty and representative government directly, from without, are not as promising as the evidence from those two cases would seem to suggest. In fact, the prospects for direct democracy-promotion in almost any country in which the United States, alone or in concert with others, is likely to take up the task—at least the prospects for doing so quickly and easily—are poor.[12]

The rhetoric surrounding democracy-promotion sometimes gives the impression that the exercise is akin to architecture, with democracy being something that can be designed and built according to a predetermined blueprint if sufficient power and political will are available. In fact, the creation of a democracy has more in common with horticulture,[13] requiring collaboration with impersonal forces that cannot readily be controlled. Like plants and flowers, moreover, democracy tends to flourish where conditions are favorable, as they were in Germany and Japan after World War II. In this sense the term "democracy-promotion" incorporates a misleading assertion, in the deceptive, and grammatically dubious, manner of a phrase used by American politicians to describe something they either claim to have done or promise to do while in office: "growing the economy."

Economic growth in market economies emerges from millions of private initiatives, not from what governments do. Similarly, genuine democracy comes about through the development, over years and even decades, of the skills, habits, and values that the practice of liberty requires. Still, the claims implied in the terms "democracy-promotion" and "growing the economy" are not entirely false. The actions of a government do affect the performance of an economy, and the outside world does affect the prospects for democracy within individual countries.

Governments provide security and order, the necessary framework for a successful economy. Governments also supply "public goods," such as roads, schools, and law enforcement, that contribute to economic growth but that the private sector ordinarily does not provide. And governments can, by implementing the appropriate fiscal and monetary policies, affect a country's overall level of economic output.

Similarly, one country can improve the chances for democracy in another by removing a major obstacle to it, a dictatorial government determined to thwart liberty and free elections, as the United States did in Afghanistan and Iraq. Financial and technical support for those living in undemocratic countries who wish to introduce democratic practices, which the United States has offered in every part of the world, can also enhance the prospects for democracy, even if only marginally.[14] The most important contributions that one country can make to the creation of democracy in another, however, and that established democracies have made to the promotion of democracy around the world, are indirect. Unlike direct, deliberate policies of democracy-promotion, these indirect contributions had a great deal to do with the rise of democracy around the world in the last quarter of the twentieth century.

In the twenty-first century, indirect democracy-promotion comes in two varieties. One of them, as it happens, has a prominent place in American history. The other has been employed by America's post-1945 democratic allies in Western Europe through the economic and political associations they formed after World War II.

In the eighteenth and nineteenth centuries, just as in the twentieth and twenty-first centuries, the United States aspired to spread its form of government to other countries. In the earlier period, however, it lacked the military and economic resources necessary for direct intervention in the affairs of others. It therefore counted on the force of the American example to impress the peoples of the rest of the world with the advantages of liberty and self-government, and thus persuade them to adopt democratic governance. Americans relied on a policy of "exemplarism" to make the world over in their image.[15]

The democratic example became increasingly potent as the world's two earliest and most important democracies, the United States and Great Britain, became increasingly powerful and prosperous, and more potent still as more and more countries, during the course of the twentieth century, adopted democratic political institutions and practices. The militarily formidable, economically prosperous, and socially cohesive community of democracies that expanded from its Anglo-American core after 1945 offered the most persuasive advertisement imaginable for liberty and representative government, one that transformed the world's political preferences, particularly in the twentieth century's last three decades.

Societies, like individuals, are subject to greater influence from what they notice than from what they are told. They are more inclined to do what they decide, on their own, serves their interests than what others try to compel them to do. For this reason, democratic exemplarism, which began as the declared policy of a series of scattered, thinly populated communities of English-speakers on the eastern seaboard of North America at the end of the eighteenth century, had become, 200 years later, the most powerful political force in the world.[16]

In the second half of the twentieth century the countries of Western Europe reinforced the democratic example with an attractive incentive for other Europeans, at least, to conduct their politics in democratic fashion. They offered membership in their economic association—founded as the European Economic Community, renamed the European Community (EC), and ultimately called the European Union (EU)—but only to fellow democracies.[17] Membership in the EU provided a route to democracy different from both the pure exemplarism of nineteenth-century American foreign policy and the direct intervention the United States occasionally practiced in the twentieth and twenty-first: it promoted democracy through positive incentives. The chief incentive was economic. Membership virtually guaranteed that the country in question would become richer, for with it came access to the markets of some of the wealthiest countries in the world as well as a certain amount of direct financial assistance dispensed from Brussels, the EU's administrative center.[18] In the 1970s and 1980s, and again in the 1990s and the first years of the twenty-first century, a series of countries, first in the southern and then in the eastern part of Europe, discarded dictatorial political systems, equipped themselves with democratic institutions, and joined first the EC and then the EU.[19]

As the twenty-first century began, EU membership was not available to countries outside Europe, and perhaps not even to some countries—Turkey and Ukraine being the most prominent examples—that considered themselves fully European and therefore eligible to join. The excluded and undemocratic countries were, however, subject to an enticement comparable to EU membership that drew them toward democracy: full participation in the international economy.

By the turn of the new millennium the desire for material betterment had become all but universal, and this was what participation in the international economy offered. By taking part in the global system of cross-border trade and receiving capital from abroad, a country could become richer and thus more powerful, and its citizens could hope to enjoy a rising standard of living. The desire to take part in the international economy and to belong to its principal associations, in particular the World Trade Organization (WTO), therefore became virtually universal.[20]

Membership of this kind, unlike membership in the EU, did not require a democratic government, and many undemocratically governed countries did in fact belong to the WTO. But admission to these international organizations, and, beyond that formal status, the capacity to take full advantage of integration into the global division of labor and international capital flows, does require the institutions and practices of a market economy. After having installed and made extensive use of these, of course, a country has taken a long step toward political democracy. Because the operation of a market economy cultivates some of the skills, habits, and values that are central to the conduct of democratic politics, the spread of the free-market economic system counts, along with the force of the democratic example, as one of the two principal causes of the remarkable twentieth-century emergence of democracy as the world's dominant form of government.[21]

The success of the democracies and the lure of the international economy affected, in the initial decade of the twenty-first century, every country in the world that did not practice democratic politics. Together, these two trends generated the global political equivalent of the force of gravity, drawing all sovereign states toward a common political destination: democracy. For the future of international politics and economics, and for the future of democracy itself, their combined impact on three countries or groups of countries will have particular importance: Russia, China, and the Arab world.

All carry considerable political and economic weight both in their home regions and in the world at large. Not only the foreign policies they adopt but also how they are governed will have consequences far beyond their borders. In the middle of the first decade of the twenty-first century, none of them—not Russia, China, or any of the Arab countries—had a genuinely democratic government.[22]

None of the governments tried to evade the global gravitational force pulling toward democracy by isolating their countries from the rest of the world, as did, for example, the dictators who ruled North Korea and Burma. The undemocratic governments of Russia, China, and the Arab world all did actively seek, however, to resist that force. The task of resistance occupied a prominent place on the political agenda of each of them. All, as it happened, could draw on resources of various kinds to mount such resistance: size, wealth, and historical experiences and cultural features that reinforced undemocratic rule. All of these countries stood as holdouts against the great global political trend of the last part of the twentieth century. They were islands in the surging twenty-first-century stream of democracy, under constant pressure from a powerful current but not necessarily fated to be swept into it.

The political histories of Russia, China, and the Arab world in the first decade of the twenty-first century and probably beyond were certain to include a clash between the forces of democracy and the rulers' efforts to keep power in their own hands. In none of these countries was the outcome of that clash predetermined. If it is not possible to know whether Russia, China, or the countries of the Arab world will become genuine democracies, however, it is possible to identify the social and political forces pressing for and against democratic governance in each case. And while it cannot be known in advance whether these countries will make the transition from dictatorship to democracy, it is possible to offer educated guesses about how such a transition, if it should take place, will come about.

Democracy in Russia

Russia at the beginning of the twenty-first century was a country that had experienced a great fall in power and status, one of the steepest on record. With the collapse of the Soviet Union, of which it had formed the core for seventy-five years, it had ceased to be, with the United States, one of the two colossi—"superpowers"—bestriding the international system. It had ceased, as well, to function as an alternative model of political and economic organization to democracy and free markets: the communist system had been thoroughly discredited. With the independence of the fourteen non-Russian republics of the

Soviet Union, the country had lost half its population and almost a quarter of its territory.

Yet post-Soviet Russia remained an important country, and its domestic political arrangements therefore a consequential feature of international politics. Despite the territorial amputations it had suffered, its borders encompassed more of the planet than any other sovereign state. Its educated population and its generous endowment of natural resources, especially its large reserves of fossil fuels, made it potentially very wealthy. The location of its vast landmass, bordering on both Europe and East Asia with close proximity to the Middle East, meant that Russia's future would affect some of the most important regions of the planet. Its possession of one of the world's two largest collections of nuclear weapons enhanced its significance for all other countries.

Russia's adoption of genuine democracy, should that come to pass, would have a particularly powerful resonance precisely because the state of which Russia had been a part for most of the twentieth century had functioned as the adversary and the antithesis of democratic government. Russian democracy would give the world as dramatic an example of political conversion as had Germany's and Japan's political trajectories after World War II. Such a development would testify to the continuing vitality into the twenty-first century of the wave of democracy-creation that had gathered momentum in the twentieth. It would add luster to democracy's already good name.

The collapse of the Soviet Union triggered three developments that augured favorably for democracy's prospects in post-Soviet Russia. Because the Soviet Union had been a multinational empire its demise meant that Russia ceased to be an imperial power, which eliminated the impulse to restrict the liberties of Russians for fear of having to grant these same liberties to non-Russians, leading to the loss of imperial control over them. Post-Soviet Russia also abandoned the communist command economy and adopted the practices and began to build the institutions of a free-market economic system. Third, and not least important, the Communist Party that had ruled the Soviet Union dictatorially lost its monopoly of power, and Russia proclaimed itself a democracy.

Fifteen years after the end of the Soviet Union and the starting point of these three revolutionary developments, however, Russia had not become a working democracy with a government limited in its powers and chosen through free and fair elections. While it had some features of democratic governance, the country was more a nominal than a genuine democracy.

Russia did conduct regular elections that were free—all adults could vote, and the level of fraud in the tallying of the ballots usually fell within the normal range for democracies—but Russian elections were not fair.[23] Russia lacked coherent, effective political parties that could represent different political ideas and economic interests, participate effectively in elections, and organize the government after elections were held.[24] Partly for this reason Russia's rulers—the Russian president and his associates—could manipulate the elections to secure the results they desired.[25]

The government's power was not circumscribed by the limits that operate in genuine democracies. The Russian president more closely resembled a traditional monarch, albeit a nominally elected one, than a modern democratic chief executive. The national legislature, the Duma, acted as a rubber stamp for the president rather than as an independent body that could check his power. While its constitution made Russia a federal state, the president chose the governors of its eighty-nine provinces. Nor was the government friendly to the kinds of independent associations that make up civil society. In 2006 the Duma enacted a law imposing strict regulations on non-governmental organizations.

Nor did the country's courts enjoy the degree of independence from interference by the executive that the rule of law requires.[26] And while the suffocating censorship of the communist era had been eased, the central authorities in Moscow did control the country's national television networks, the principal source of information for most Russians.[27] Moreover, although the communist economic system, in which the government owned all major economic assets and made all major decisions concerning investment and production, had vanished into history, the Russian government played an increasingly intrusive role in the economy and had moved to reassume control over its most valuable component, the energy sector.

In sum, twenty-first-century Russia had the forms, but not the substance, of democracy. Russian democracy resembled columns carved into modern buildings in order to give them a classical appearance, columns that, unlike the free-standing columns of Roman and Greek temples and many neoclassical edifices modeled after them, in fact do nothing to support the building. Russia's democratic institutions served decorative rather than functional purposes.

Russia did not fail to become a genuine democracy because an alternative set of political ideas established themselves as the basis of governance. Communism was defunct and no other undemocratic ideology appeared to replace it.[28] Nor did democracy's failure stem from the skill, determination, and cohesion of the elite that held power. The group that surrounded

Vladimir Putin, who presided over Russia's "managed" version of democracy, was distinguished more for the personal cupidity of its members than for their daring in gaining power, determination in holding it, or zeal in using it.

Nor was the failure of democracy in Russia principally the result of the country's immediate post-Soviet experience. To be sure, that experience did not fortify democracy's prospects, at least in the short term. With the breakup of the Soviet Union and the abrupt shift from a planned to a market economy, many Russians suffered a decline in their living standards.[29] The transfer of property from the state to private hands that accompanied the shift to the market took place out of public view and beyond public control, and made a few well-connected people extremely wealthy. It appeared to be an exercise in high-level looting. The government in power when these misfortunes and outrages took place called itself democratic, and while it scarcely qualified as a model of democratic governance, this description did serve to discredit the concept of democracy in the eyes of many Russians.[30] A decade and a half after the collapse of communism, democracy did not have a particularly good name in Russia.

To add insult to injury, the Western countries, led by the United States, took advantage of Russia's weakness to expand their military alliance, the North Atlantic Treaty Organization (NATO), eastward to Russia's western border, over the objections of the Russian government and contrary to assurances that the leaders of the Soviet Union had received during the final years of that country's existence.[31] NATO expansion marked the Western countries, above all the United States, as duplicitous and aggressive in Russian eyes. Insofar as Russians associated the democratic form of government with these countries, democracy's good name was further tarnished in Russia.

While these post–Cold War misadventures hardly assisted the cause of democracy in Russia, however, neither did they bear the decisive responsibility for the failure to establish it after the Soviet Union collapsed. That responsibility belongs not to Boris Yeltsin or Vladimir Putin, or to the feckless American advocates of NATO expansion, but rather to Vladimir Lenin and Joseph Stalin, the architects of the communist system under which Russians lived from 1917 to 1991. The legacy of that system did more to thwart the creation of a working democracy in Russia than any policy carried out after 1991 by the Russian or any other government.

The collapse of the Soviet Union was almost entirely unanticipated, and little thought had been given to what might follow such an implausible event. When it happened, it was initially widely assumed—naively and entirely incorrectly—that post-Soviet Russia could and would exchange one political and economic system for another, in the manner of someone changing clothes or like a politician switching from one political party to another. This proved impossible because post-Soviet Russia lacked the social bases for democracy. It lacked them because the Communist regime had smashed, repressed, or stifled all of the institutions, all of the practices, and all of the values that democracy requires.

In theory and in practice, communism opposed both principal features of democracy. It denied the claim of popular sovereignty on the grounds that the Communist Party, with its privileged access to the laws of history based on the teachings of Marx and Lenin, was better suited to rule—in the name and on behalf of the people—than the people themselves. It suppressed liberty because the Party, which dominated the government, had the right and the duty to exercise strict control over every facet of political and economic life. The Communist Party's impressively successful effort to achieve total control earned for the communist system the descriptive title "totalitarianism."

The government's control extended to the economy, which it owned and managed by administrative fiat. Private transactions based on calculations of profit and loss, which form the heart of a market economy, had no place under communism. Nor was private property, which had never thrived in pre-communist Russia, permitted. Communism in Russia, as elsewhere, branded as "class enemies" and sought to destroy capitalists—that is, investors and owners of enterprises—landlords, and even peasants tilling their own small plots. In democracies, private property is an essential institution. Under communism, possessing it became a capital offense. Its absence meant that Communist Russia lacked a major form of liberty, an opportunity to cultivate the habits of sovereignty, and a protected sector of society that could serve as a redoubt for independent political activity.[32]

The steamroller that was communism flattened everything in its path, squashing in particular any and all organized activity independent of the state itself. The oldest and in many places the sturdiest element of civil society, organized religion, came in for special attention in the officially atheist Soviet Union. It was forcibly suppressed, with clergy and believers harassed and persecuted. In general, the ruling Communist Party sought to prevent horizontal social ties from forming between and among people and groups, and to confine social and political life to a series of vertical links between the authorities and individuals. The Communists wanted the inhabitants of the Soviet Union to spend their time gazing upward, in fear and respect, at the juggernaut that ruled over them, and not, as is normal in democratically governed societies, in making connections of all kinds with their fellow citizens outside the surveillance and beyond the reach of the state.

The bleak social landscape that communism created was evident to any attentive observer of Soviet life. Less visible, but just as harmful to the prospects for democracy in post-Soviet Russia, was the impact of Communist rule on the psychology of the Russian people. It inculcated habits and values antithetical to those that democracy requires.[33] Because individual initiative of any kind could attract the malevolent attention of the Soviet authorities, Russians under communism learned to be passive and quiescent; but citizens must take an active part in public life for democracy to operate. Because communist societies were riddled with spies and informers who reported even the faintest hint of political deviance to the regime, Russians learned to trust no one outside their small circles of immediate family and close friends; but democratic political systems (and free-market economies) require extensive trust and cooperation.[34] Because the Party-dominated government owned and managed everything, Russians under communism did not feel responsible for anything beyond their small circles; but genuine democracy requires that citizens have a sense of responsibility for the well-being of their community and their country.

The ancient Greek historian Tacitus said of the aftermath of a particularly destructive war, "They made a desert and called it peace." The Communist Party of the Soviet Union made Russia a desert and called it socialism. That desert was communism's legacy to post-Soviet Russia. Gardens do not flourish in deserts, and democracy could not take root in the social conditions that seventy-five years of communism in Russia, following centuries of authoritarian tsarist rule, had created.

Vladimir Putin, Russia's second post-Soviet president, paid far less rhetorical homage to Western-style political institutions and practices than had his predecessor, Boris Yeltsin. Putin's time in office did not truly mark a retreat from democracy, however, because democracy was a destination that Russia under Yeltsin had not reached—and, given the country's lack of the social foundations on which democracy must rest, could not have reached. Yeltsin's achievement was to complete the destruction of communism. Neither he nor anyone else could have built democracy in Russia in the immediate aftermath of its destruction. Reviving Russia's social landscape to make it fertile soil for liberty and representative government would have to be the work of a generation, or more. In the first decade and a half after the end of communism, such a revival began.

It could begin because the system of government responsible for creating the desert had disappeared, never to return. The communist steamroller was disassembled and its parts consigned to the junkyard of history. The Russian regime that succeeded it did not conform to the standards of democracy, but neither did it set about, deliberately and relentlessly, to eradicate any and all bases for democratic government. The new Russian government's goal was simply to keep power and enrich the powerholders.

Sigmund Freud once said that the purpose of the therapeutic technique he pioneered, psychoanalysis, was to transform neurotic misery into ordinary unhappiness. The collapse of the Soviet Union had the political equivalent of that transforming effect on Russia. It delivered the Russian people from the stifling grip of full-blown totalitarianism to the softer rule of ordinary authoritarianism. In political terms, twenty-first-century Russia stood about as far from—and therefore approximately as close to—genuine democracy as had the dictatorially ruled countries of Latin America and East Asia in the 1960s.

Democracy's long-term prospects in Russia seemed relatively bright, as well, because Russia was free of one of the legacies of its pre-Soviet past, which had carried over into the communist period: the sense that the country was marked out for a unique cultural and political destiny, one different from and superior to the paths followed by other countries. This sense of Russian exceptionalism dates back at least to the fifteenth century, when a monk speaking for the tsar proclaimed Moscow to be "the Third Rome," destined to be the last and mightiest center of a world empire.[35] In the centuries that followed, two opposing currents of political opinion and cultural affinity regularly competed for primacy in Russia: one embracing the idea of an exceptional destiny and deriding the value, as a model for Russia, of the experiences of other countries; the other believing in the wisdom of following in the political and economic footsteps of the countries to the West—believing, that is, that Russia was a European country and should govern itself in a European manner.[36]

With its declared intention to bring into being a new and superior civilization, communism in Russia represented the historical high point of the first tradition. The collapse of the Communist state, and with it Communist ideology, left no model of a non-Western terrestrial paradise for Russians to build upon, and dealt a sharp and possibly fatal blow to the very idea of trying to build any such thing. However problematic they found the idea that their country should seek to emulate the West might be in the initial decade of the twenty-first century, for the first time in many centuries Russians had no alternative idea available to them.

In the years following the end of communism, moreover, Russia did begin to refashion itself along Western lines. The ownership of private property became legal. A market economy began to emerge, and along with it came the beginnings of one of its modern offshoots, which often serves as the social backbone of democracy: a property-owning, consumer-goods-purchasing middle class.[37]

Three other features of the country and the world respectively at the outset of the twenty-first century made the long-term prospects for democracy in Russia far brighter than ever before. First, the population of the country no longer consisted, as it had until the industrialization and urbanization that the Communist regime forcibly imposed from the 1920s to the 1960s, largely of illiterate peasants and landless agricultural workers, whose ancestors had been serfs before being freed in the 1860s. By the twenty-first century the average Russian was literate, educated, and lived in a city, and was therefore the kind of person more likely to find democracy appealing and dictatorship unacceptable than his or her rural forebears.

Second, the revolutions in transportation and communication had made it far more difficult for Russia's rulers to close the country off from the outside world, and in particular from awareness of the ideas and institutions of the democracies, than they had during the centuries when absolute monarchs had ruled the country and for most of the communist period. Indeed, in the age of the Internet, satellite relays for telephones, and regular long-distance travel by jet aircraft, sealing Russia off from democratic examples abroad had become all but impossible, and the post-Soviet government, however hostile its attitude toward democracy, did not seriously attempt this.[38]

Third, Russia in the twenty-first century faced far less danger of attack by its neighbors than ever before. Monarchs and commissars from the sixteenth century through most of the twentieth had justified gathering and exercising unlimited power on the grounds that this was necessary to protect the country from its enemies. The dramatic decline in the intensity of great-power competition in Europe in the last years of the twentieth century deprived that rationale of much of its force.[39]

Against these harbingers of a more democratic political future than Russia has ever had, however, had to be set a countervailing force. The country's large reserves of energy threatened to tilt it in the direction of autocratic government of the kind with which other, similarly endowed countries were encumbered. Post-Soviet Russia had the unhappy potential to become a petro-state.[40]

The energy resources that the new Russia inherited made it the world's biggest exporter of natural gas and the second largest exporter of oil. Among all countries, it had the largest reserves of natural gas and the eighth largest reserves of oil, and a large fraction of the Russian government's revenues came from the sale of energy.[41] These energy riches created in Russia, as in other similarly endowed countries, the temptation to seize and hold political power in order to capture the wealth they generated, and the trends in Russian public life in the first decade of the twenty-first century gave evidence of this.

The central government extended its control over the energy sector, and associates of the president assumed positions in which they could appropriate generous shares of its revenues for themselves. Another feature of a petro-state, a swollen, heavy-handed bureaucracy (which had been integral as well to the communist economic system), also appeared in post-Soviet Russia. Besides dictatorial government and an out-sized, smothering bureaucracy, Russia ran the risk of develop-ing the third problem typical of petro-states: weak economic performance outside the energy sector.

Yet none of these three afflictions was inevitable. The coun-try is not necessarily destined to become a large, northern, Slavic version of Saudi Arabia. Some sovereign states rich in energy have managed to avoid these pitfalls because their po-litical institutions and economic practices were established be-fore they received the financial benefits of their natural resources, or because those resources were not large enough to obviate the need to build a productive economy outside the energy sector, or because of wise political and economic choices, often the result of skilled and far-sighted leadership. The United States is a major oil producer, for example, yet it has never come close to developing the distinguishing features of a petro-state.

Russia's twenty-first-century political fate is likely, there-fore, to be determined by a contest between two broad and conflicting trends: the slow growth of a market economy with a middle class and the multiple institutions of civil society, which strongly incline a country to democracy, on the one hand, and the political and economic patterns that large-scale energy wealth encourages, which often underwrite undemo-cratic governance, on the other. If the first trend should prove to be more deeply rooted, more enduring, and generally more powerful than the second, Russia will have the opportunity to acquire a government chosen through free elections and scrupulous about the protection of liberty. How might this come about?

One obvious way for democracy to come to Russia is the manner in which it came to so many other countries in the last three decades of the twentieth century: peaceful public demonstrations by large numbers of citizens leading eventually to free elections that install a government committed to safeguarding liberty. This peaceful method of transferring power from dictators to democrats counts as the most important political innovation of the last third of the twentieth century. It is more or less the way in which communism in Russia came to an end. Boris Yeltsin inspired demonstrations against the regime, elements of which were trying to mount a coup in August 1991. The regime failed to master the challenge that the demonstrations represented and disintegrated.[42] Two years earlier the Soviet-installed Communist governments of Eastern Europe had fallen in the same way. And in the middle of the first decade of the twenty-first century, peaceful demonstrations unseated three governments in recently independent countries that had once been provinces of the Soviet Union: the "Rose Revolution" in Georgia in 2003, the "Orange Revolution" in Ukraine in 2004, and the "Tulip Revolution" in Kyrgyzstan in 2005.

As the mechanism for establishing democracy in Russia, massive, peaceful demonstrations of the kind that became familiar in Russia's geographic neighborhood have, however, two drawbacks. The Russian government took note of the "color revolutions" and took steps to ward off a similar development in its own country. While official opposition did not present an insuperable, perhaps not even a particularly formidable, long-term obstacle to anti-government demonstrations in Russia, the new governments that such demonstrations brought to power in Georgia, Ukraine, and Kyrgyzstan—and this is the second drawback—did not immediately establish themselves as genuine working democracies with a full complement of liberties and the protection of the rule of law available to all citizens. Like Russia, they lacked the infrastructure of democracy.

Moreover, another, more gradual, less dramatic scenario for the advent of a democratic political system in Russia is possible. The country might, in effect, grow into democracy. Over time, as the social underpinnings of liberty and representative government expand, the institutions of democracy with which the new Russia equipped itself, initially largely decorative, might ultimately become functional. The British monarch once ruled the United Kingdom, but over the centuries steadily yielded effective power to the parliament and, by the twenty-first century, played a purely symbolic role in public affairs. Russia's political institutions might, in the course of the new century, follow the opposite trajectory.

Its political parties might attract members in significant numbers from Russian society and begin to free themselves from the tutelage of the central authorities. Elections might become genuinely competitive exercises, with several candidates representing different interests and points of view having a serious chance to win office. The State Duma and the provincial governments might come to exercise real authority and serve as counterweights to the Russian president, as the country's constitution intends that they do. The courts might escape the undue influence of the political authorities and adjudicate cases according to the law, protecting the political and economic rights even of those lacking political power or connections to those who hold it.

The Russian political system in the early years of the twenty-first century could be compared to a ghost town. It had the equivalent of the buildings necessary for a thriving community but not the people. With the passage of time, the growth of a market economy, and the independent organizations of civil society as well as a prolonged and intense exposure to the example of successful democracies, the town might come to be repopulated—or rather, in the case of Russian democracy, populated for the first time.

While the rulers of Russia would likely oppose a trend toward "creeping democracy," they are unlikely to have the political skills, the discipline and solidarity in their own ranks, or the public support to be able to mount powerful and unyielding resistance to it. The same could not be said, however, of the other large country that had, near the end of the twentieth century, abandoned orthodox communism but had not, in the early years of the twenty first, established democracy: the People's Republic of China.

Democracy in China

"Let China sleep," Napoleon once said. "When she wakes up, the world will be sorry." In the final two decades of the twentieth century China awakened. A series of reforms that brought some of the features of the free market to what had been a communist-style centrally planned economy set in motion a remarkable burst of nearly double-digit annual growth. Between 1978 and 2005, the Chinese people experienced a sevenfold increase in their material standard of living.[43] During that period, China became a major recipient of investment from abroad and an important participant in the global trading system. Its foreign trade, worth $20 billion in 1979, had by 2005 grown to a value of $1 trillion.[44] The world's most populous country, the owner of the third-largest nuclear arsenal on the planet, was on course to have, at some point in the twenty-first century, the world's largest economy.

China was therefore destined to be a major international presence, perhaps the equal in power and influence of the United States itself. Whether the world would be sorry for China's rise depended, at least in part, on what kind of government it came to have. The country loomed as perhaps the most significant potential test of the democratic peace theory.[45] Since China did not, in the early years of the twenty-first century, have a democratic government, the optimal condition for such a test was the advent of democracy, which would permit a comparison between the foreign policies of democratic and non-democratic governments of the same country. Whether China would provide such a test seemed, in turn, to depend on the validity of another theory about political life in the contemporary era, one for which the supporting evidence was almost as plentiful, and which had achieved almost as much currency in academic and political circles as the link between democratic government and a peaceful foreign policy: the connection between market-generated wealth and democratic politics.

In 1996, an article in a journal of international affairs began with the question "When will China become a democracy?" and then proceeded to give a strikingly specific response: "The answer is around the year 2015."[46] Embedded in that answer were two assumptions, one about China, the other about democracy. The author assumed that China's rapid economic growth would continue, as indeed it did over the course of the succeeding decade. He assumed as well that when this surging growth lifted the country's per capita income to between $7,000 and $8,000 annually, which he calculated would occur in about the year 2015, the pressures for democratic government in China would become all but irresistible, as they had in other Asian countries that had reached this level of well-being.

The connection between democracy and wealth is a close one.[47] While poor democracies were found in increasing numbers as this form of government spread around the world, with the exception of political communities grown rich from oil, there were very few wealthy dictatorships.[48] Economic growth, the history of the modern era has demonstrated, puts in place the foundations of democratic politics; and the breakneck pace of China's growth began to create, at a very rapid rate, the conditions for liberty and representative government in a society that had never known either.

Two and a half decades after the introduction of economic reforms, China had a booming market economy.[49] True, large parts of the planned economy that communism had built after 1949 persisted. Tens of millions of Chinese were employed in enterprises owned and managed by the state, many of them unprofitable.[50] But the private part of the Chinese economy, in which the major decisions were made on the basis of calculations of profit and loss rather than the whims of politically appointed planners, was far more dynamic, accounting for 50 percent of the country's total output and virtually all of its growth.[51]

The galloping pace of economic growth had created, by the first decade of the twenty-first century, a middle class. As a proportion of China's huge population it remained small,[52] but its numbers were increasing rapidly. More and more Chinese lived in cities, became well educated, and earned their livings in ways that provided them with both a degree of independence on the job and the income and sufficient leisure time for pursuits away from work. More and more Chinese used their rising incomes to acquire consumer goods. The shopping mall, the contemporary Western focus and symbol of private consumption, was exported to China and thrived there.[53]

The core institution of the free-market economy, private property, was not fully established in China even after a quarter-century of economic reform.[54] Urban dwellers could own their own homes and rural Chinese could lease the land they were cultivating for as long as thirty years, neither of which had been possible through the 1970s. But Chinese people did not have a secure right to property formally protected by law, of the kind that anchors Western market economies.[55] The precise location of ownership rights in China was sometimes difficult to specify. Formal control of many large businesses, for example, was vested in amorphous local bodies, seemingly partly private and partly public, known as "township and village enterprises." Nor did China have a legal system fully capable of adjudicating competing claims on property and protecting individuals' rights to it. While it is a common American complaint that the United States has too many lawyers, China plainly had too few.[56] Yet even without secure property rights and the rule of law, which Western economists generally consider to be crucial for the kind of behavior that produces economic growth,[57] China's economy surged.

Along with the growth of the economy, in the era of economic reform, the independent groups that make up civil society proliferated in China. In 2005, 285,000 non-governmental groups were officially registered with the government—a tiny number for a country with a population of more than 1.3 billion—but estimates of the number of unofficial groups ran as high as 8 million.[58] Among the non-governmental groups were many congregations, some of them very small, most of them formally illegal, of practicing Christians, of whom there were perhaps 70 million.[59] The severe pollution of China's air and water began to inspire the formation of groups dedicated to protecting the country's environment.[60]

Economic growth created distinct and sometimes conflicting economic interests in China, and while formally organized and politically active economically based interest groups of the kind that are integral to democratic political systems did not exist, the differing preferences on matters of public policy did find expression within the councils of government.[61] Gradually, beneath the surface of public events, China began to acquire the feature of Western political systems generally known as pluralism.

Furthermore, twenty-first-century China emphatically fulfilled one of the historical conditions for democracy: it was open to the world. The founding leader of Communist China, Mao Zedong, who ruled from the Communist conquest of power in 1949 until his death in 1976, sought, with considerable success, to wall the country off from what he regarded as the corrupting influence of the outside world. His successors opened the country's doors and welcomed what Mao had tried to keep out. The Chinese government joined 130 international organizations and signed more than 150 international treaties.[62] In the quarter-century after 1980, the volume of China's trade with other countries rose seventyfold, trade's share of China's overall output increased fivefold, and the country's proportion of world trade as a whole climbed from 0.8 percent to 7.7 percent.[63] In 2002, the total of Chinese tourists abroad reached 6 million, and 400,000 Chinese had studied abroad.[64]

The Internet, to which an estimated 111 million Chinese had access in 2005,[65] did double duty in laying the foundations of political democracy. It connected to the rest of the world millions of Chinese who had never traveled beyond the country's borders and had perhaps never even met a foreigner. At the same time, it connected individual Chinese to one another, as do the organizations of civil society, outside the purview of the government. It helped to create the horizontal social linkages that typify democracies and that undemocratic governments seek to discourage, restrict, or control.[66]

While the conditions in which liberty and representative government can arise and flourish were growing rapidly in twenty-first-century China, the country did not have the formal structures of democracy. It lacked, in addition to private property and a full-fledged legal system to protect it, genuine political parties, contested and meaningful elections for national office, and any mechanism for securing religious liberty and political rights. Yet even in political terms, China was no longer the anti-democratic desert that it had been the achievement of orthodox communism to create there as well as in Russia.

The ruling Communist Party had ceased to be the monolith dominated by a single tyrannical figure over which Mao had presided.[67] Different currents of opinion were represented in the ranks of its members, including the opinion that the government of China should become more democratic. Officials at the village and neighborhood levels were selected by election, although the Party controlled the choice of candidates and the elected officials generally wielded little real power.[68] Perhaps most importantly, by the middle of the first decade of the new century, the idea that citizens have rights, that there exist areas of social and political life on which the government must not impinge, had spread beyond the very small circle of Western-oriented intellectuals to Chinese throughout the country. Workers and farmers—certainly not all of them but a significant number—became seized with "rights consciousness," which is, of course, a fundamental feature of democratically governed societies.[69]

The dizzying change that a quarter-century of economic reform and its consequences brought to China therefore installed, in a relatively short period of time, many of the building blocks of political democracy. As Chinese economic growth proceeded, as the ranks of the country's middle class expanded, and civil society spread, the pressure for democratic change in its governance was sure to increase. As it did, however, it was just as certain to encounter formidable resistance from the ruling Communist Party.

While abandoning the Maoist project of exerting control over every aspect of social and political life, the Party remained determined, as the economic reforms proceeded, to retain its monopoly of political power, and it adopted a number of measures for doing so. It squelched any sign of organized political opposition to its rule. No other political party was permitted to operate in China.[70] It attacked, as well, organized groups that it deemed politically threatening, even if they had no political agenda: the exercise and meditation movement Falun Gong, for example, became the target of a harsh campaign of repression that drove it underground.[71]

The Chinese government also practiced selective censorship. Many subjects that could not be discussed publicly during the Maoist era ceased to be forbidden, but explicit expressions of political dissent and, above all, any questioning of the role of the Communist Party were prohibited. Journalists whose reporting strayed into what the authorities considered dangerous territory found themselves subject to harassment and sometimes prosecution and imprisonment. In this way the Party made plain the limits of its tolerance.[72] It

also undertook the difficult task of censoring the Internet, trying to shut down or block access to politically heretical web-
sites. For this purpose, the Chinese government reportedly
employed 30,000 people and managed to secure limited cooperation from Western Internet companies that operated in
China.[73]

The Party had reason to worry about its grip on power. Beyond the rapid social and economic changes that made democracy an increasingly plausible form of government for China
and an increasingly attractive one to the Chinese people, it
had, by its retreat from the orthodox version of communism
that Mao had imposed, given up the original rationale for its
exercise of power in China—the claim that, guided by the laws
of history that Marx had discovered and the understanding of
which first Lenin and then Mao had refined, it was building a
new and glorious socialist community. Still, the Chinese Communists did not suffer from the same large deficit of political
legitimacy that had, at the end of the 1980s and the beginning
of the 1990s, created the conditions for the end of communism in Eastern Europe and the Soviet Union.[74]

They had presided over a far more successful economy than
had their European and Soviet counterparts. The years before
Mikhail Gorbachev took power in Moscow and inaugurated
the changes that ultimately led to communism's collapse, came
to be known—referring to the economic sluggishness that
characterized them—as "the era of stagnation." In the twenty-
five years after the introduction of economic reform, the
Chinese, by contrast, experienced the opposite of stagnation.
The sweeping changes that took place in those years made
several hundred million Chinese richer and, within limits,
freer than they had been before. This was one reason that the
ruling Communists could count on the tacit support—perhaps

indulgence is a more accurate word—of many Chinese who had no particular fondness for the Party and did not believe that it had the right to govern China in perpetuity without limits on its authority.

Popular indulgence of Communist rule had another source: the fear of something worse. Recurrent periods of violent chaos scar China's twentieth-century history: the rule of regional warlords after the fall of the last dynasty in 1911, the brutal Japanese invasion and occupation in the 1930s and 1940s, the civil war between the Communists and the Kuomintang after the defeat of Japan, and Mao's nationwide campaigns of upheaval and repression, notably the Great Leap Forward of the 1950s and the Great Proletarian Cultural Revolution of the 1960s. Although by the twenty-first century almost none of them had lived through every one of these cataclysms and the younger generation had escaped all of them, the Chinese people were aware of their country's potential for bouts of large-scale murder and destruction. Understandably, they wished to avoid any more of them. If the price of stability was the continuation of the dictatorial rule of the Communist Party, this was perhaps a price worth paying.

The millions who had done particularly well in the quarter-century of reform, moreover, many of them educated, cosmopolitan, and living in the cities of the country's coastal provinces, had reason to be wary of the resentment of the many more mainly rural residents of inland China whose well-being the economic boom had not enhanced. The beneficiaries might well calculate that Party rule protected them and their gains.

The regime could also tap a widespread and potent popular sentiment to reinforce its position: nationalism. The government assiduously publicized its claim to control Taiwan, a

claim that seemingly enjoyed wide popularity on the mainland,[75] and made known the military measures it was prepared
to take if the island's democratically elected government
should ever declare formal independence.[76] In addition, the
Party did not openly say, but many Chinese surely understood,
that if it fell from power the non-Han-Chinese ethnic and religious minorities of western China might become restive. Indeed, the Buddhists of Tibet and the Muslims of Xinjiang
might take the opportunity, especially if confusion, turmoil,
and a political vacuum followed Communist rule, to break
away from the Chinese state, which they had never voted to
join and which they had good reason to regard as the instrument
of imperial oppression.[77] In China, as in other countries, the
advent of democracy would bring with it the risk of civil strife.

The ideology of Marxism-Leninism-Maoism commanded
virtually no allegiance in twenty-first-century China, not even,
as far as could be determined, in the ranks of the Communist
Party itself; but Chinese patriotism, defined as the determination to control all the territory claimed by the Communist
government after 1949—even when, as in the case of Taiwan,
the mainland authorities did not actually exercise control and
had not done so for more than 100 years—was a sentiment
that many if not most Chinese apparently shared and about
which some were passionate.[78]

Given the broad and deep social forces pressing, directly
and indirectly, for greater freedom and a system of genuine
self-government, therefore, but with the presence, as well, of a
ruling party with both strong determination to prevent the advent of such political changes and access to considerable economic and political resources for this purpose, how might
democracy come to China?

Although the immediate pressures for democracy were greater than in Russia, because of more rapid economic expansion over a longer period, China was not likely to grow into a democratic political system gradually and peacefully, as was possible in Russia. China lacked Russia's formal democratic institutions, and the ruling group had deeper roots in the society and greater means at its disposal for remaining in power. The more likely route for democracy to come to the Chinese mainland, if it should do so, is through the kind of massive peaceful demonstrations, triggering a political crisis and ultimately the abdication of the ruling group, that have brought about political transformations in so many countries around the world. China itself was the scene of such an uprising in the spring of 1989, when demonstrators gathered in Tiananmen Square in Beijing and in other cities throughout the country. Using the army, the government broke up the demonstrations violently, jailed or exiled many of the demonstrators, and thus retained its monopoly of power.[79] Such a moment, with Chinese taking to the streets in large numbers to protest government policies, could well come again.

By the middle of the first decade of the twenty-first century, public demonstrations, occasionally violent ones to express discontent over a range of issues, had become a familiar feature of Chinese life. The number of such demonstrations was on the increase and by one estimate 74,000 of them, involving 3.6 million people, took place in 2004 alone.[80] Several kinds of issues drove Chinese to active protest, in particular the blatant and widespread corruption of Party officials and the government's arbitrary practice of seizing land and closing factories, often without warning and without compensation to those injured by these initiatives, who had no way of stopping them.[81]

Because the Communist Party's monopoly of power lends itself to offenses of this kind, they are unlikely to end, despite the government's regular promises to end them.

Although increasingly frequent, the protests tended to remain local in scope, focused on specific grievances rather than on the political system as a whole, and isolated from one another; and the Chinese government made every effort to keep individual demonstrations from spreading.[82] If, however, the pace of economic growth, the principal source of the Party's popularity and legitimacy, begins to slacken, the resulting discontent could create political conditions in which episodes of protest become larger, more frequent, and ultimately regional or national in scope. Protracted large-scale protests across China could pose a serious challenge to the regime of the kind it faced in the spring of 1989.[83]

The outcome of such a crisis cannot be predicted with any confidence. In 1989, a few Party elders, led by Deng Xiaoping, ordered the crackdown on the demonstrators.[84] A similar twenty-first-century crisis might produce a different result: it might lead to the political ascendance of pro-democracy forces and a transition from communism to democratic rule.[85] The circle of people who would decide how to respond to such an event has probably widened since 1989, and pro-democracy sentiment is probably more strongly represented in the ranks of the Party.[86] Certainly, the conditions for democratic government—a market economy, a middle class, the institution of private property, openness to ideas and examples from the rest of the world—became more widely and deeply established in the years following the Tiananmen episode. In a crisis, these cumulative changes might well weigh heavily (but even then, not necessarily decisively) against a forcible reassertion of Communist control over Chinese society.[87]

In general, Communist rule in China in its early twenty-first-century form seems unlikely to persist over the long term for two reasons. First, the strategy that the Communist Party has adopted for governing China contains a fundamental contradiction. The regime has geared its policies to promoting economic growth, on which it counts to sustain political stability and build support for, or at least tolerance of, Communist rule. Economic growth, however, creates the basis both for popular opposition and for a democratic alternative to dictatorial government.

Second, the Communist system was made for different circumstances than those of the twenty-first century. It took hold in backward peasant societies that could be isolated from the rest of the world at a time when the teachings of Marx, Lenin, and Mao seemed plausible guides to national power and social improvement. Twenty-first-century China has none of these features. To be sure, the Communist Party has adapted to the ongoing changes in the country and the world. Specifically, it has practiced a form of appeasement toward the society it governs, giving up much of the authority that Mao had asserted over a range of economic and social matters in order to keep control of the country's political life.[88]

Whether, and for how long, it can continue this strategy, and how far it can conduct an orderly retreat without surrendering its monopoly of power, are questions to which only China's twenty-first-century history can provide the answers. What is clear is that in China, as, with a somewhat lower probability, in Russia, economic growth is likely, over the long term, to proceed, and as it does the pressures for limited and freely elected government will mount. In this crucial respect Russia and China differ from a region the political direction of which will also affect countries elsewhere, that also, midway through the first decade of the twenty-first century, lacked democratic government, but where the prospects for democracy were less promising: the Arab Middle East.

DEMOCRACY IN THE ARAB WORLD

The predominantly Muslim and Arabic-speaking countries that stretch from the Mediterranean Sea to the Indian Ocean and across the northern rim of the African continent affect the rest of the world through two principal exports: terrorism and oil. Were these countries to become democracies, the world could anticipate receiving less of the first and having more reliable access to the second.

The Arab countries might seem to be better candidates than Russia or China to adopt liberty-protecting governments chosen by free elections. They have no history of communist rule pulverizing the institutions and repressing the practices on which democracy rests. They had a longer twentieth-century history than either of the two formerly orthodox communist giants of continuous exposure to and direct contact with Western democracies. Moreover, in the first decade of the twenty-first century most Arab governments proclaimed a commitment to political reform of some kind.[89] These seeming advantages notwithstanding, however, the early twenty-first-century prospects for democracy in the Arab Middle East are distinctly poor.

While Russia could look to neighbors to the West—in Central and Eastern Europe and the Baltic region—for examples of successful transition to democratic governance, and while China's geographic neighborhood includes a number of democracies, including an ethnic Chinese one on the offshore island of Taiwan, none of the twenty-two members of the Arab League has ever had a genuinely democratic government.[90] And whereas twenty-first-century Russia and China harbor social and economic trends favorable to the rise of democracy, such trends in the Arab world, insofar as they exist at all, are considerably weaker.

Furthermore, a number of features of Arab society and political life work against the advent of democratic government. None of these features, at the outset of the twenty-first century, was exclusive to the Middle East. Each was to be found in other parts of the world in some form or other. Nowhere else, however, were these anti-democratic social forces all present, and in such strength. These forces, which in combination made for a formidable barrier to the spread of democracy even in an era in which that form of government was ascendant around the world, included the ethnic and religious heterogeneity of the countries of the region, an abundance of oil, the influence of Islam, and a long history in which the home of democracy, the Christian West, was the chief adversary.

Because human beings have a tendency to repose greater trust in those who resemble them in ways they deem important than in those who differ from them, countries composed of peoples with the same ethnic or national or religious affiliations adopt and sustain democracy more readily than those in which different groups live together.[91] In a homogeneous country people are less likely to mount efforts to secede, which often leads to violence and, even short of that, makes full-fledged democracy difficult to sustain, than they are in multiethnic, multinational, or religiously diverse societies. Where several groups reside within the same sovereign borders, one of them often forcibly dominates the others. Such countries become "empires in miniature."[92] For the ruling group, democracy is a danger to be resisted, which jeopardizes its privileges and threatens to usher in anarchy or civil war.[93]

Since the middle of the twentieth century, the Arab countries have projected to the world an image of homogeneity and solidarity. They speak a single language and, for the most part, profess a single faith. They have their own political group—the Arab League. They have periodically subscribed, at least rhetorically, to the idea that all Arabs belong to a single nation.[94] In fact, however, virtually every Arab country is sharply divided along the lines of tribe, ethnicity, and religion, with the most significant religious split being that between the two major branches of Islam, the Sunni and the Shia. The invocation of Arab solidarity has often served as a cover for the autocratic rule of one group over others. In general, the many divisions of the Arab states have obstructed free elections and the protection of liberty throughout the Arab Middle East.[95]

Iraq, for example, was cobbled together by Great Britain after World War I out of three former provinces of the Ottoman Empire, each dominated by a different group: Sunnis, Shias, and Kurds—who are Sunni Muslims but not Arabs. The Sunnis, who by the outset of the twenty-first century numbered only about 20 percent of the country's population, managed to get political control of Iraq and kept it by dictatorial rule, which reached its zenith of murderous brutality under Saddam Hussein.[96] In Syria, a group making up an even smaller proportion of the population, the Alawis, an offshoot (and to some Muslims, a heresy) of Islam, seized power and kept it in the same way the Sunnis of Iraq did. Democracy would have put an end to their reign, and they therefore opposed it.[97]

In neighboring Lebanon, a political system that had struck a delicate balance among Sunni and Shia Muslims, Christians, and other groups collapsed in the 1970s into civil war, which ended only when Syria intervened to impose order by force. In many of the Arab states of the Persian Gulf, including the largest, Saudi Arabia, the ruling Sunnis denied the Shias, along with all other inhabitants, the right to political participation, which would have led to the Shias' receiving a larger share of these countries' revenues from the sale of oil than the Sunni rulers cared to give them. The kingdom of Jordan consisted of an elite descended from the Bedouin of the Arabian peninsula governing a largely Palestinian society. In North Africa, Arabs coexisted uneasily with Berbers. Even Egypt, the largest and most homogeneous Arab country and therefore the one most closely resembling a European nation-state, had a Coptic Christian minority that numbered approximately 10 percent of the population. In each of these cases distrust among the different groups contributed to the suppression of liberty and representative government.

The presence of different ethnic, national, and religious groups in a single country obstructed the twenty-first-century progress of democracy outside the Middle East, as well—in the Balkans, for example, and in many parts of Africa. But another feature of the Arab world—indeed for most non-Arab countries its most important feature—posed an additional obstacle: oil.[98]

The largest reserves of readily accessible oil on the planet are located in the Middle East, most of it in countries on or near the Persian Gulf. Several of the thirteen members of the Organization of Petroleum Exporting Countries (OPEC), the main association of oil-producing countries, are Arab states, and a number of other Arab countries not belonging to OPEC exported oil at the outset of the twenty-first century or had done so in the latter stages of the twentieth.[99]

In these countries, whose economic dependence on the sale of hydrocarbons ranged from heavy to almost exclusive,[100] the wealth accruing from the extraction of oil has had the effect of discouraging other forms of economic activity. The total output of all Arab countries fell short of that of a single medium-sized European country—Spain.[101] The total value of all manufactured goods exported from the Arab world did not match that of Finland.[102] The Arab countries therefore did not have independent entrepreneurs and proprietors. Their businessmen depended on the government for patronage, which stemmed ultimately from oil wealth.[103] Partly for this reason, these countries lacked the social stratum closely associated with democracy—a genuine middle class.

In the Arab world, as elsewhere, the enormous riches that energy reserves supplied created powerful incentives to capture and retain power, which brings with it control of those riches. Rather than being separated, as in democracies, wealth and political power, in the Arab world, go together. Their enormous oil wealth, moreover, has given Arab governments not only the motive but also the means to monopolize power indefinitely. They have used part of the revenues they have received to build effective apparatuses of repression, on the one hand, and to buy off the populations they govern with generous welfare benefits, on the other. In some of the smaller oil sheikhdoms of the Persian Gulf most members of the dominant group, the Sunni Arabs, do not have to hold jobs: they live comfortably on government stipends and rely on foreigners to do the work that the society requires.

Oil wealth inhibited the growth of democracy in other parts of the world, of course. But it had a particularly pronounced anti-democratic impact on the Arab Middle East because it operated in concert with a basic feature of Arab societies that also worked against the impulse for democracy: their Islamic faith.

Islam is not wholly incompatible with democracy. For one thing, there is no simple, standard version of the faith but rather, like Christianity, many different varieties found in many different countries around the world. For another, some predominantly Muslim countries, such as Turkey, Indonesia, and Mali had, in the first decade of the twenty-first century, working if imperfect democratic governments. Most predominantly Muslim countries did not have democratic governments,[104] but this was not always and everywhere exclusively because of the religion practiced within their borders. Moreover, virtually all religions have at some point in their histories made claims to authority that conflicted with democratic norms. This was certainly the case in the cradle of democracy, the Christian West. Such claims were, however, unusually strong in the Arab version of Islam, and their strength stemmed from the religion's founding design.

From the beginning, faith and power, the divine law and worldly governance, were fused. Muhammad was not only a prophet, he was also a ruler.[105] Christianity, by contrast, began as a faith outside the established structure of power—that of the Roman Empire. The phrase "render unto Caesar that which is Caesar's; render unto God that which is God's" stems from the faith's early experience. From that experience came the basis for the distinction in the Christian world between civil and religious life—that is, secularism—which is integral to the societies that practice democracy.

In Islam, however, the two realms were not originally, and did not develop as, separate entities. The fusion of the two creates a bias against liberty. Placing the limits that protect freedom in democracies on a government that is carrying out the divine will seems not only unnecessary but an act of impiety. The fusion of faith and power in Islam also calls into question popular sovereignty. The task of government for a devout Muslim is to apply God's law, on which human legislators, whom free elections empower for this purpose, cannot and therefore should not attempt to improve.[106]

The singularly political character of Islam, and the unusually powerful attachment of the Arabs to that faith,[107] make it a kind of competitor of, and alternative to, democracy in that part of the world. Indeed, during the last three decades of the twentieth century, the most dynamic political trend in the Middle East was not democracy, as was the case elsewhere, but a political form of Islam that often employed violence to try to impose what its adherents deemed original, authentic Islamic institutions and practices.[108] The various Islamic movements, sometimes termed "fundamentalist" or "Islamist," did not, when they took power, govern in democratic fashion. This was so even when, as in the case of Hamas (the Islamic Resistance Movement) in the Palestinian territories, they came to power through elections. Like other such groups, Hamas did not accept the limits on state power and the independence of important areas of social, political, and economic life that liberty requires.[109] Nor, however, did radical Muslim groups in power create a full-fledged modern ideology to rival democracy of the kind that fascism and communism had been during the twentieth century, because these groups did not provide a plausible design for governing a modern state, as the twentieth century ideologies had done.[110]

Still, if Islam did not furnish a practical blueprint for twenty-first-century governance, it did supply a focus of political loyalty other than the principles of democracy. Almost all the Arab countries gave the religion an exclusive official status in their constitutions.[111] Unlike the small number of politically isolated individuals who advocated liberty and representative government in those countries,[112] moreover, the Islamic movements commanded too much loyalty and legitimacy among Arabs for the governments to repress them entirely. Instead, these governments used Islam, and its political adherents, in two different ways to bolster their own undemocratic rule.

They employed the threat of fundamentalism in power that these movements posed to appeal for support from Western governments, on the grounds that the Islamists were the only alternatives to the incumbent dictatorships— that is themselves—and that however offensive to their values the governments of the West found the regimes of the region, the Islamic radicals in power would be worse: they would attack Western interests. This was not a hollow claim.

The Egyptian government could point to the Muslim Brothers, the only significant source of organized opposition to its rule, as a reason that it deserved Western political and economic support.[113] Saudi Arabia had an even more alarming aspirant to power to cite to persuade the world that the cupidity and religious extremism of the al-Saud tribe was preferable to the likely alternative to it: Osama bin Laden, the leader of the al-Qaeda network that had mounted the terrorist attacks of September 11, 2001. Every Arab government, to justify its dictatorial rule, could invoke the events in Algeria in the 1990s, when a challenge to the regime by a powerful Islamic group led to a bloody civil war that carried on for a decade and cost 100,000 lives.[114]

At the same time, Arab rulers sought to use Islam to enhance their own standing in the eyes of those they governed. Saddam Hussein, a secular tyrant for most of his bloody career in power, was given, in his final years, to ostentatious displays of piety. The most thoroughgoing and, for the rest of the world, the most dangerous embrace of Islam as a basis of political legitimacy took place in Saudi Arabia.

The Saudi state was established at the beginning of the twentieth century as a partnership between the al-Saud tribe and an unusually severe and militant form of Islam[115] originally advanced in the eighteenth century by a preacher named Ibn Abd al-Wahhab, and thus widely known as Wahhabism. The ruling tribe justified its monopoly of power, and the flood of wealth from the country's oil that came with it, as a means to enforce the tenets of Wahhabism on the Arabian peninsula. With the oil wealth that their political power brought them, the Saudi rulers also sought to spread their version of the faith through financial support for mosques and religious schools all over the world.[116] From these mosques and schools, in Saudi Arabia itself but also in Pakistan and Western Europe, emerged some of the terrorists who conducted murderous attacks on civilians in the first decade of the twenty-first century.

Islam suffused the history, and the sense of identity, of the Arab world. For much of that history Arab Muslims saw themselves as engaged in an epic battle for global supremacy with the Christian West.[117] This version of the past also created resistance to democracy in the twenty-first-century Arab Middle East.

In the centuries after its founding, Islam spread far beyond its point of origin on the Arabian peninsula, often by military conquest. Eventually, however, the faith suffered a reversal of fortune, which has continued to the present day.[118] In the fifteenth century, Muslim rule on the Iberian peninsula ended. In 1683 the armies of the greatest of all Islamic powers, the Ottoman Empire, which controlled Anatolia, much of the

Arab world, parts of the Caucasus and North Africa, as well as the Balkan peninsula, reached the gates of Vienna, but were stopped there by European Christian forces. Thereafter the Ottoman Empire became steadily weaker than its European rivals, coming to be known as the "sick man of Europe." At the end of the eighteenth century European power penetrated to the heart of the Middle East, when a French army led by Napoleon occupied Egypt. In the nineteenth and twentieth centuries Britain and France established their rule over much of North Africa and what had once been the Arab provinces of the Ottoman Empire.[119]

The historical memory of rivalry with and, over the course of 400 years, defeat by the Christian West still resonated in the Arab Middle East in the twenty-first century, long after most of the relevant events had taken place.[120] That historical memory served as a source of popular anger and resentment throughout the region and thereby blocked the progress of democracy in two ways.[121] First, those sentiments made it possible for the ruling dictatorships to mobilize support for themselves as the stalwart defenders of the Arabs against the cultural and political onslaught of the West and its local surrogate, Israel.[122] This assertion gained credence not because it was true but because it was consistent with what Arabs had been taught was the dominant pattern of their own past. Second, resentment of the West helped to discredit everything of Western origin, including its dominant political system. In the Middle East, democracy lacked the good name that it enjoyed elsewhere. Liberty and free elections had far less favorable reputations in the Middle East than in the rest of the world by virtue of their common association with the civilization that was persistently declared to be the historic adversary of Arab Muslims.[123]

To be sure, Russia and China also had histories of rivalry with the countries that became the world's leading centers of democracy. The regimes that had conducted the rivalry in each case, however—traditional empires and then orthodox communist states—had disappeared. The conflict between the Arab world and the West, by contrast, had had at its core, at least initially, the religious differences between the two sides, and the Islamic faith remains central to the life of the Arabs in the twenty-first century.

In the Arab Middle East, the combination of ethnic and religious pluralism, oil, Islam, and the historical legacy of rivalry with the West severely weakens the impact both of the major external sources of pressure for democracy—the power of the democratic example—and of the principal internal source—a market economy. The opportunity for bringing liberty and representative government to the region, such as it is, lies in the fact that there are many Arab countries. If one of them were to become a democracy, this would provide an example that could not readily be discredited on the grounds that it was alien and irrelevant to local circumstances. A genuine Arab democracy would demonstrate that a government that is neither an autocracy nor a would-be theocracy can take root in the local soil, which would make a stronger and more favorable impression on Arabs than do democracies in Europe, North America, and East Asia.

Under the protection of an American military presence, the United States intended for Iraq to become the first Arab democracy, the country that would show the rest of the Arab Middle East the possibility and the advantages of establishing a liberty-protecting government chosen by the people. This is not what happened. Instead, over the course of the four years following the overthrow of Saddam Hussein's regime, Iraq came to exemplify the difficulties of implanting democratic government—both those that any such enterprise faces and the particular features of the Arab world that obstruct it—as well as the risks that such an effort entails.

As with virtually every other foreign policy of the United States, democracy-promotion was not the principal purpose of the American invasion of Iraq in 2003. Rather, the major goal was to deprive Saddam Hussein's regime of the weapons of mass destruction, in this case chemical, not nuclear, armaments, that it was widely and apparently genuinely—although not, as it turned out, accurately—believed to possess and that several United Nations resolutions had demanded that it relinquish. The American government initially planned to withdraw its troops a few months after toppling Saddam, which would have given it no effective means to implant a political system of liberty and popular sovereignty. It was only when and because the fall of Saddam precipitated the collapse of Iraq's entire political and administrative structure that the United States assumed responsibility for governing the country.

The initial American and allied invasion force was a relatively small one, numbering 150,000 soldiers, in contrast to the army three times that size that the United States had sent twelve years earlier to evict Saddam's army from Kuwait. The smaller size was in keeping with Secretary of Defense Donald Rumsfeld's conviction that America could accomplish its twenty-first-century military missions with fewer troops than it had routinely mustered for comparable operations in the previous century. For the task of deposing Saddam Hussein, Rumsfeld was proven correct. But for the very different task of controlling Iraq and so being able to nurture democratic politics there, a far larger force was needed. This became clear immediately after the overthrow of Saddam's regime, but the administration of George W. Bush, for all its rhetorical embrace of the goal of building an Iraqi democracy, never supplied the additional soldiers that were needed, which bespoke a less-than-wholehearted commitment to democracy-promotion there.

Even if the United States had made a larger and more sophisticated attempt to implant democracy in Iraq, however, success would have been, at best, difficult to achieve. The country lacked virtually all the social preconditions of liberty and popular sovereignty. The habits of trust and compromise that underpin democratic politics, for example, were almost nonexistent. During the Saddam Hussein era, as during the communist period in Russia, to trust anyone except relatives and close friends in a society thick with secret police and their informers was to court imprisonment or death. In Iraqi public life, moreover, compromise was unknown. Those who held political power sought to monopolize it indefinitely and to crush all opponents, actual or potential.

Nor did Iraq possess the institutions of civil society that make representative government and individual liberty possible. Like the Communist rulers of the Soviet Union, Saddam Hussein aspired to total control of the society he governed and worked to snuff out any and all independent political activity. This was made easier by the presence in Iraq, as in other Arab countries, of large reserves of oil. That oil provided Saddam with considerable wealth without the need for a robust private economy, which, had it existed, could have formed the core of an Iraqi civil society.

With the fall of Saddam's regime, groups independent of the governing authorities did appear, but the most prominent and powerful of them were not the kind that foster liberty. Post-Saddam Iraq's independent sector was dominated by the followers of radical Muslim clergy, sectarian militias, bands of criminals, and death squads.

Had the United States occupied Iraq in the nineteenth century, it might have been able to pacify the country and govern it for decades, as the British did in India, creating the circumstances in which the institutions and the values that democracy requires could gradually establish themselves. Eventually, the Iraqi equivalent of India's Nehru might have appeared, a leader with commanding authority and a deep commitment to liberty and popular sovereignty. In the first decade of the twenty-first century, however, this kind of imperial tutelage had become impossible. Even if the American public had been willing to supply it, neither the people of Iraq nor the inhabitants of any other country would accept it.

Standing in the way of the establishment of democracy in Iraq was another feature of many Arab (as well as non-Arab) countries: religious and ethnic divisions. The Sunni Arabs who had dominated the country under Saddam Hussein and indeed in all the years since the British had formed Iraq out of three former provinces of the Ottoman Empire in 1921, launched a bloody insurgency against the American occupation and the largely Shia government to which the American authorities transferred power. When the Shia began to fight back, the result was a virtual civil war, which was hardly a propitious setting for the development of liberty and popular sovereignty. Meanwhile, the country's third principal group, the Kurds, effectively seceded from Iraq. They governed themselves more or less independently of the other two, as they had been doing since 1991 when, in the wake of its first war against Saddam Hussein's regime, the United States deployed military forces to protect the Kurdish homeland in the northern part of the country from Saddam's army. Increasingly, the Kurds used their own Kurdish language, while Arabic, the official language of Iraq, fell into disuse among them.

In these circumstances, the elections that were held in the country, although free and fair, served to emphasize and to aggravate Iraq's divisions: Sunnis, Shia, and Kurds voted overwhelmingly for members of their own groups, prompting the observation that the voting more closely resembled a census than an election. As in other polarized societies, elections in Iraq, in the absence of a broad consensus among its three constituent groups on the most basic political issues and without the institutions of liberty, served to increase rather than reduce the level of violence.

To these formidable obstacles to democracy was added, after Saddam was deposed, yet another condition unfavorable to it, one for which the United States bore considerable responsibility: the absence of order in the country. Keeping order is the first duty of any government. It was the legal responsibility of the United States in Iraq from April 2003, when its armed forces ousted the existing government, until June 2004, when power was formally transferred to a new Iraqi government—and it continued to be an informal American responsibility for months thereafter. Yet the duty of keeping order was one that the United States conspicuously failed to fulfill.

The robberies, the kidnappings, the assassinations, the bombs exploding in crowded urban areas, the forcible evictions from their homes of Sunnis by Shias and vice versa, and the religiously inspired oppression visited on the inhabitants of cities and towns in both Sunni and Shia areas made personal insecurity the overwhelming fact of everyday life for many Iraqis, perhaps a majority of them. Tens of thousands were killed and several million fled the country; the refugees undoubtedly included many of those most committed to democratic norms and most capable of operating the institutions of democracy.

Iraq came, in no small part through American failures, to resemble the state of nature that the seventeenth-century English philosopher Thomas Hobbes described, in which life for everyone is "nasty, brutish, and short." In such a setting, personal safety becomes the highest priority, while liberty and popular sovereignty have far less value, if they have any value at all.[124] Rather than a showcase for democracy, therefore, the overthrow of Iraq's dictatorship turned the country into a cautionary example of the difficulties and dangers of trying to build one quickly and from scratch in conditions powerfully unfavorable to its establishment.

The country with perhaps the best prospects for democracy in the Arab world was Egypt. It was the oldest and most homogeneous one: its Christian minority made up only 10 percent of the population and did not threaten the Muslim majority. Egypt did conduct elections in 2005 in which the names of candidates not chosen by the regime were permitted to appear on the ballots. They were not, however, permitted to win. Effective power remained the monopoly of the dictatorship, and in the wake of the election the opposition candidate for president was harassed and jailed.[125]

Another relatively promising candidate for democracy was Lebanon, the Arab country with proportionately the largest middle class, the closest and friendliest connections to the West, and a history, from the 1930s to the 1970s, of a degree of harmony among different religious communities unusual in the region. There, in 2004, the assassination of a popular former prime minister, widely believed to have taken place at the

behest of Syria, sparked a series of large, peaceful demonstrations in protest. Reminiscent of the demonstrations that
had toppled dictators in Europe and East Asia, they gave rise
to the hope that Syria would release its imperial grip on its
neighbor and that Lebanon could then find a way to govern
itself as a democracy. But one of the country's constituent
groups, the Shia, maintained a political organization,
Hezbollah, that was provided with an independent military
force by Syria and Iran. Hezbollah used its military arm to
carry out, without the consent of the central government,
acts of terror against neighboring Israel. In July 2006, one
such act triggered a war. Because the Lebanese government
did not control all of the territory it claimed, two years after
demonstrations had filled the streets of the capital, Beirut,
Lebanon was not a fully sovereign state, let alone a genuinely
democratic one.

     While the autocrats of the Arab world had a wide array of
resources on which to draw to resist pressures for democracy,
they did have to mount active resistance in order to remain in
power. They did not have the option of simply ignoring the
challenge to their preferred form of governance that the remarkable rise of global democracy posed. None could shield
the countries they ruled from the powerful democratic current
at large in the world in the first decade of the twenty-first century. The force of that current put the question of democracy
on the political agenda of every undemocratic country, where
it would remain as long as the richest and most powerful sovereign states governed themselves in democratic fashion. The
prospects for global democracy depend heavily, therefore, on
how long this defining condition of twenty-first-century international politics persists.

Democracy in the Democracies

The good name that democracy enjoyed at the outset of the twenty-first century rested on the fact that it was practiced throughout Western Europe and North America and also in Japan. The end of democracy in these places would have something like the effect on its prospects elsewhere that the extinction of the sun would have on the rest of the solar system. The disappearance of democracy from the wealthy countries that formed its heartland seems an extremely improbable contingency. The discussion of democracy in these countries and around the world has largely concerned speculation about the places to which it might expand, not those from which it might retreat.

Still, nothing lasts forever. In several billion years, according to some estimates, the light of the sun will go out, it will no longer radiate heat, and life on Earth will presumably end. Within a much shorter period of time, the disappearance of democracy from its strongholds is not entirely unimaginable. For most of recorded history, after all, no political community governed itself in a democratic manner, and even when it first appeared, democracy did not immediately become the majority preference on the planet, attaining that status only at the end of the twentieth century. As recently as the 1970s it seemed to some observers a beleaguered form of political organization, one that was hardly likely to take hold beyond its Western base.[126]

In the foreseeable future, democracy is unlikely to retreat from the countries in which it has been firmly established, however, because each of its two major constituent parts is closely tied to prominent and seemingly durable features of modern life. Popular sovereignty is the logical consequence of the idea of equality.[127] Liberty appears necessary for the effective operation of advanced, complex, and productive free-market economies.

Over the course of the twentieth century, the idea that all people are created equal and that a political system must incorporate this idea in order to be legitimate came to be the subject of an unprecedented and remarkably broad consensus. More specifically, inequality based on inherited characteristics, the principle on which governments had been based from time immemorial, fell into terminal disrepute.[128]

By the twenty-first century monarchy and empire, regimes based on inequality, had all but disappeared in the West. The universal practice of popular sovereignty through representative government in Western Europe, North America, and Japan was the result. Political inequality in the form of undemocratic governments persisted elsewhere, of course, but dictatorships practiced inequality furtively rather than embracing it forthrightly as had been common until the middle of the twentieth century. Inequality may have been alive and well, but the idea of inequality was not.

In the Western democracies alternatives, or even challenges, to political equality ceased even to be discussed. Political debate concerned how to implement equality, in particular whether certain groups deserved special treatment to compensate for past disadvantages, not whether to do so at all. No one suggested that the government not be chosen by elections, or that not every adult be eligible to vote in those elections. This marked an extraordinary transformation in the intellectual basis of political life. In the course of less than a century the status of the principle of inequality went from axiomatic to taboo.

Just as intellectual life changed in ways that made political equality, and therefore popular sovereignty, unassailable, so, over roughly the same period, economic life changed in ways that made liberty indispensable. The richest countries in the world derive their wealth from their extraordinarily productive market economies. In these economies most people are engaged in the provision of services of various kinds rather than in agriculture or manufacturing, economic activity relies heavily on the use of information, and economic growth comes through innovation—making new products and finding new and more efficient ways to make existing ones.

Economies of this sort require at least one of the varieties of liberty—the economic kind—to function effectively. An advanced industrial economy must have secure property rights, without which innovation is rare because innovators cannot be confident of reaping the benefits of their inventions. More broadly, a secure legal framework is necessary for the successful operation of an economy advanced by the standards of the twenty-first century because in such an economy millions of separate transactions take place daily and they will not go forward without the assurance, which the law provides, that they will be completed. Such an economy depends as well on the free movement of individuals and information, which the establishment of political liberty guarantees and which liberty-denying dictatorships routinely impede.[129]

To be sure, the economies of countries in which liberty is absent can and do grow rapidly. Undemocratic China achieved higher annual rates of growth in the quarter-century following the introduction of economic reforms than did the Western democracies. China was able to do this because it started from a low level of economic output and because of the particular stage of economic development it had reached when the reforms began. It could expand its economy by shifting labor on a large scale from agricultural tasks in the countryside to factory work in the cities, where former peasants could be employed more productively.[130] Moreover, during the period of explosive growth, China had no need to innovate. It imported machinery and techniques of production that had already been developed in the West.

China expanded its economy by what economists call the "extensive" method of growth, which involves raising output by increasing the volume of inputs. When underutilized inputs—labor, for example—become scarce, as they were in the West by the last decades of the twentieth century, growth must proceed by "intensive" methods—by making more efficient use of a given volume of inputs. Intensive growth requires innovation and innovation requires liberty. The material well-being of the planet's most economically advanced countries—and some day, presumably, of China as well—therefore depends on the practice of democracy's second component part. This means that the established democracies are just as unlikely to discard liberty as they are, because of the powerful consensus in favor of political equality that obtains in each of them, to abandon popular sovereignty.

Still, circumstances can be imagined in which they would be moved to jettison democratic institutions and practices. At least three scenarios for the end of democracy in the democracies are possible, although not, in the foreseeable future, at all probable. In the first scenario, the democracies lose what democratic government has had greater success than any other kind in providing: prosperity. In the other two, democratic political systems fail to provide what every government must furnish: order.

The economies of the Western democracies could conceivably suffer contractions on the scale that they experienced during the Great Depression of the 1930s. The American stock market crash of 1929 set in motion a sharp decline in output in North America and Western Europe that persisted for the better part of a decade, ending only with the economic mobilization occasioned by World War II. The sharp rise in unemployment that accompanied it, which made more than 40 percent of the industrial workforce jobless in some countries,[131] along with the Western governments' apparent helplessness in the face of these calamities, caused a loss of faith in the political system that presided over them. Political radicalism of various stripes gained popularity on both sides of the Atlantic Ocean, as well as in Japan. Fascism arose, and communism attracted followers, during and because of the greatest economic crisis of the industrial age.

A comparable economic failure in the twenty-first century would surely have similar effects. It would, at the least, shake confidence in the political and economic system that had produced it. If it were sufficiently severe and prolonged, it might well trigger a search for, and perhaps even the embrace of, a different, non-democratic method of governance that promised a superior economic performance.[132]

Democracy in the democracies could also, conceivably, fall victim to an epidemic of terrorism, or to a series of environmental disasters that cripple or destroy the networks of commerce, transportation, and communication on which daily life in the wealthiest countries has come to depend.[133] Such crises, in the worst case, could create violent disorder in societies that, in the first decade of the twenty-first century, were models of social peace.

The breakdown of order would bring to Western societies the conditions of Hobbes's state of nature: poverty, uncertainty, insecurity, and the fears to which they give rise. To restore the minimum conditions of safety and security without which life becomes unbearable, people would be willing to hand power, without democratic limits, to those who could guarantee them—as many seemed willing to do in Iraq four years after the American invasion. The loss of liberty and the surrender of the prerogative of choosing the government might well seem a reasonable price to pay for relief from the consequences of terrorism or environmental collapse.

None of these scenarios violates the laws of nature or falls outside the known boundaries of human experience. Any of them could therefore occur. Indeed, the forces that could bring them about were in evidence at the outset of the twenty-first century. The global economy had become larger and more complicated, its different parts more closely interconnected, than ever before. Its workings were not fully understood, and it certainly could not be controlled by any single government or international organization, no matter how powerful. Through an external shock or internal malfunction it could break down and be difficult to repair. Cells of terrorists around the world plotted to do as much damage as they could to the countries of the democratic West uninhibited by moral scruples or military threats. By their very successes in steadily expanding their outputs, the economies of the Western democracies as well, increasingly, as those of China, India, and other non-Western countries, have put stress on the planet's environment. The continuation of the early-twenty-first-century rate of resource consumption and waste production—in particular the "greenhouse gases" that raise the Earth's temperature and thus threaten to alter its climate—by some reckonings will ultimately bring about large changes in the physical conditions of life on the planet inconsistent with comfortable human existence.

The democracies, however, were well aware of the problems that these features of twenty-first-century life portended, and worked to forestall them. Since the Great Depression, advances in the understanding of modern economics and the experience of trying to apply what was learned to the management of these economics has yielded a body of knowledge and an arsenal of policies that have prevented an economic disaster on the scale of the 1930s.

As for international terrorism, in the wake of the attacks of September 11, 2001, governments all over the world charged their police forces and intelligence-gathering services with tracking, and arresting or eliminating, those seeking to perpetrate similar assaults. The threat that human activity posed to the Earth's environment was hardly a secret. Scientific studies, programs and laws in many countries, as well as international treaties were devoted to preventing or mitigating the damage to the planet's air, water, vegetation, animal life, and atmosphere.

Because of the flexibility with which liberty and popular sovereignty endow countries by protecting discussion and debate on all subjects and making possible changes of policy through changes in the composition of the government, democracies may well be better suited to coping successfully with these problems than undemocratically governed countries.[134] Democracy may prove as successful in meeting the challenges of the twenty-first century as it did in meeting those of the twentieth. And even if the democracies do not succeed in preventing all economic downturns, or stopping every terrorist attack, or avoiding environmental degradation in any form—and they surely will not achieve complete success in any of these areas—these misfortunes would have to occur on a very large scale to dislodge democratic government from Europe, North America, and Japan. They would have to occur in many countries, not only one or two, and cause severe hardship to hundreds of millions of people in order to dissolve the attachment that the people of these countries have formed, over the decades and indeed centuries, to liberty and popular sovereignty.

It would take, that is, massive discontinuity in their social and economic lives for the established democracies to abandon democracy. That this is so testifies to how firmly established democratic government had become in these countries by the beginning of the twenty-first century. During most of the twentieth century, by contrast, the West did not lack widely heeded predictions that the continuation of the trends of the day would lead inevitably to the triumph of entirely different political forms. This was the confident expectation at the heart of Marxism, an ideology that attracted, at one time or another during its career, millions of believers. The dystopias presented by the English writers Aldous Huxley and George Orwell, in their novels *Brave New World* and *Nineteen Eighty-four*, both of them widely read and discussed in the middle decades of the twentieth century, depicted the principal scientific and political currents of that era as bringing into being a world in which liberty and self-government had all but disappeared.

In the twenty-first century, however, a straight-line projection of the present into the future, the continuation of the principal social, political, and economic conditions, will reinforce the dominant status that democracy has come to enjoy. For in that case the most powerful and successful countries will remain democracies. They, and their democratic political systems, will continue to be the objects of admiration and emulation around the world. Democracy will retain its good name, and its example will generate pressure on all undemocratic governments to submit themselves to the judgment of the people they govern and to accept the limits on their powers that allow liberty to flourish. Without a major dislocation in the life of the planet, and in particular in the social, economic, and political conditions prevailing in the wealthiest and freest of its societies, therefore, the rise of global democracy, which has its origins in the eighteenth century, which began in earnest in the nineteenth and accelerated in the twentieth, is likely to continue well into the twenty-first.

Notes

Chapter 1

1. Quoted in Walter Russell Mead, *Special Providence: American Foreign Policy and How It Changed the World*, New York: Knopf, 2001, 46–47.

2. George W. Bush, "Inaugural Address," *The New York Times*, January 21, 2005, A12.

3. "In the early 1970s, there were about 40 democracies in the world. . . . As the 20th century ended, there were around 120 democracies in the world." George W. Bush, "Remarks by the President at the 20th Anniversary of the National Endowment for Democracy," United States Chamber of Commerce, November 6, 2003, available at www.whitehouse.gov/news/releases/2003.

4. The number for 1975 is taken from Samuel P. Huntington, *The Third Wave: Democratization in the Late Twentieth Century*, Norman, OK: The University of Oklahoma Press, 1999, 14, 26. The number for 2005 is from Aili Piano and Arch Puddington, editors, *Freedom in the World 2005, The Annual Survey of Political Rights and Civil Liberties*, Lanham, MD: Rowman and Littlefield, 2005, 789.

5. George W. Bush, "Inaugural Address."

6. Ibid.

7. Ibid.

8. Ibid.

9. Thus Woodrow Wilson said of Russia in 1917 (in a statement with which no scholar of that country's history would agree and for which neither the Russian experience before or after 1917 provided any convincing evidence): "Russia was known by those who knew it best to have been always in fact democratic at heart, in all the vital habits of her thought, in all the intimate relationships of her people that spoke to their natural instinct, their habitual attitude toward life." Quoted in Tony Smith, *America's Mission: The United States and the Worldwide Struggle for Democracy in the Twentieth Century*, Princeton, NJ: Princeton University Press, 1994, 89. Thus John F. Kennedy: "Democracy is the destiny of humanity." Quoted in ibid., 214. Ronald Reagan: "[M]an's instinctive desire for freedom and self-determination surfaces again and again." Quoted in ibid., 266. George H. W. Bush: "Make no mistake. Nothing can stand in the way of freedom's march." Quoted in ibid., 314.

10. George W. Bush, "Inaugural Address."

11. These words appear in the opening paragraph of perhaps the most influential of all American writings on politics and government, *The Federalist Papers*, edited by Clinton Rossiter, New York: Mentor Books, 1961, 33. Hamilton continues, "If there be any truth to the remark, the crisis at which we are arrived may with propriety be regarded as the era in which that decision is to be made." Ibid. In Federalist 14, another of the founders, James Madison, makes the same assertion: "[P]osterity will be indebted for the possession, and the world for the example, of the numerous innovations displayed on the American theater in favor of private rights and public happiness." Ibid., 104.

12. For a graphic depiction of the progress—and regression—of democracy, see Huntington, op. cit., 14.

13. Ibid., 17.

14. Ibid., 18–19.

15. George F. Kennan, *The Cloud of Danger*, Boston: Little, Brown, 1977, 41–42. "[D]emocracy didn't seem to be in good shape in 1975. Many democracies or near-democracies had recently been taken over by authoritarian forces, including Greece in 1967, the Philippines in

1972, and two of Latin America's oldest democracies, Chile and Uruguay, in 1973. Then in 1975 democratic Lebanon descended into virulent civil war, and India, the world's largest democracy, became an authoritarian state (only for a couple of years, as it turned out), while communism, substantially contained since 1949, began to gain market share: it picked up Cambodia, Vietnam, and Laos in 1975 and was to add Angola in 1976, Mozambique and Ethiopia in 1977, South Yemen and Afghanistan in 1978, and Nicaragua and Grenada in 1979." John Mueller, *Capitalism, Democracy, and Ralph's Pretty Good Grocery*, Princeton, NJ: Princeton University Press, 1999, 214.

16. George W. Bush, "Inaugural Address."

17. These differences partly correspond to the distinction, influential in the history of political thought, drawn by the nineteenth-century French writer Benjamin Constant between modern liberty, which involves areas in which the individual may do as he or she wishes, and ancient liberty, which had involved the opportunity to participate actively in public decisions. The ancients, however, did not accord all adults this kind of liberty. See John Dunn, *Setting the People Free: The Story of Democracy*, London: Atlantic Books, 2005, 63.

18. Fareed Zakaria, *The Future of Freedom: Illiberal Democracy at Home and Abroad*, New York: W. W. Norton, 2003, 31.

19. David Hackett Fischer, "Freedom's Not Just Another Word," *The New York Times*, February 27, 2005, A27.

20. Finer, *A History of Government from the Earliest Times*. Volume I: *Ancient Monarchies and Empires*, Oxford: Oxford University Press, 1997, 91, 388.

21. Finer, *The History of Government from the Earliest Times*. Volume II: *The Intermediate Ages*, Oxford: Oxford University Press, 1997, 866–70.

22. Guido de Ruggiero, *The History of European Liberalism*, translated by R. G. Collingwood, Boston: The Beacon Press, 1959, 1–4. Thus the witticism, "In democracy it is your vote that counts. In feudalism, it is your count that votes."

23. Richard Pipes, *Property and Freedom*, New York: Knopf, 2000, 104–5. By some accounts, private property was known previously in ancient Greece.

24. "Freedom . . . must be . . . sustained by the rule of law." George W. Bush, "Inaugural Address."

25. de Ruggiero, op. cit., 365–66. Historically, law is closely associated with property. Pipes, op. cit., 103–4; Tom Bethell, *The Noblest Triumph: Property and Prosperity through the Ages*, New York: St. Martin's Press, 1998, 7.

26. Finer, *The History of Government from the Earliest Times*. Volume III: *Empires, Monarchies, and the Modern State*, Oxford: Oxford University Press, 1997, 1570–71.

27. Linda Colley, *Britons: Forging the Nation, 1707–1837*, New Haven, CT: Yale University Press, 1992, 196. In Poland, the parliament, the *sejm*, was considerably stronger than the monarch, which it, in fact, chose. But Polish independence came to an end with the partition of its territory among neighboring empires in the late eighteenth century. Finer, *Empires, Monarchies, and Modern States*, 1369–72.

28. The monarchs were William and Mary, imported from the Netherlands because they were considered more respectful of liberty and of the Protestant religion.

29. This is a central theme of Alan Macfarlane, *The Origins of English Individualism*, Oxford: Blackwell, 1978.

30. Ian Buruma, *Anglomania: A European Love Affair*, New York: Random House, 2000, ch. 1, especially 21 and 35.

31. Finer, *Empires, Monarchies, and Modern States*, 1398, 1488–89.

32. The framers of the American Constitution were influenced by the writings of Charles de Secondat, Baron de Montesquieu, who had admired the British political system and imputed the liberty that the British people enjoyed to what he took to be the separation of powers within their government. The Americans thus imitated the British system by way of a French interpretation of it. Zakaria, op. cit., 44–45; Gay, op. cit., 324–25.

33. This was in keeping with the pre-Revolutionary practices in many of the colonies. Diarmaid MacCulloch, *The Reformation: A History*, New York: Viking, 2003, 521–25.

34. There was a major exception: the property of those who remained loyal to the crown and fled to Canada or England was in many cases expropriated after the Revolution.

35. "Article XVII. Property, being an inviolable and sacred right, can in no sense be taken away except where public necessity, legally determined, clearly demands it, and always on condition of a preceding indemnity." Quoted in de Ruggiero, op. cit., 68.

36. "The French Revolution is the most important single event in the entire history of government." Finer, *Empires, Monarchies, and Modern States*, 1517.

37. Quoted in de Ruggiero, op. cit., 66.

38. Dunn, op. cit., 33–35.

39. Finer, *Ancient Monarchies and Empires*, 46; Finer, *The Intermediate Ages*, 1024–27; MacCulloch, op. cit., 171.

40. The intellectual attack on hierarchy preceded the French Revolution. See Gay, op. cit., 399. On the impact of ideas on international politics see John Mueller, *Quiet Cataclysm: Reflections on the Recent Transformation of World Politics*, New York: HarperCollins, 1995, chs. 9 and 10.

41. Finer, *Empires, Monarchies, and the Modern State*, 1607.

42. C. A. Bayly, *The Birth of the Modern World, 1780–1914*, Oxford: Blackwell, 2004, 190, 409, 444.

43. "[W]hatever the continued inequalities, there is now a widespread belief in the universal equality of humans at birth." Alan Macfarlane, *The Riddle of the Modern World: Of Liberty, Wealth, and Equality*, New York: St. Martin's Press, 2000, 5.

44. Finer, *Empires, Monarchies, and the Modern State*, 1478.

45. The literature on the causes of nationalism is voluminous. A useful overview of it appears in Bayly, op. cit., 199–219.

46. Woodrow Wilson, who played a major role at the Paris Conference, believed that "no right anywhere exists to hand peoples about

from sovereignty to sovereignty as if they were property." Quoted in Smith, op. cit., 88.

47. de Ruggiero, op. cit., 93, 104.

48. For "almost two thousand years of its history as a word," democracy, as "it was overwhelmingly judged by most who used the term, had proved grossly illegitimate in theory and every bit as disastrous in practice." Dunn, op. cit., 15.

49. Finer, *Ancient Monarchies and Empires*, 362.

50. Gay, op. cit., 498, 519; Finer, *Empires, Monarchies, and the Modern State*, 1497; Sean Wilentz, *The Rise of American Democracy: Jefferson to Lincoln*, New York: W. W. Norton, 2005, xvii, xviii, 7, 114.

51. Finer, *Ancient Monarchies and Empires*, 46–47. On the criticisms of Athenian democracy, justified and unjustified, see ibid., 62–68.

52. On the Enlightenment view of the capacities of the common man, see Gay, op. cit., 519. In nineteenth-century Russia, "Echoing the thoughts of many a British or French colonial administrator or American slave-owner, a Russian bureaucrat rejected reform on the grounds that the peasants' 'capacity to reason is in a child-like state.'" Bayly, op. cit., 416.

53. The phrase was coined by Fareed Zakaria. See his article "The Rise of Illiberal Democracy," *Foreign Affairs* 76, no. 6, November–December 1997.

54. The two men in fact corresponded with each other about their common interests and concerns. Harvey C. Mansfield and Delba Winthrop, "Editors' Introduction," in Alexis de Tocqueville, *Democracy in America*, Chicago: University of Chicago Press, 2000, xxviii–xxix.

55. Tocqueville hoped that an independent judiciary, local self-government, and the many civic associations he observed in America would preserve liberty there. Mill advocated a system of proportional representation for the British Parliament to assure a hearing for minority views.

56. Tocqueville, op. cit., 55.

57. Finer, *Empires, Monarchies, and the Modern State*, 1575.

58. The figures are from Zakaria, *The Future of Freedom*, 50. Slightly different figures are given in Finer, *Ancient Monarchies and Empires*, 44.

59. Huntington, op. cit., 16.

60. Alexander Keyssar, *The Right to Vote: The Contested History of Democracy in the United States*, New York: Basic Books, 2000, 78–80.

61. The value of the property needed to qualify for the vote varied from country to country and over time. Nineteenth-century British electoral reform consisted in part of lowering the value of the property a man (only men were eligible) had to own in order to vote.

62. Keyssar, op. cit., 47–48; Wilentz, op. cit., 5, 8.

63. Bayly, op. cit., 303; Colley, op. cit., 345.

64. Keyssar, op. cit., 48; Wilentz, op. cit., 343–44, 485.

65. Karl Marx and Friedrich Engels, *The Communist Manifesto*, with an Introduction by Eric Hobsbawm, London: Verso, 1998, first published in 1848, 52. "It was this fear of being expropriated that Marx was talking about in 1848 when he said that Europe was 'haunted by the spectre of Communism': it was not 'communism' as we have known it today in the least, but the fear of losing one's property." Finer, *Empires, Monarchies, and the Modern State*, 1583.

66. The role of land reform as a prerequisite for democracy is an important theme of Smith, op. cit. See, in particular, 50–59 and 162–63. Not all twentieth-century efforts at land reform succeeded either in redistributing cultivable property or in paving the way for democracy. On this point, see Bethell, op. cit., 208–21.

67. For a brief overview of Marx's errors of economic analysis, see Robert Skidelsky, "What's Left of Marx?" *The New York Review of Books*, November 16, 2000, 26–27.

68. Moreover, whereas all working Americans must contribute to the Social Security fund because it is supported by the tax payments of non-beneficiaries, most recipients, upon retirement, have received more in benefits than they have paid in taxes to this fund.

69. On the elevation of social welfare to something like a third entitlement of modern citizenship, along with liberty and political participation, see T. H. Marshall, "Citizenship and Social Class," in *Citizenship and Social Class and Other Essays*, Cambridge, UK: Cambridge University Press, 1950.

70. Michael Mandelbaum, "The Future of Nationalism," in Raju G. C. Thomas, editor, *Yugoslavia Unraveled: Sovereignty, Self-Determination, Intervention*, Lanham, MD: Lexington Books, 2003, 44.

71. The phrase is from Michael Howard, *The Lessons of History*, New Haven, CT: Yale University Press, 1991, 33.

72. Multinational states in which one national group dominates and represses others embody a version of what Tocqueville and Mill feared: the tyranny of the majority. Sunni-dominated Iraq exemplified something different: tyranny of an ethnic minority. The Sunnis, especially during the rule of Saddam Hussein, exercised particularly tyrannical control precisely because non-Sunnis heavily outnumbered them.

73. Zakaria, *The Future of Freedom*, 114–15.

74. The United States, however, does not fit this description. While certainly a democracy, it is not a multinational state. With the exception of Americans of African descent, it is populated by people who came, or whose forebears came, to North America from elsewhere voluntarily, as individuals, and so tacitly accepted the local—American—nationality. The multinational states of Europe and other parts of the world, by contrast, came into being when people who had lived in the same place for generations found themselves part of new political units together with other groups by virtue of borders being redrawn, almost invariably without their being consulted.

75. "Protection of individual rights does not satisfy the demands of groups for protection, preservation of a separate identity, and power." Marina Ottaway, "Iraq: Without Consensus, Democracy Is Not the Answer," Policy Brief 36, Carnegie Endowment for International Peace, Washington, D.C., March 2005, 3. See also Mandelbaum, "The Future of Nationalism," 49–50.

76. The Athenians regarded election as an insufficiently democratic method of selecting officials and instead chose them by drawing lots. Finer, *Ancient Monarchies and Empires*, 345.

77. This is the subject of Federalist 10, written by James Madison.

78. Lewis Carroll, *Through the Looking Glass*, in *The Annotated Alice*, Martin Gardner, editor. Cleveland: World Publishing Company, 1963, 269.

79. By one estimate, "the total approaches 100 million killed." Stephane Courtois, "The Crimes of Communism," in Courtois, Nicholas Werth, Jean-Louis Panne, Andrzej Paczkowski, Karel Bartosek, and Jean-Louis Margolin, *The Black Book of Communism: Crimes, Terror, Repression*, translated by Jonathan Murphy and Mark Kramer, Cambridge, MA: Harvard University Press, 1999, 4.

80. "[T]oday 'democracy' is universally held up to be desirable, indispensable, imperative. Hence no regime would dare to call itself anything else. So we have seen a row of military dictators calling their regimes respectively 'presidential democracy,' 'basic democracy,' 'guided democracy,' 'organic democracy,' 'selective democracy,' or 'neo-democracy.'" Finer, *Ancient Monarchies and Empires*, 384.

81. It is conceivable that a genetic component underlies this pattern. A study of four prominent social theorists, Montesquieu, Adam Smith, Alexis de Tocqueville, and the twentieth-century anthropologist and philosopher Ernest Gellner, found that "all were agreed that alongside sexual and intellectual drives, the desire to dominate and exert power over others was a basic human instinct." Macfarlane, *The Riddle of the Modern World*, 273.

82. Finer, *Empires, Monarchies, and the Modern State*, 1559.

83. Finer, *The Man on Horseback: The Role of the Military in Politics*, 2nd rev. ed., Boulder, CO: Westview Press, 1988, 191, 241.

84. Ibid., 190.

85. Ibid., 189.

86. The original Latin is *Sed quis custodiet ipsos custodies?* Quoted in Gay, op. cit., 565.

87. Stephen Holmes and Cass Sunstein, *The Cost of Rights: Why Liberty Depends on Taxes*, New York: W. W. Norton, 1999, 61.

88. Clinton Rossiter, editor, *The Federalist Papers*, 322.

89. Madison recognized that the root of the problem lay in human nature itself: "It may be a reflection on human nature that such devices should be necessary to control the abuses of government. But what is government itself but the greatest of all reflections on human nature? If men were angels, no government would be necessary. If angels were to

govern men, neither external nor internal controls on government would be necessary." Ibid.

90. "By [1914, the state] could widely deploy more men, more authority, more resources, and more destructive power against its own citizens and against other states than it had done earlier. It had, in many areas, though not all, gained a more effective control of reserves of manpower and money. It was able to deploy new symbols to enforce its authority, and it had created larger and more efficient bureaucracies, archives, and survey departments to aid it in these tasks." Bayly, op. cit., 265. See also Finer, *Empires, Monarchies, and the Modern State*, 1423–24, 1480–81, 1610–11, 1624.

91. Bayly, op. cit., 33.

92. On the negative correlation between violence attending a transfer of political power and the establishment of stable democracy, see Huntington, op. cit., 207.

93. The peaceful transitions of the 1970s and 1980s, which he terms the "third wave" of democracy-creation in world history, are analyzed in Huntington, op. cit., on which the discussion that follows relies.

94. The countries were Poland, Hungary, Czechoslovakia, Bulgaria, Romania, and East Germany, which was subsequently absorbed by West Germany.

95. The new countries were Estonia, Latvia, Lithuania, Belarus, Ukraine, Russia, Moldova, Georgia, Armenia, Azerbaijan, Kazakhstan, Uzbekistan, Kyrgyzstan, Turkmenistan, and Tajikistan.

96. In Romania, the Communist leader and his wife were killed. The great exception to the pattern of peaceful political change in Communist-ruled countries was Yugoslavia, the dissolution of which occasioned considerable bloodshed.

97. Huntington, op. cit., 125.

98. Huntington divides the peaceful transfers of power into three categories. In what he calls "transformations," "those in power take the lead and play the decisive role in ending that regime and changing it into a democratic system." Huntington, op. cit., 124. In "replacements," democracy "results from the opposition gaining strength and the government losing strength until the government collapses or is

overthrown." Ibid., 142. In "transplacements," "democratization is produced by the combined actions of government and opposition." Ibid., 151. He notes that in most of the transitions he studied, some measure of cooperation by the regime in power was the norm. Ibid., 142.

By one largely schematic, rather than empirical, account, democracy, defined as popular sovereignty through free elections, comes about when elites, fearing mass violence that will dispossess them of their wealth, concede changes in the political system in order to avoid this violence. Permitting elections as the method of choosing the government forestalls violence when other kinds of concessions would not do so, according to this argument, because it is a measure that cannot easily be revoked. It therefore counts as a credible concession in the eyes of those to whom it is made. Daron Acemoglu and James Robinson, *The Economic Origins of Democracy and Dictatorship*, New York: Cambridge University Press, 2006.

99. "Americans move forward in every generation by reaffirming all that is good and true that came before—ideals of justice and conduct that are the same yesterday, today, and forever." George W. Bush, "Inaugural Address."

CHAPTER 2

1. The term apparently comes from the American practice of "branding" cattle—burning into the animal's skin with a red-hot iron a particular pattern to identify its owner. For a discussion of democracy as a product promoted by the equivalent of a marketing campaign, see John Mueller, *Capitalism, Democracy, and Ralph's Pretty Good Grocery*, Princeton, NJ: Princeton University Press, 1999, 202–12.

2. Some brands gain such popularity that the brand name becomes a generic term for the product itself: "Kleenex" for paper tissue and "Xerox" for a photocopy in the United States, and "Biro" for ball-point pen and "Hoover" for vacuum cleaner in England. While democracy had not become a term for government itself in the twenty-first century, in the last decade of the twentieth, a sign of its dominance was the meaning of the word "transition," which was widely used to refer to the set

of economic and political tasks formerly Communist countries were undertaking after the end of Communist rule. It was understood to connote a transition to democracy. (Not every post-Communist government arrived at this political destination, however, or had even managed, by the middle of the first decade of the new century, to make noticeable progress toward it.)

3. Samuel P. Huntington, *The Third Wave: Democratization in the Late Twentieth Century*, Norman, OK: The University of Oklahoma Press, 1991, 101–3.

4. Ibid., 104–5.

5. The singular features of English history are the subject of Alan Macfarlane, *The Origins of English Individualism: The Family, Property, and Social Transition*, Oxford: Blackwell, 1978.

6. Ibid.

7. Alan Macfarlane, *The Riddle of the Modern World: Of Liberty, Wealth, and Equality*, New York: St. Martin's Press, 2000, 282–83. See also James Q. Wilson, "Democracy for All?" *Commentary*, March 2000, 26.

8. See below, 81–82, and chapter 5, 237–239.

9. On these questions see Joel Mokyr, ed., *The British Industrial Revolution: An Economic Perspective*, Boulder, CO: Westview Press, 1999.

10. Douglass North, a Nobel laureate in economics, has placed particular emphasis on this point. See, for example, Douglass C. North and Robert Paul Thomas, *The Rise of the Western World: A New Economic History*, New York: Cambridge University Press, 1973. The fact that land was freely marketable also helped make the Industrial Revolution possible, because it contributed to the production of an agricultural surplus. C. A. Bayly, *The Birth of the Modern World, 1780–1914*, Oxford: Blackwell, 2004, 174.

11. "England gave people elbow room." David Landes, *The Wealth and Poverty of Nations: Why Some Are So Rich and Some So Poor*, New York: W. W. Norton, 1998, 220.

12. Ronald Hyam, "The British Empire in the Edwardian Age," in Judith M. Brown and Wm. Roger Louis, editors, *The Oxford History of*

the British Empire, Volume IV: *The Twentieth Century,* Oxford: Oxford University Press, 1999, 48.

13. The phrase comes from a period before the empire attained its greatest size: "Sir George Macartney—later, as Lord Macartney, an Imperial administrator in many parts of the world—wrote in 1773 of 'this vast empire on which the sun never sets and whose bounds nature has not yet ascertained.'" P. J. Marshall, "Introduction," in Marshall, editor, *The Oxford History of the British Empire,* Volume II: *The Eighteenth Century,* Oxford: Oxford University Press, 1999, 8.

14. This is the theme of Paul M. Kennedy, *The Rise and Fall of British Naval Mastery,* Amherst, New York: Humanitas Books, 1998, first published 1976. See especially Parts I and II.

15. This is a major theme of Paul Kennedy, *The Rise and Fall of the Great Powers: Economic Change and Military Conflict from 1500 to 2000,* New York: Random House, 1987, for example, 76–86, and of Niall Ferguson, *The Cash Nexus: Money and Power in the Modern World, 1700–2000,* New York: Basic Books, as on 14–16. On the characteristics of democracies that inspire trust in others, with political as well as financial consequences, see Charles Lipson, *Reliable Partners: How Democracies Have Made a Separate Peace,* Princeton, NJ: Princeton University Press, 2003.

16. "During the eighteenth century the volume of Irish and Scottish emigration to British America was much larger than English emigration." Marshall, op. cit., 9.

17. Ibid., 10; S. E. Finer, *The History of Government from the Earliest Times,* Volume III: *Empires, Monarchies, and the Modern State,* Oxford: Oxford University Press, 1997, 1394–1405.

18. Peter Burroughs, "Imperial Institutions and the Government of Empire," in Andrew Porter, editor, *The Oxford History of the British Empire,* Volume III: *The Nineteenth Century,* Oxford: Oxford University Press, 1999, 187–89.

19. By Huntington's count, five of the ten were former colonies, and the sixth was Britain itself. Huntington, op. cit., 14–15.

20. The volume of the *Oxford History of the British Empire* devoted to the principal themes of imperial history includes forty-one essays on

such subjects as "Science, Medicine, and the British Empire," "Art and Empire," and "Architecture in the British Empire," but none on democracy. Robin W. Winks, editor, *The Oxford History of the British Empire*, Volume V: *Historiography*, Oxford: Oxford University Press, 1999.

21. "Englishmen escaped democracy and high taxation by establishing themselves in Kenya as territorial aristocrats." A. J. P. Taylor, *English History, 1914–1945*, Harmondsworth, UK: Penguin, 1970, first published 1965, 202.

22. On the motives of the first British conquerors in India, see Laurence James, *Raj: The Making and Unmaking of British India*, New York: St. Martin's Press, 1998, Part I. On the strategic motives for imperial expansion, the *locus classicus* is Ronald Robinson and John Gallagher, *Africa and the Victorians: The Climax of Imperialism*, Garden City, NY: Doubleday Anchor Books, 1968, first published 1961. On the need for bases, see Kennedy, *British Naval Mastery*, 154–56.

23. On this point, see Andrew Porter, "Trusteeship, Anti-Slavery, and Humanitarianism," in Porter, editor, op. cit.

24. Hyam, op. cit., 54; Judith Brown, "India," in Brown and Louis, editors, op. cit., 430. The British usually sought to keep the costs of imperial rule as low as possible, which often caused them to retain indigenous, and undemocratic, systems of authority. Burroughs, op. cit., 190, 196.

25. Leonard Woolf's memoir of his time as an official in Ceylon at the beginning of the twentieth century provides a vivid picture of how imperial rule operated. Woolf, *Growing: An Autobiography of the Years 1904–1911*, New York: Harcourt Brace and World, 1961.

26. Wm. Roger Louis, "Introduction," in Brown and Louis, editors, op. cit., 22, 37.

27. The most impressive democratic legacy of the British Empire is independent India, which became, with the end of British rule in 1947, the world's largest democracy, and has remained, except for a brief period in the 1970s, a representative democracy for six decades.

28. Louis, "Introduction," in Brown and Louis, editors, op. cit., 42, 44.

29. See, for example, Joseph Ellis, *His Excellency: George Washington*, New York: Knopf, 2005, among many studies of the life of the first American president.

30. John Lukacs, *Five Days in London: May 1940*, New Haven, CT: Yale University Press, 1999.

31. On Gorbachev, see Archie Brown, *The Gorbachev Factor*, New York: Oxford University Press, 1996.

32. Fareed Zakaria, *The Future of Freedom: Illiberal Democracy at Home and Abroad*, New York: W. W. Norton, 2003, 107.

33. The secondary school at which Nehru was educated, Harrow, was the same one that, a decade earlier, Winston Churchill—as it happened, a vigorous opponent of Indian independence for most of his political career—had attended. Nehru went on to university in England, at Trinity College, Cambridge.

34. Quoted in Burroughs, op. cit., 181.

35. The Seven Years' War was "the most dramatically successful war the British ever fought." Linda Colley, *Britons: Forging the Nation, 1707–1837*, New Haven, CT: Yale University Press, 1992, 101.

36. Bayly, op. cit., 428, 467.

37. At the Paris Peace Conference, "a young kitchen assistant at the Ritz [Hotel] sent in a petition asking for independence from France for his little country. Ho Chi Minh—and Vietnam—were too obscure even to receive an answer." Margaret MacMillan, *Paris 1919: Six Months That Changed the World*, New York: Random House, 2001, 59. Thirty-five years later, Ho led the successful Vietnamese war for independence from France.

38. The United States had made its debut as an imperial power and a major presence in the Pacific with its victory over Spain and annexation of the Spanish-ruled Philippine Islands in 1898.

39. See this chapter, 82–92.

40. The relationship between democracy and peace is the subject of chapter 4.

41. Macmillan, op. cit., offers a useful account of the peace conference.

42. Wilson said in 1918, "Democracy seems about universally to prevail. . . . The spread of democratic institutions . . . promise[s] to reduce politics to a single form . . . by reducing all forms of government to Democracy." Quoted in Niall Ferguson, "To Withdraw Now Would Be Folly," *The Wall Street Journal*, February 9, 2005, A10.

43. Huntington, op. cit., 16–18.

44. Lukacs, op. cit.

45. Tony Smith, *America's Mission: The United States and the World-wide Struggle for Democracy in the Twentieth Century*, Princeton, NJ: Princeton University Press, 1994, 154.

46. The Cold War had a similar effect on the political outlook of the Catholic Church. An institution rooted in tradition, it had not wholeheartedly endorsed democratic politics before the second half of the twentieth century. But the fact that democracies opposed the greatest twentieth-century threat to the church, the resolutely anti-religious Communist powers, as well as other effects of the modern world, instilled a more favorable attitude toward liberty and popular sovereignty, which church doctrine and policies came to reflect. These in turn helped to spread democracy to mainly Catholic countries in Europe and Latin America. Huntington, op. cit., 75–85.

47. Smith, op. cit., 172.

48. Huntington, op. cit., 87–89.

49. "The European Commission [the executive of the EU] has become a highly skilled manager of the accession process. It has written the book on member-state-building. Any country that truly wants to adopt a European model, and is prepared to give that project a clear run of five years or so, under the tutelage of Brussels, can reasonably expect success." Robert Cottrell, "Meet the neighbours: a survey of the EU's eastern borders," *The Economist*, June 25, 2005, 15.

50. "The Turkish parliament passed thirty-four constitutional amendments in October 2001 to bring itself in line with EU standards." Fareed Zakaria, *The Future of Freedom: Illiberal Democracy at Home and Abroad*, New York: W. W. Norton, 2003, 80. In 2004, "the EU declared itself ready to open negotiations [for membership] with Turkey . . . so long as Turkey met some last pre-conditions, mainly by

bringing an amended penal code into force and extending its customs-union agreement with the EU to cover all the new members, including Cyprus. Turkey duly amended the code." Cottrell, op. cit., 12.

51. Quoted in Michael Mandelbaum, *The Ideas That Conquered the World: Peace, Democracy, and Free Markets in the Twenty-first Century*, New York: PublicAffairs, 2002, 47.

52. Sunil Khilnani, *The Idea of India*, New York: Farrar, Straus, and Giroux, 1997, ch. 2.

53. An owner has an incentive to increase the value of what he or she owns because the benefits of the increase belong to him or her.

54. This is the subject of chapter 3.

55. This is the title of a book on post–Cold War American foreign policy by Robert J. Lieber, *The American Era: Power and Strategy for the 21st Century*, New York: Cambridge University Press, 2005.

56. Samuel P. Huntington, "The U.S.—Decline or Renewal?" *Foreign Affairs*, Winter 1988/1989, 82.

57. This is a major theme of H. W. Brands, *What America Owes the World*, New York: Cambridge University Press, 1998.

58. The various ways that the United States sought to foster democracy abroad during the Cold War are described and discussed in Joshua Muravchik, *Exporting Democracy: Fulfilling America's Destiny*, Washington, DC: The American Enterprise Institute, 1991.

59. Michael Mandelbaum, *The Case for Goliath: How America Acts as the World's Government in the Twenty-first Century*, New York: PublicAffairs, 2006, 88–94.

60. See chapter 3.

61. Huntington, op. cit., 97; Smith, op. cit., 280–81.

62. Huntington, op. cit., 95, 234, 238.

63. In 2004–2005, the European Union played something like the American role as facilitator in the peaceful political transition in Ukraine.

64. Wilson's name has come to be associated with the strain in American foreign policy that emphasizes the national mission to spread liberty throughout the world. Smith, op. cit., xv, 84; Walter Russell

Mead, *Special Providence: American Foreign Policy and How It Changed the World*, New York: Alfred A. Knopf, 2001, ch. 4.

65. Smith, op. cit., 297.

66. Richard Reeves, *President Reagan: The Triumph of Imagination*, New York: Simon and Schuster, 2005, 108–10.

67. Theodore Draper, "Mission Impossible," *The New York Review of Books*, October 6, 1994.

68. Winston Churchill, *The Grand Alliance*, Boston: Houghton Mifflin, 1950, 370.

69. Daniel Pipes and Adam Garfinkle, editors, *Friendly Tyrants: An American Dilemma*, New York: St. Martin's Press, 1991.

70. President John F. Kennedy stated the dilemma in 1961 when the pro-American dictator of the Dominican Republic, Rafael Trujillo, was assassinated, and the United States had to decide how to approach the question of who would succeed him: "There are three possibilities, in descending order of preference: a decent democratic regime, a continuation of the Trujillo regime, or a Castro regime. We ought to aim at the first, but we really can't renounce the second until we are sure that we can avoid the third." Quoted in Arthur M. Schlesinger, Jr., *A Thousand Days: John F. Kennedy in the White House*, Boston: Houghton Mifflin, 1965, 769.

71. Woodrow Wilson recognized this: "Democracy, like every other form of government, depended for its success upon qualities and conditions which it did not itself create, but only obeyed." Quoted in Smith, op. cit., 79.

CHAPTER 3

1. Quoted in Peter Gay, *The Enlightenment: An Interpretation: A New Science of Freedom*, New York: W. W. Norton, 1977, first published 1969, 24.

2. Robert Dahl, *On Democracy*, New Haven, CT: Yale University Press, 1998, 166–67.

3. In the African country of Guinea, to take one example, after independence from France in 1958, the country's leader, Ahmed Sekou

Toure, replaced independent traders with "a huge state trading corpo-ration; new state industries were launched as part of an ambitious in-dustrialisation programme; agricultural cooperatives were established; and public works expanded." Martin Meredith, *The Fate of Africa: From the Hopes of Freedom to the Heart of Despair: A History of Fifty Years of In-dependence*, New York: PublicAffairs, 2005, 273.

4. Nor have they invariably supported free markets. According to Adam Smith, "People of the same trade seldom meet together, even for merriment and diversion, but the conversation ends in a conspiracy against the public, or in some contrivance to raise prices." Smith, *The Wealth of Nations*, New York: The Modern Library, 1994, first pub-lished 1776, 148.

5. "For several decades in the last century the free market became so repugnant to the intelligentsia that only professional economists—and by no means all of them—could bear to study its workings in any depth, let alone with any sympathy." Ferdinand Mount, "Net present values," *TLS*, May 27, 2005, 10. On the reputation of the market in literature, see "Cents and sensibility," *The Economist*, January 6, 2001, 51, and Clive Crook, "The good company: a survey of corporate social respon-sibility," *The Economist*, January 22, 2005, 10–11.

6. "The problem of the world's poorest countries, it appears, is not that they are exploited by multinationals, but rather that they are ig-nored by them." Martin Wolf, *Why Globalization Works*, New Haven, CT: Yale University Press, 2004, 115. See also ibid., 242.

7. "The market economy is the most powerful mechanism for dis-mantling equality that humans have ever fashioned." John Dunn, *Set-ting the People Free: The Story of Democracy*, London: Atlantic Books, 2005, 137.

8. John Mueller, *Capitalism, Socialism, and Ralph's Pretty Good Grocery*, Princeton, NJ: Princeton University Press, 1999, 13, 47–48.

9. Ibid., 61.

10. "It is not from the benevolence of the butcher, the brewer, or the baker that we expect our dinner, but from their regard to their own in-terest. We address ourselves, not to their humanity but to their self-love,

and never talk to them of our own necessities but of their advantages."
Smith, op. cit., 15.

11. Mueller, op. cit., 65.

12. Martin Malia, *The Soviet Tragedy: A History of Socialism in Russia,
1917–1991*, New York: The Free Press, 1994, 33, 494.

13. Quoted in Smith, op. cit., 79.

14. By one estimate liberal democracies constitute 45 percent of the
world's population and generate 89 percent of its economic output.
Adrian Karatnycky, "The Democratic Imperative," *The National Interest*, Summer 2004, 108.

15. See chapter 3, 128–131.

16. There is also "a positive relationship between the political rights
and civil liberties that different countries' citizens enjoy today and the
prior quarter-century's growth of per capita income." Benjamin Friedman, *The Moral Consequences of Economic Growth*, New York: Knopf,
2005, 315–16. China is a conspicuous exception to this pattern.

17. Adam Przeworski, Michael E. Alvarez, Jose Antonio Chelbub,
and Fernando Limongi, *Democracy and Development: Political Institutions
and Well-Being in the World, 1950–1990*, New York: Cambridge University Press, 1997, 78–79. "Few relationships between social, economic,
and political phenomena are stronger than that between level of economic development and existence of democratic politics." Samuel P.
Huntington, *The Third Wave: Democratization in the Late Twentieth Century*, Norman, OK: The University of Oklahoma Press, 1991, 311.
While economic success clearly promotes political freedom, the reverse
relationship is not strongly established. In general, democracy seems
neither distinctly better nor markedly worse for economic growth, as
measured by per capita income, than other forms of government. Przeworski et al., op. cit., 178. See also Robert J. Barro, "Democracy and
Growth," Working Paper No. 4909, National Bureau of Economic Research, Cambridge, Massachusetts, October 1994. Explanations for the
more rapid rate of economic growth in China than in India sometimes
cite Indian democracy as an impediment to economic progress. Guy de
Jonquieres, "India must turn good economics into good politics," *Financial Times*, March 22, 2005, 17.

18. At least two different explanations are possible for the observation that as countries become richer they are more likely to be democracies. One is that, at a certain point, the generation of wealth triggers the movement toward political democracy. Economic growth, according to this explanation, reaches a "tipping point" that sets in motion political change. The other explanation is that such triggers have various sources but that, once democratic government has been established, it is likely to endure to the extent that the country in question is affluent. This second explanation is offered in Przeworski et al., op. cit.: "[W]hereas economic development under dictatorship has at most a non-linear relationship to the emergence of democracies, once they are established, democracies are much more likely to endure in more highly developed countries." Ibid., 103.

19. Ibid., 273; Huntington, op. cit., 61–63; Fareed Zakaria, *The Future of Freedom: Illiberal Democracy at Home and Abroad*, New York: W. W. Norton, 2003, 69–70.

20. One of the most often cited phrases in the history of political theory is Jeremy Bentham's assertion, in *The Theory of Legislation*, that "Property and law are born together and die together. Before the laws there was no property; take away the laws, all property ceases." See, for example, Stephen Holmes and Cass Sunstein, *The Cost of Rights: Why Liberty Depends on Taxes*, New York: W. W. Norton, 1999, 59. On the relationship of property and law, see also Richard Pipes, *Property and Freedom*, New York: Alfred A. Knopf, 2000, 130–31.

21. Benjamin Friedman, op. cit., 29, 335.

22. Huntington, op. cit., 64. Not all democracies have high rates of literacy. India's, for example, is low. On Indian ballots, each political party has its own symbol to make it possible for illiterates to vote. But India became, and remained, a democracy despite, not because of, the sizable percentage of its population that cannot read or write. The very large number of poor and illiterate Indians are susceptible to political manipulation. They form what have become known as "vote banks," sizable blocs of people whose votes their landlords or employers or caste or tribal leaders can deliver, en masse, to the highest bidder.

23. Affluence underwrites popular sovereignty in yet another way. It provides resources that can be divided among different groups, which is a method of resolving conflicts through compromise rather than violence. Poor countries have fewer resources and thus experience greater difficulty in keeping political participation peaceful. Benjamin Friedman, op. cit., 306–7.

24. Civil society is "the social residue left when the state is subtracted." Ernest Gellner, *Conditions of Liberty: Civil Society and Its Rivals*, New York: Penguin, 1994, 212.

25. Ibid., 146, 171, 211.

26. "Civil society is that set of diverse non-governmental institutions which is strong enough to counterbalance the state and, while not preventing the state from fulfilling its role of keeper of the peace and arbitrator between major interests, can nevertheless prevent it from dominating and atomizing the rest of society." Ibid., 5.

27. Harvey C. Mansfield and Delba Winthrop, "Editors' Introduction," in Alexis de Tocqueville, *Democracy in America*, Chicago: University of Chicago Press, 2000, lxxi. Traditional societies had (and where they persist still have) well-developed, powerful, partly autonomous associations below the level of the state, but these were based on kinship. Membership was not voluntary, and liberty did not, on the whole, flourish within them. Gellner, op. cit., 6–7.

28. The political party "lent a political shape to communities of residence or occupation, helped to define a sense of shared interest across them, and established salient outlines for political conflict over the exercise of governmental power." Dunn, op. cit., 184.

29. Charles S. Maier, "Democracy since the French Revolution," in John Dunn, editor, *Democracy: The Unfinished Journey*, Oxford: Oxford University Press, 1992, 134–35.

30. C. A. Bayly, *The Birth of the Modern World, 1780–1914*, Oxford: Blackwell, 2004, 74.

31. Gay, op. cit., 468; Alan Macfarlane, *The Riddle of the Modern World: Of Liberty, Wealth, and Equality*, New York: St. Martin's Press, 2000, 178.

32. Gellner, op. cit., 13, 134. Communist countries did have organizations of various kinds, but they did not operate independently of the ruling authorities. The Communist regimes created and supervised them and used them for a purpose that directly contradicts the democratic principle of popular control of the government. Communist associations of workers and writers served as the instruments by which the government controlled the people. They acted as "transmission belts" for conveying the authorities' instructions to the public.

33. Gellner, *Nations and Nationalism*, Oxford: Blackwell, 1983, 138.

34. Ibid., 48. See also Eric Hobsbawm, *Nations and Nationalism since 1870: Programme, Myth, Reality*, Cambridge, UK: Cambridge University Press, 1992, first published 1990.

35. Ibid., 86, 140.

36. Ibid., 36, 142.

37. Gellner, *Conditions of Liberty*, 113. See also Gellner, *Nations and Nationalism*, 55.

38. Gellner, *Conditions of Liberty*, 107–8.

39. Michael Mandelbaum, *The Ideas That Conquered the World: Peace, Democracy, and Free Markets in the Twenty-first Century*, New York: PublicAffairs, 2002, ch. 5.

40. Dahl, op. cit., 150–51.

41. Both the free market and democratic political systems therefore involve peaceful competition that penalizes some—the losers of elections and firms that fail to turn a profit—but benefits the society as a whole.

42. "[S]urveys have repeatedly shown that the prevailing level of interpersonal trust is greater in countries where incomes on average are higher." Benjamin Friedman, op. cit., 308.

43. Mueller, op. cit., 6, 21, 23.

44. Of course, the example of government intervention in any individual case can, and is intended to, deter misconduct in many others.

45. "'I am a proud communist,' Mr. [Buddhadeb] Bhattacharjee [the chief minister of the Indian state of West Bengal] says. 'I believe in Marx's world outlook, in the fundamental contradiction between labour and capital and in the class struggle. I know Americans will not write

the last chapter of human civilisation but I am also a realist. The world is changing. The lesson from the collapse of the Soviet Union and from China is that we reform, perform, or perish." Jo Johnson, "Bengal Tiger: Calcutta is transformed from Marxist redoubt into India's latest hotspot," *Financial Times*, October 20, 2005, 11.

46. Huntington, op. cit., 51.

47. "As Dmitry Shlapentokh has observed, were it not for Andropov's kidney disease communism would still be around." Vladimir Kontorovich, "The Economic Fallacy," *The National Interest*, Spring 1993, 44.

48. Andrew J. Nathan, "Introduction: The Documents and Their Significance," in *The Tiananmen Papers*, compiled by Zhang Liang, edited by Andrew J. Nathan and Perry Link, New York: PublicAffairs, 2002, first published 2001, xxxvi, xlix.

49. On the crucial question of whether to introduce martial law, in the Standing Committee of the Politburo, the highest decision-making body of the Communist Party, the vote was two in favor and two opposed, with one abstention. It was this deadlock that triggered Deng's decision to use force. Ibid., lvii.

50. Ibid., xliii.

51. "The documents reveal that if left to their own preferences, the three-man majority of the Politburo Standing Committee would have voted to persist in dialogue with the students instead of declaring martial law. Had they done so, China's recent history and its relations with the West would have been very different. Dialogue with the students would have tipped the balance toward political reform, and China today might well be an open society or even an electoral democracy, possibly under the rule of a reformed Communist Party." Ibid., xxxviii.

52. When Communists took power, they destroyed existing free-market systems more quickly than such systems could be rebuilt after communism ended, a point made by the Polish saying that it is easier to turn an aquarium into fish soup than vice versa.

53. These countries had implemented limited market reforms during the Communist period, which eased their transitions to full-fledged

free-market economies. See Jeffry Frieden, *Global Capitalism: Its Fall and Rise in the Twentieth Century*, New York: W. W. Norton, 2006, 431.

54. Terry Lynn Karl, *The Paradox of Plenty: Oil Booms and Petro-States*, Berkeley: The University of California Press, 1997, 5–6.

55. Thomas L. Friedman, *The World Is Flat: A Brief History of the Twenty-first Century*, New York: Farrar, Straus, and Giroux, 2005, 460. See also Thomas L. Friedman, "The First Law of Petropolitics," *Foreign Policy*, May–June 2006.

56. Ibid., 40, 42, 52–54.

57. Ibid., 41, 61; Zakaria, op. cit., 139. "Almost two-thirds of Kuwaitis are under 20 and will soon want jobs. They'll expect to find them with Kuwait's employer of first and last resort, the government, which promises a salary to any citizen who wants one. Almost all Kuwaitis who work are on the public payroll." Yasmine El-Rashidi, "In Kuwait, Gush of Oil Wealth Dulls Economic Change," *The Wall Street Journal*, November 4, 2005, A20.

58. "When a government is the direct beneficiary of a centrally controlled major revenue stream and is therefore not reliant on domestic taxation or a diversified economy to function, those who rule the state have unique opportunities for self-enrichment and corruption, particularly if there is no transparency in the management of revenues. Because achieving political power often becomes the primary avenue for achieving wealth, the incentive to seize power and hold on to it indefinitely is great." From a Human Rights Watch report on oil-rich Angola, quoted in Meredith, op. cit., 614.

59. Ibid., 616.

60. Smith, op. cit., 18, 52.

61. Macfarlane, op. cit., 269–71. See also Gellner, *Conditions of Liberty*, 64, 72.

62. In the 1970s, Mobutu was said to have fully one-third of the country's revenues at his disposal. By the time he was evicted from power, the country (subsequently renamed the Congo), which had once been rich in minerals, had become a failed state, its people destitute. Meredith, op. cit., 298, 393.

63. Gellner, *Conditions of Liberty*, 92.

64. Corruption and taxation differ in a fundamental way. While both can act as a drag on economic activity, taxes, unlike bribes, also make positive contributions to economic life. They pay for public investments, such as schooling, that make a society more productive economically, and for social welfare programs that make it more stable politically.

65. Meredith, op. cit., 526, 686.

66. Ibid., 170, 172–73, 370.

67. Ibid., 375.

68. Ibid., 580, 382–83.

69. "By the end of the 1980s, not a single African head of state in three decades had allowed himself to be voted out of office." Ibid., 378–79. "In twenty-nine countries [in Africa], over the course of 150 elections held between 1960 and 1989, opposition parties were never allowed to win a single seat." Ibid., 385–86.

70. On the reasons for petro-states' poor economic performances outside the oil sector, see Sebastian Mallaby, "The Democracy Trap," *The Washington Post*, April 25, 2005, A19.

Chapter 4

1. Quoted in Tony Smith, *America's Mission: The United States and the Worldwide Struggle for Democracy in the Twentieth Century*, Princeton, NJ: Princeton University Press, 1994, 271.

2. A summary and synthesis of the relevant studies is in Charles Lipson, *Reliable Partners: How Democracies Have Made a Separate Peace*, Princeton, NJ: Princeton University Press, 2003.

3. Jack Levy, "Domestic Politics and War," *Journal of Interdisciplinary History* 18, no. 4, Spring 1998, 662.

4. *Human Security Report 2005: War and Peace in the 21st Century*, Human Security Centre, The University of British Columbia, Canada, New York: Oxford University Press, 2005, 2. On the obsolescence of major war, see Michael Mandelbaum, "Is Major War Obsolete?" *Survival*, Winter 1998–1999, especially 34–35.

5. This is a principal finding of Monty G. Marshall and Ted Robert Gurr, *Peace and Conflict 2005*, College Park, MD: Center for International Development and Conflict Management, University of Maryland, 2005. See chs. 2 and 3. "By 2003, there were 40 percent fewer conflicts than in 1992. The deadliest conflicts—those with 1,000 or more battle-deaths—fell by some 80 percent. The number of genocides and other mass slaughters of civilians also dropped by 80 percent." Andrew Mack, "Peace on Earth? Increasingly, Yes," *The Washington Post*, December 28, 2005, A21.

6. This is the main thesis of John Mueller, *The Remnants of War*, Ithaca, NY: Cornell University Press, 2005. See also Martin Meredith, *The Fate of Africa: From the Hopes of Freedom to the Heart of Despair: A History of 50 Years of Independence*, New York: PublicAffairs, 2005, 472.

7. *Human Security Report*, 147.

8. "Between 1946 and 1991 the number of state-based armed conflicts being fought worldwide trebled . . . But today, 15 years after the end of the Cold War, the number of international crises is just a small fraction of the 1981 high point." Ibid., 3.

9. The idea that commerce in general, whether between or within countries, has a pacifying effect on the people who practice it, dates at least from the eighteenth century. Montesquieu and Adam Smith believed it, as did Voltaire and Tom Paine. See John Mueller, *Capitalism, Democracy, and Ralph's Pretty Good Grocery*, Princeton, NJ: Princeton University Press, 1999, 69, 83–84; Peter Gay, *The Enlightenment: Volume II: The Science of Freedom*, New York: W. W. Norton, 1969, 50; Benjamin M. Friedman, *The Moral Consequences of Economic Growth*, New York: Knopf, 2005, 41.

10. On Cobden see A. J. P. Taylor, *The Troublemakers*, London: Pimlico, 1993, first published 1957, ch. 2, and Anthony Howe, *Free Trade and Liberal England, 1846–1946*, Oxford: The Clarendon Press, 1997, ch. 3. Cobden also favored international arbitration and disarmament as mechanisms to promote peace. Martin Ceadel, *The Origins of War Prevention: The British Peace Movement and International Relations, 1730–1854*, Oxford: Oxford University Press, 1996, ch. 10.

11. "It is commerce which is rapidly rendering war obsolete, by strengthening and multiplying the personal interests which act in natural opposition to it." Quoted in Michael Howard, *War and the Liberal Conscience*, New Brunswick, NJ: Rutgers University Press, 1986, first published 1978, 37. Tocqueville concurred: "Trade is the natural enemy of all violent passions. Trade loves moderation, delights in compromise, and is most careful to avoid anger." Quoted in Alan Macfarlane, *The Riddle of the Modern World: Of Liberty, Wealth, and Equality*, New York: St. Martin's Press, 2000, 174.

12. This idea is belied by civil wars, which take place between and among people who ordinarily trade a good deal. The causes of civil wars are evidently powerful enough to override the natural, normal desire for prosperity. Mueller, *Grocery*, 117.

13. Mueller, *Retreat from Doomsday: The Obsolescence of Major War*, New York: Basic Books, 1989, 27–28, 50.

14. The Austrian-American economist Joseph Schumpeter believed that trade, and more importantly capitalism in general, was conducive to peace. He explained the persistence of war and the similarly economically irrational practice of imperialism by the presence, in otherwise modern, capitalist countries, of groups and practices, he termed "atavisms," which had originated in the precapitalist era, prominent among them the aristocracy. Schumpeter, "The Sociology of Imperialisms," in Schumpeter, *Imperialism and Social Classes*, Cleveland, OH: The World Publishing Company, 1955.

15. On the empirical evidence for the post-1945 connection between trade and peace, see Lipson, op. cit., 68.

16. Thomas L. Friedman, *The World Is Flat: A Brief History of the Twenty-first Century*, New York: Farrar, Straus, and Giroux, 2005, 419–29.

17. Ibid., 423–29. See also Thomas L. Friedman, *The Lexus and the Olive Tree: Understanding Globalization*, New York: Farrar, Straus, and Giroux, 1999, 402.

18. Macfarlane, *Riddle*, 274; Michael Mandelbaum, *The Ideas That Conquered the World: Peace, Democracy, and Free Markets in the Twenty-first Century*, New York: PublicAffairs, 2002, 122.

19. The principle of comparative advantage, the theoretical justification for free trade, applies to agriculture as well as to manufacturing. But the gains from trade became far greater, and therefore more obvious, as a result of the Industrial Revolution.

20. Mueller, *Grocery*, 111–12.

21. See Richard Rosecrance, *The Rise of the Trading State: Commerce and Conquest in the Modern World*, New York: Basic Books, 1986. At the same time, sovereign states and territories, such as Hong Kong, Singapore, the Benelux countries, and Switzerland, that were small, lacked natural resources, and had no hope of mustering significant military power, managed, through active participation in the international trading system, to become, in per capita terms, very wealthy.

To be sure, their common status as trading states depended on the military power of the United States, which protected them from real and potential adversaries and provided a secure framework for global commerce after 1945. See Michael Mandelbaum, *The Case for Goliath: How the United States Acts as the World's Government in the Twenty-first Century*, New York: PublicAffairs, 2006, chs. 2 and 3.

22. Preindustrial wars may have been more destructive than modern ones when measured by the proportion of the population killed and of property destroyed. The two world wars of the twentieth century were, however, more destructive in absolute terms and far more destructive than any war that Europe had seen for several centuries. John Mueller, *Quiet Cataclysm: Reflections on the Recent Transformation of World Politics*, New York: HarperCollins College Publishers, 1995, 130, 142.

23. Mandelbaum, "Obsolete?" 21.

24. This is the thesis of Mueller, *Retreat from Doomsday*, which argues that a third world war would probably not have taken place even if nuclear weapons had never been invented.

25. "The firepower carried by one submarine equipped with nuclear-tipped ballistic missiles could inflict more damage on any of the Second World War's belligerent powers than all the destruction any of them suffered during the course of that conflict." Mandelbaum, "Obsolete?" 22.

26. Michael Howard, *The Invention of Peace*, London: Profile Books, 2000.

27. On the rise of this attitude, see Mandelbaum, *The Ideas That Conquered the World*, 121–28 and Mueller, *Cataclysm*, 131.

28. Mueller, *Retreat from Doomsday*, 240–42.

29. "Europe (and the developed world) has experienced an almost complete absence of international warfare since 1945. Jack Levy calculates that 'the probability of no war occurring between the handful of leading states in the system' for such a long time is about .005." Mueller, *Quiet Cataclysm*, 127. "What [is] the probability . . . that the absence of wars between well-established democracies is a mere accident? The answer: less than one chance in a thousand. That is a level of certainty not often achieved with laboratory rats, let alone in studies of international relations." Spencer Weart, *Never at War: Why Democracies Will Not Fight One Another*, New Haven, CT: Yale University Press, 1998, 4.

30. "If the consent of the citizens is required in order to decide that war should be declared . . . nothing is more natural than that they would be very cautious in commencing such a poor game, decreeing for themselves all the calamities of war. Among the latter would be: having to fight, having to pay the costs of war from their own resources, having painfully to repair the devastation war leaves behind, and, to fill up the measure of evils, load themselves with a heavy national debt that would embitter peace itself and that can never be liquidated on account of constant wars in the future." Immanuel Kant, *Perpetual Peace*, Indianapolis: Bobbs-Merrill, 1957, 5–6.

31. Woodrow Wilson told the Congress of the United States in 1917, in asking for a declaration of war, that the people of Germany had not been consulted by their rulers on the decision to go to war. This was not entirely correct. What was true was that each of the belligerent governments in 1914, including the German one, sought to portray its country as the victim of aggression by others since responding to an attack is a universally accepted justification for war.

32. This is a major theme of Edward D. Mansfield and Jack Snyder, *Electing to Fight: Why Emerging Democracies Go to War*, Cambridge, MA:

MIT Press, 2005. See especially ch. 6. On the presence of this pattern in Africa, see Meredith, op. cit., 389, 608.

33. Mansfield and Snyder, op. cit., 10–11. On the problem of determining borders, see Michael Mandelbaum, "The Future of Nationalism," in Raju G. C. Thomas, editor, *Yugoslavia Unraveled: Sovereignty, Self-Determination, Intervention*, Lanham, MD: Lexington Books, 2003, 47–49.

34. Jack Snyder, *From Voting to Violence: Democratization and Nationalist Conflict*, New York: W. W. Norton, 2000, 19, 32, 69. This is the case both for people previously excluded from power and for members of the old elite who risk losing power in the new, more open political system. Ibid., 83, 181.

35. See chapter 1, 16–23.

36. Kant, it should be noted, believed that the habits of liberty and economic interdependence also promoted peace. Michael Doyle, *Ways of War and Peace*, New York: W. W. Norton, 1997, 286–87.

37. Weart, op. cit., 77, 89, 294.

38. This is the principal explanation for the democratic peace offered by Weart. Ibid. See also John M. Owen IV, *Liberal Peace, Liberal War*, Ithaca, NY: Cornell University Press, 1998.

39. It has also been argued, notably by Natan Sharansky in *The Case for Democracy*, New York: PublicAffairs, 2004, that dictatorships are prone to war because of their own distinctive internal political norms, habits, and institutions.

40. Weart, op. cit., 112.

41. This feature of democracy discourages civil as well as interstate wars. It inclines governments to make concessions to dissatisfied groups that, without such concessions, might seek to secede through the use of force. In this way, for example, independent and democratic India has weathered political conflicts, without large-scale violence, of the kind that have led to civil wars in undemocratic countries. To be sure, democratic political forms and procedures do not always prevent civil war, as the American experience from 1861 to 1865 demonstrates.

42. Sharansky, op. cit., 3; Richard Pipes, *Vixi: Memoirs of a Non-Belonger*, New Haven, CT: Yale University Press, 2003, 214.

43. Lipson, op. cit., 36–44. The great Western Cold War military alliance, the North Atlantic Treaty Organization (NATO), was grounded in the political habits that liberty had fostered within them applied to relations among the member states. John Lewis Gaddis, *We Now Know: Rethinking Cold War History*, New York: Oxford University Press, 1997, 199–201, 288–89.

44. See Arthur M. Schlesinger Jr., *The Imperial Presidency*, Boston: Houghton Mifflin, 1973, especially chs. 3–7.

45. Weart, op. cit., 90.

46. Michael Mandelbaum, *The Fate of Nations: The Search for National Security in the Nineteenth and Twentieth Centuries*, New York: Cambridge University Press, 1988, ch. 5; Mandelbaum, *The Ideas That Conquered the World*, 112.

47. Lipson, op. cit., 10–11.

48. See Michael Mandelbaum, *The Nuclear Question: The United States and Nuclear Weapons, 1946–1976*, New York: Cambridge University Press, 1979, 195–96.

49. Michael Mandelbaum, *The Dawn of Peace in Europe*, New York: The Twentieth Century Fund, 1996, 98–99.

50. This is a principal theme of Lipson, op. cit.

51. This is a major theme of Snyder, op. cit. See, for example, 15, 20, 25, 79.

52. "No ruling group likes to admit that it can govern its people only by regarding and treating them as criminals. For this reason there is always a tendency to justify internal oppression by pointing to the menacing iniquity of the outside world. And the outside world must be portrayed, in these circumstances, as very iniquitous indeed—iniquitous to the point of caricature." George F. Kennan, "America and the Russian Future," *Foreign Affairs*, Spring 1990, first published 1951, 162.

53. Mansfield and Snyder, op. cit., 46.

54. Ernest Gellner, *Conditions of Liberty: Civil Society and Its Rivals*, New York: Allen Lane, The Penguin Press, 1994, 176–77. In waging wars dictatorships labor under a handicap that does not affect democracies: the armed forces of undemocratic regimes are often configured to suppress internal dissent rather than to defeat foreign enemies.

55. According to Tocqueville, "[A]ll nations that have had to engage in great wars have been led, almost in spite of themselves, to increase the powers of the government. Those which have not succeeded in this have been conquered. A long war almost always faces nations with this sad choice: either defeat will lead them to destruction or victory will bring them to despotism." Quoted in Alan Macfarlane, *The Riddle of the Modern World*, New York: St. Martin's, 2000, 219.

56. *The Man on Horseback* is the title of a book by S. E. Finer about the seizure of political power by military figures, Boulder, CO: Westview Press, 1988, second edition.

57. Mansfield and Snyder, op. cit., 36.

58. This is the theme of Arno J. Mayer, *The Persistence of the Old Regime: Europe to the Great War*, New York: Pantheon, 1981. See, for example, 4, 15, 284, 290, 298, 300, 304–5.

59. Ibid., 305.

60. Paul Kennedy, *The Rise of the Anglo-German Antagonism, 1860–1914*, London: George Allen and Unwin, 1982, 326, 359–60.

61. Michael Mandelbaum, *The Nuclear Revolution: International Politics Before and After Hiroshima*, New York: Cambridge University Press, 1979, 114–15.

62. Kennedy, op. cit., 428. In his authoritative study of Anglo-German relations before World War I, Kennedy concludes that while domestic considerations had something to do with the coming of war, no single explanation suffices to account for it, and that in the hierarchy of causes, "the elemental German push to change the existing distribution of power" stands highest. Ibid., 469.

63. Martin Malia, *The Soviet Tragedy: A History of Socialism in Russia, 1917–1991*, New York: The Free Press, 1994, 110.

64. Snyder, op. cit., 236; Peter Baker and Susan Glasser, *Kremlin Rising: Vladimir Putin's Russia and the End of Revolution*, New York: Scribner's, 2005, 30, 35, 37, 371–72. Putin's aides accused those who protested his accumulation of power beyond what democratic norms would permit of being in league with foreign powers. Ibid., 374–75.

65. Presumably for the same reason, the Communist government in Beijing also deliberately sought to keep alive Chinese resentment of

Japan for the Japanese conquest of and atrocities committed in mainland China during World War II.

66. "A World Bank report, *Claiming the Future* (1995), put the economic dislocation of the Muslim Middle East and North Africa in stark
terms. These lands, with a population of 260 million people, exported
fewer manufactured goods than Finland with its 5 million people."
Fouad Ajami, *The Dream Palace of the Arabs: A Generation's Odyssey*, New
York: Pantheon Books, 1998, 275. See also Thomas Friedman, *The
World Is Flat*, 401.

67. "Meanwhile the blame game—the Turks, the Mongols, the im-
perialists, the Jews, the Americans—continues, and shows little sign of
abating. For the governments, at once oppressive and ineffectual, that
rule much of the Middle East, this game serves a useful, indeed an essential purpose—to explain the poverty that they have failed to alleviate
and to justify the tyranny that they have intensified. In this way they
seek to deflect the mounting anger of their unhappy subjects against
other, outer targets." Bernard Lewis, *What Went Wrong? Western Impact
and Middle Eastern Response*, New York: Oxford University Press, 2002,
159. This is a major theme of Barry Rubin, *The Long War for Freedom:
The Arab Struggle for Democracy in the Middle East*, New York: Wiley
and Sons, 2006. See, for example, 45, 86, 98, 128.

68. To cite a specific example of the governments of the region incit-
ing popular hostility to the West, the demonstrations and violence in
the Islamic world at the beginning of 2006 in protest against cartoons
depicting the prophet Muhammad in a Danish newspaper were encouraged, and in some cases orchestrated, by officials in the countries where
they took place. See Andrew Higgins, "How Muslim Clerics Stirred
Arab World against Denmark," *The Wall Street Journal*, February 7,
2006, A25, and Hassan M. Fattah, "At Mecca Meeting, Cartoon Out-
rage Crystallized," *The New York Times*, February 9, 2006, A1.

69. Ajami, op. cit., 285; Rubin, op. cit., 92, 94.

70. Rubin, op. cit., 19–20, 46, 289. The phrase that Fouad Ajami
uses to describe this feature of Arab political culture is "an incendiary
mix of victimology and wrath." Ajami, *The Foreigner's Gift: The Ameri-*

cans, the Arabs, and the Iraqis in Iraq, New York: The Free Press, 2006, 78, 165, 211.

71. Ajami, *Dream Palace*, 285, 294.

72. In the Arab press, for example, "the eight-year-long effort of President Bill Clinton to bring a negotiated peace and create a Palestinian state is literally never mentioned." Rubin, op. cit., 135.

73. Ibid., 62, 64, 244.

74. Ibid., 142, 146.

75. The Saudi regime publicly opposed, but privately supported, the 2003 American war in Iraq. Ajami, *Foreigner's Gift*, 72–73. The importance to the world of Saudi Arabia's reserves of oil, access to which, successive American administrations calculated, required the continuation in power of the al-Saud dynasty, made the United States willing to tolerate the Saudi government's anti-American activities. The American indulgence of similar Egyptian policies stemmed from the desire to support that country's formal peace with Israel.

76. Rubin, op. cit., 151.

77. Ajami, *Dream Palace*, 280–81.

78. Rubin, op. cit., 71–72, 83–84, 88.

79. The Arabs who lived within the 1967 boundaries of Israel did have rights of citizenship, including the right to vote in free, fair, regular elections and political, economic, and religious liberty, none of which was available to anyone living in an Arab-governed country.

80. See Michael Doran, *Pan-Arabism before Nasser: Egyptian Power Politics and the Palestine Question*, New York: Oxford University Press, 1999. For all their insistence on the need for a Palestinian state, moreover, the Arab regimes had never taken any steps to create one when they had the opportunity to do so. From 1948 to 1967, the territory that the Arabs often said should form such a state (while at other times declaring that Arab "Palestine" should include all of Israel, which should therefore disappear) was under the control of Jordan and Egypt. Neither country showed any interest in granting these territories independence, and no other Arab government ventured the opinion that they should.

81. Barry Rubin, *The Arab States and the Palestine Conflict*, Syracuse, NY: Syracuse University Press, 1981, xiii, xvii.

82. Dennis Ross, *The Missing Peace: The Inside Story of the Fight for Middle East Peace*, New York: Farrar, Straus, and Giroux, 2004.

83. Rubin, *Long War for Freedom*, 155, 164. See also Hala Mustafa, "Blaming Hamas sidesteps regional realities," *Financial Times*, May 17, 2006, 13.

84. This was not new. Many, if not most, terrorists of the past had been willing to sacrifice their own lives to carry out their missions. Walter Laqueur, *No End to War: Terrorism in the Twenty-first Century*, New York: Continuum, 2003, 71–72. What was new in the twenty-first century was that terrorist organizations—or at least al-Qaeda—operated on a genuinely global scale. Ibid., 49, 68.

85. Ibid., 226–27.

86. Mary R. Habeck, *Knowing the Enemy: Jihadist Ideology and the War on Terror*, New Haven, CT: Yale University Press, 2006, 174. The conflict that the events of September 11 triggered (or more accurately highlighted, since the anti-American side had been waging it for some time) pitted the United States, the West, and the global forces of economic and political liberalism against a radical form of Islam sometimes called "Islamic fundamentalism" or "Islamism." In his 2006 State of the Union address, President George W. Bush cited as a principal source of danger in the world "radical Islam, the perversion by a few of a noble faith into an ideology of terror and death." George W. Bush, "State of the Union Address," *The New York Times*, February 1, 2006, A20.

87. Laqueur, *The New Terrorism: Fanaticism and the Arms of Mass Destruction*, New York: Oxford University Press, 1999, 43.

88. Habeck, op. cit., 14, 164.

89. Laqueur, op. cit., ch. 2.

90. President George W. Bush said so explicitly. "Ultimately, the only way to defeat the terrorists is to defeat their dark vision of hatred and fear by offering the hopeful alternative of political freedom and peaceful change." Bush, "State of the Union Address."

91. Sharansky, op. cit., 22. For the assertion that democracy offers a cure for terrorism, see Habeck, op. cit., 176–77, Amir Taheri, "Bush Is

Right: Democracy Is the Answer," in Adam Garfinkle, editor, *A Practical Guide to Winning the War on Terrorism*, Stanford, CA: Hoover Institution Press, 2004, and Graham Fuller, "Terrorism: Source and Cures," in Garfinkle, editor, op. cit., 22–23.

92. This argument is described, although not endorsed, in Gerard Alexander, "The Authoritarian Illusion," *The National Interest*, Fall 2004, 80.

93. This is the theme of Robert Pape, *Dying to Win: The Strategic Logic of Suicide Terrorism*, New York: Random House, 2005. The terrorist attacks launched by Chechen rebels against Russia arguably fit into this category, and a case could be made for including the terrorist activities of the Tamil separatists in Sri Lanka in it as well. For reservations about the validity of Pape's thesis, see Martin Kramer and Robert Pape, "Suicide Terrorism in the Middle East: Origins and Response," Policy-Watch 1050, Washington Institute for Near East Policy, Washington, D.C., November 16, 2005, and Laqueur, "What Makes Them Tick?" *The Washington Post Book World*, July 24, 2005, 7.

94. Laqueur, *No End to War*, 13, 23. The personal motive for terrorism is well put in the description of the terrorist known as "the Professor" in Joseph Conrad's 1905 novel *The Secret Agent*, still the most acutely observed account of the psychology of terrorism ever written: "The way of even the most justifiable revolutions is prepared by personal impulses disguised into creeds. The Professor's indignation found in itself a final cause that absolved him from the sin of turning to destruction as the agent of his ambition. . . . By exercising his agency with ruthless defiance he procured for himself the appearances of power and personal prestige." Ware, Hertfordshire, UK: Wordsworth Editions, 1993, 76–77.

95. The legitimacy of the Islamist ideology in the eyes of its adherents, like that of Marxism-Leninism for its proponents, did not rest on its capacity to command majority support. Both groups of believers considered themselves to be in possession of a superior truth, which they were therefore justified in using any means, including terrorism, to put into practice. See Habeck, op. cit., 162.

96. Laqueur, *No End to War*, 14–15. Islamist terrorists in Western Europe spread their message and organized their networks in mosques, which the democratic principle of free exercise of religion made safe havens for them. Ibid., 69.

97. "There was no terrorism under Hitler and Stalin, except of course terror from above; there was little if any terrorism under Gen. Franco and the Greek colonels. If Chechens had engaged in terrorism under Stalin or his successors, those surviving the journey would soon have found themselves on the wrong side of the Arctic Circle. Under Ottoman rule, Arab insurgents would have fared no better than did the Armenians." Laqueur, "What Makes Them Tick?" 7.

98. On state-sponsored terrorism see Daniel Byman, *Deadly Connections: States That Sponsor Terrorism*, New York: Cambridge University Press, 2005.

99. The most notable of these was the Islamic Republic of Iran. "In at least thirty Muslim countries, terrorism, practiced either by the state or its opponents, is an integral part of political life." Taheri, op. cit., 7.

100. The decline of war may itself contribute to an increase in the incidence of terrorism, which can become an attractive tactic to countries that seek to advance their goals by the use of force and lack the means, or the nerve, to wage full-scale war. "[T]he war against terrorism will not be won in our time in any case. Terrorism is the contemporary form of violent conflict, as major wars have become too costly and conflict won't disappear from the face of the earth in the foreseeable future." Laqueur, "The Danger That Lies in Our Midst," *The Wall Street Journal*, July 12, 2005, A16.

CHAPTER 5

1. "President Bush Discusses Freedom in Iraq and Middle East." Remarks by the president at the twentieth anniversary of the National Endowment for Democracy, United States Chamber of Commerce, Washington, D.C., November 6, 2003, available at www.whitehouse.gov /news/releases/2003.

2. "In the world today, the fundamental character of regimes matters as much as the distribution of power among them. The goal of our statecraft is to help create a world of democratic, well-governed states that can meet the needs of their citizens and conduct themselves responsibly in the international system. This is the best way to provide enduring security for the American people." *The National Security Strategy of the United States*, March, 2006, 1, available at www.white house.gov/nsc/nss/2006.

3. In 2004, the United States also persuaded the countries, most of them European, that belong to the Group of Eight (G-8) to commit themselves to a "Partnership of Progress and a Common Future with the Region of the Broader Middle East and North Africa" and to a "Democracy Assistance Dialogue" sponsored by Turkey, Yemen, and Italy. See Paula Dobriansky, "Advancing Democracy," *The National Interest*, Fall 2004, 76. The European commitment to promoting democracy in the Middle East had tended to be more rhetorical than substantive. In the year following the attacks on New York and Washington, D.C., the European Union gave "over twenty times more money for the preservation of historical sites in the Middle East than for democracy building." Richard Youngs, "Europe's Uncertain Pursuit of Middle East Reform," *Carnegie Papers* 45, June 2004, 10.

4. See chapter 2, 82.

5. See chapter 2, 89–90.

6. The post-Soviet countries of Central Asia, ruled by dictators and acting as potential or actual havens for terrorist groups, also belonged to this category.

7. This was also the case in two undemocratically governed but oil-rich countries that had once been provinces of the Soviet Union, Azerbaijan and Kazakhstan. "Vice President Cheney . . . blasted Russian commitment to democracy internally and on its borders when he made a swing through Europe and Central Asia. . . . But one day later he was in Astana, the Kazakh capital, where he praised the country for the progress it had made since the fall of the Soviet Union—even though by all accounts its human rights record is worse than Russia's." Glenn

Kessler, "Oil Wealth Colors the U.S. Push for Democracy," *The Washington Post*, May 14, 2006, A18.

8. The United States resumed full diplomatic ties with the dictatorial government of Libya in 2005, following a quarter-century without them, after that government publicly abandoned its nuclear weapons program. Libya also exports oil.

9. "One of the main dilemmas for proponents of democracy assistance is to figure out how to do in two years what Britain did in two hundred, and like Britain, how to do it in the right sequence." Jack Snyder, *From Voting to Violence: Democratization and Nationalist Conflict*, New York: W. W. Norton, 2000, 185. On the general requirement of time for one of democracy's principal habits, trust, to take hold, see Charles Lipson, *Reliable Partners: How Democracies Have Made a Separate Peace*, Princeton, NJ: Princeton University Press, 2003, 9–10.

10. See chapter 2, 72–79.

11. On the relevance of the German and Japanese cases see James Kurth, "Ignoring History: U.S. Democratization in the Muslim World," *Orbis*, Spring 2005, 307–10.

12. "Some people appear to believe that if enough people in Washington decide the Middle East needs to become democratic, democratization will happen, just by the force of the American will alone. Yet the most basic, consistent lesson coming out of the experience of democracy promotion in other regions is that external actors, even very determined ones employing significant resources, rarely have a decisive impact on the political direction of other societies." Thomas Carothers and Marina Ottaway, "The New Democracy Imperative," in Carothers and Ottaway, editors, *Uncharted Journey: Promoting Democracy in the Middle East*, Washington, DC: Carnegie Endowment for International Peace, 2005, 10.

13. See chapter 1, 44–45.

14. See Thomas Carothers, *Aiding Democracy Abroad: The Learning Curve*, Washington, DC: Carnegie Endowment for International Peace, 1999.

15. American exemplarism is a major theme of H. W. Brands, *What America Owes the World: The Struggle for the Soul of Foreign Policy*, New

York: Cambridge University Press, 1998. In his Farewell Address in 1796, the first American president, George Washington, declared, "It will be worthy of a free, enlightened, and at no distant period a great nation to give to mankind the magnanimous and too novel example of a people always guided by an exalted justice and benevolence." Ibid., 3. The fourth president, James Madison, wrote, "The free system of government we have established is so congenial with reason, with commonsense, and with a universal feeling, that it must produce approbation and a desire of imitation." Ibid., 5.

16. This is the subject of chapter 2.

17. See chapter 2, 75–77. On the requirement of democracy for EU membership, see Mark Leonard, *Why Europe Will Run the 21st Century*, New York: PublicAffairs, 2005, 18, 45, 56.

18. After Greece joined the European Community in 1981, it received particularly generous funding. "For Athens, EC membership amounted to a second Marshall Plan: in the years 1985–1989 alone, Greece received $7.9 billion from EC funds, proportionately more than any other country." Tony Judt, *Postwar: A History of Europe since 1945*, New York: The Penguin Press, 2005, 528. To be sure, the incentives to join were not only economic. After the Cold War ended, the formerly Communist countries sought membership not only to improve their economic conditions but also to "stabilize their domestic polities, lock themselves into 'the West' . . . [and] head off the temptation of a retreat into national Communism." Ibid., 717. Moreover, by the last quarter of the twentieth century, the democratic example had become so powerful, especially in Europe, that the southern and eastern Europeans might well have adopted democratic governance even without the lure of the economic rewards of EU membership. On the attractions of EU membership, see also chapter 2, 76–77, and chapter 3, 127–128.

19. Greece joined in 1981, Spain and Portugal in 1986, eight formerly Communist Eastern European countries—Hungary, Poland, Slovakia, Latvia, Estonia, Lithuania, Slovenia, and the Czech Republic, along with Malta and Cyprus—in 2004, and Bulgaria and Romania in 2007.

20. Michael Mandelbaum, *The Ideas That Conquered the World: Peace, Democracy, and Free Markets in the Twenty-first Century*, New York: PublicAffairs, 2002, 321–23.

21. This is the subject of chapter 3.

22. All, as it happened, had also been the targets, in the post–Cold War period, of deliberate, but not conspicuously successful, campaigns of democracy-promotion by the United States: a program of economic assistance and advice after the collapse of the Soviet Union in the case of Russia; an effort during the 1990s to tie trade to the protection of certain political liberties in China; and the Middle East initiatives launched in the wake of the terrorist attacks of September 11, 2001.

23. This was the verdict on the 2003 parliamentary elections of the independent election observers of the Organization for Security and Cooperation in Europe (OSCE). Peter Baker and Susan Glasser, *Kremlin Rising: Vladimir Putin's Russia and the End of Revolution*, New York: Scribner, 2005, 311.

24. The political associations that Russia did have were sometimes jokingly called "couch parties" because all of the members could fit on a single piece of furniture.

25. The methods by which these manipulations were accomplished are described in Andrew Wilson, *Virtual Politics: Faking Democracy in the Post-Soviet World*, New Haven, CT: Yale University Press, 2005.

26. The 2004–2005 legal proceedings against Mikhail Khodorkovsky, the principal owner of the country's largest oil company, Yukos, which led to his jailing and the transfer of control of the company's assets to the government, had an obvious political motive and did not, to put it mildly, conform to Western standards of jurisprudence. The government in effect expropriated the wealth of a private individual. To be sure, the manner in which Khodorkovsky had acquired these assets in the first place, through a private arrangement with President Boris Yeltsin, also departed sharply from normal Western business practices.

27. Baker and Glasser, op. cit., 78, 90.

28. Ibid., 6.

29. Richard Pipes, *Property and Freedom*, New York: Knopf, 2000, 217. On the decline in output in Russia and other post-Communist

countries following the collapse of communism, see Anders Aslund, *Building Capitalism: The Transformation of the Former Soviet Bloc*, New York: Cambridge University Press, 2002, ch. 4.

30. "Not surprisingly, many Russians came to identify 'democracy' with poverty and degradation." Geoffrey Hosking, *Rulers and Victims: The Russians in the Soviet Union*, Cambridge, MA: The Belknap Press of Harvard University, 2006, 392. "[T]he very word [*democracy*] had been discredited, an epithet that had come to be associated with upheaval rather than opportunity." Baker and Glasser, op. cit., 3.

31. Michael Mandelbaum, *The Dawn of Peace in Europe*, New York: The Twentieth Century Fund, 1996, ch. 3. See also Michael Mandelbaum, *NATO Expansion: A Bridge to the Nineteenth Century*, Chevy Chase, MD: The Center for Political and Strategic Studies, 1997. NATO's military interventions in Bosnia and Kosovo in the Balkans in the 1990s, both without Russian approval, also offended many Russians.

32. See chapter 3, 101, 106.

33. "[T]he most debilitating and antipodean aspect of Sovietism has been its effect on the population's mentality. It left behind an envious egalitarianism, a suspicion that entrepreneurship is 'speculation,' the reflex of responding to administrative commands rather than to market incentives, and the dulling pall cast by Marxist-Leninist dogma over habits of critical thought." Martin Malia, *The Soviet Tragedy: A History of Socialism in Russia, 1917–1991*, New York: The Free Press, 1994, 510. See also Richard Pipes, "Why the Bear Growls," *The Wall Street Journal*, March 1, 2006, A14.

34. See chapter 3, 115–117.

35. Martin Malia, *Russia under Western Eyes: From the Bronze Horseman to the Lenin Mausoleum*, Cambridge, MA: Harvard University Press, 2000, 5. The first Rome was Rome itself, the second, Constantinople, for centuries the seat of Eastern Christianity.

36. See, for example, ibid., 143–44.

37. Baker and Glasser, op. cit., 144–46. Estimates of the number of Russians who counted as part of the country's new middle class varied considerably. A very large number of those who qualified, whatever the

standard, lived in the capital, Moscow, because that was where much of the country's wealth was concentrated. Stephen Kotkin, "Gasputin," *The New Republic*, May 29, 2006, 37. Still, a Russian middle class was beginning to appear outside the capital city. "What is happening in Voronezh, 300 miles south of Moscow, is a powerful new phenomenon. Western-style retailing and international brands, largely confined a decade ago to metropolitan Moscow and St. Petersburg, are spreading to cities across Russia. After the hardships of the 1990s, Russia is finally witnessing the rise of a prosperous post-Soviet middle class." Neil Buckley, "From shock therapy to retail therapy: Russia's middle class starts spreading," *Financial Times*, October 31, 2006, 13.

38. For example, foreign direct investment in Russia, which totaled $20 billion in the course of the 1990s, reached $16 billion for the year 2005 alone. *Russia's Wrong Direction*, New York: The Council on Foreign Relations, 2006, 12.

39. See Mandelbaum, *The Dawn of Peace in Europe*, 69–109, and Mandelbaum, *The Ideas That Conquered the World*, ch. 4.

40. See chapter 3, 128–130.

41. "[W]ell over half the increase in industrial output since 1998 [in Russia] has been in the resource-intensive sectors." Martin Wolf, "Russia must be helped to be a 'normal democracy,'" *Financial Times*, May 11, 2005, 13.

42. Michael Mandelbaum, "Coup de Grace: The End of the Soviet Union," *Foreign Affairs: America and the World, 1991/92* 71, no. 1.

43. Benjamin Friedman, *The Moral Consequences of Economic Growth*, New York: Knopf, 2005, 11.

44. Minxin Pei, "China is stagnating in its 'trapped transition,'" *Financial Times*, February 24, 2006, 15.

45. For speculation on how democracy would affect China's foreign policy, see Arthur Waldron, "How Would Democracy Change China?" *Orbis*, Spring 2004.

46. Henry S. Rowen, "The Short March," *The National Interest*, Fall 1996, 61. By another, later estimate, the year 2020 will be crucial for Chinese democracy because the country will then have a per capita gross domestic product of $10,000. Bruce Gilley, *China's Democratic Fu-*

ture: How It Will Happen and Where It Will Lead, New York: Columbia University Press, 1996, 154–55.

47. See chapter 3, 100–103.

48. Perhaps the most conspicuous example of wealth combined with the absence of political democracy was the tiny Southeast Asian city-state of Singapore. The government of Singapore, however, while it was not chosen through free and fair elections, did protect private property and did provide, more broadly, the rule of law in economic affairs, without which it would not have become wealthy.

49. According to a professor at the government's top training school, "Through the experience of markets, there is a basis for civic consciousness and political participation. The power for democratization grows. People begin to think of paying their votes in return for the services of politicians, who are expected to engage in open competition among rivals to prove their worth, and win office. In the end, people demand to be full citizens, not subjects, in politics just as they are in the economy. . . . In China, the principle of competition is leaking into the political system." Gilley, op. cit., 93.

50. "The state still owns nearly 60 percent of fixed assets and dominates vital industrial sectors, from financial services to energy." Pei, op. cit.

51. At the turn of the twenty-first century, "there were two million private companies and 100 million people in the private sector accounting for 50 percent of the GDP." Gilley, op. cit., 66.

52. Gilley estimates the Chinese middle class at between 10 and 15 percent of the country's population. Ibid., 64.

53. "In the race to build the biggest malls, China is winning. Half of the 10 biggest malls in the world are in China, and two more are being built that will tie for No. 1 when they are completed." David Barboza, "China, Now a Land of Shoppers, Builds Malls on Gigantic Scale," *The New York Times*, May 25, 2005, C7.

54. The Center for Strategic and International Studies and the Institute for International Economics, *China: The Balance Sheet*, New York: PublicAffairs, 2006, 107.

55. James Miles, "Balancing act: a survey of China," *The Economist*, March 25, 2006, 4, 8.

56. In a population of 1.3 billion people, there were, in 2005, 120,000 certified lawyers. In 1979, there had been fewer than 2,000. *China: The Balance Sheet*, 8.

57. Robert Skidelsky, "The Chinese Shadow: II," *The New York Review of Books*, December 1, 2005, 34; Douglass C. North, "The Chinese Menu (for Development)," *The Wall Street Journal*, April 7, 2005, A14.

58. *China: The Balance Sheet*, 61.

59. Ibid., 7.

60. "Green activism, which hardly existed in China a decade ago, is spurring the development of a civil society." "How to make China even richer," *The Economist*, March 25, 2006, 11. On the problem of pollution in China, see Elizabeth Economy, *The River Runs Black: The Environmental Challenge to China's Future*, Ithaca, NY: Cornell University Press, 2004. The economic reforms also made possible private educational institutions, which had not existed in the Maoist era. By 2004, China had 78,500 such institutions enrolling 17 million students. *China: The Balance Sheet*, 70.

61. David M. Lampton, *Same Bed, Different Dreams*, Berkeley: University of California Press, 2002, 288–89; "Lobbyists in China Raise Their Voices," *The Wall Street Journal*, March 10, 2006, A4.

62. *China: The Balance Sheet*, 140.

63. Martin Wolf, "China should stick to trial and error—but risk bolder trials," *Financial Times*, June 7, 2006, 13.

64. Gilley, op. cit., 70.

65. "The party, the people, and the power of cyber-talk," *The Economist*, April 29, 2006, 28. China also had an estimated 390 million mobile phone subscribers. *China: The Balance Sheet*, 7.

66. When a small democracy movement appeared in China in 1978 and 1979, it spread its message via hand-drawn, large-character posters mounted on walls in Beijing. A decade later, the demonstrators in Tiananmen Square in the Chinese capital could communicate by photocopying and fax machines. The Internet has multiplied many times over the number of people with whom direct communication is rela-

tively easy. Merle Goldman, *From Comrade to Citizen: The Struggle for Political Rights in China*, Cambridge, MA: Harvard University Press, 2005, 8.

67. Gilley, op. cit., 88.

68. "In 1987 China began elections for village head and village council; by the late 1990s these elections were held in nearly 80 percent of China's almost one million rural villages." Goldman, op. cit., 1. See also Alexandra Harney, "China puts democracy to test," *Financial Times*, July 19, 2005, 2. Perhaps the closest thing to a national election in China not controlled by the Communist Party took place in 2005 when Chinese viewers voted for the winner of a televised singing contest by sending text messages through their mobile phones. More than 400 million people were said to have watched the show's final episode, of whom 8 million actually voted. Jim Yardley, "The Chinese Get the Vote, if Only for 'Super Girl,'" *The New York Times*, September 4, 2005, Week in Review, 3; "Democracy idol," *The Economist*, September 10, 2005, 42.

69. This is a major theme of Goldman, op. cit. See, for example, 9, 224.

70. Ibid., ch. 6.

71. Ibid., 217–21.

72. Ian Buruma, "China in Cyberspace," *The New York Review of Books*, November 4, 1999, 11.

73. Microsoft, Google, Yahoo!, and Cisco Systems cooperated with the Chinese government's efforts at censorship. "A setback for free speech in China," *Financial Times*, January 26, 2006, 12; Tom Zeller Jr., "China, Still Winning against the Web," *The New York Times*, January 15, 2006, Week in Review, 4. The effectiveness of those efforts was unclear. See Nicholas D. Kristof, "In China It's ******** vs. Netizens," *The New York Times*, June 20, 2006, A21.

74. "Opinion surveys suggest that despite frequent public protests in the countryside as well as in the cities, the central government still enjoys a considerable degree of support." Miles, op. cit., 15.

75. *China: The Balance Sheet*, 135. See also chapter 3, 111–112, and chapter 4, 164–165.

76. Gilley, op. cit., 114.

77. Ibid., 115, 144, 170. If the fall of communism did trigger movements for independence from China in Taiwan or Tibet or Xinjiang, or some of all of those places, the competitors for power in the post-Communist period might well use an appeal to nationalism based on the promise to resist the "fragmentation" of China as a tactic to acquire it. Ibid., 232–33, 240. This occurred in the former Yugoslavia after the fall of communism and in other places around the world as well, often leading to war.

78. The Communist regime also used resentment of Japan for its twentieth-century invasion and occupation of China to stir nationalist sentiment and so, at least indirectly, encourage support for itself. Ian Buruma, "China's persistent Japan syndrome," *Financial Times*, April 14, 2005, 13.

79. See chapter 3, 124–125.

80. Richard McGregor, "Cultivating the countryside: Hu takes pains to keep China free from a peasants' revolt," *Financial Times*, September 8, 2005, 13. By another estimate, 87,000 such incidents took place in 2005. *China: The Balance Sheet*, 40.

81. "Between 1997 and 2004, 50 million Chinese workers lost jobs in state-owned and collective firms. The result has been major gains in market-based productivity and income increases. The cost is anger, social tension, demonstrations, and riots." Albert Keidel, "China's Growing Pains Shouldn't Hurt Us," *The Washington Post*, "Outlook," July 24, 2005, B5. On a Chinese website on which people could post their views, "Messages complained about corruption, the privatisation of state-owned enterprises, and the hardships of unemployed workers." "The Party, the People, and the Power of Cyber-Talk," 27.

82. McGregor, op. cit.

83. "Should China's growth falter, the country's ability to maintain social and political stability would be in great doubt. A prolonged slump in property prices would confront homeowners with their first taste of negative equity and banks with a millstone of bad loans. Urban unemployment would rise perilously. Bottled-up grievances over corruption and poor governance could set off open unrest with support

from an urban middle class no longer so enamoured of the status quo."
Miles, op. cit., 12.

84. See chapter 3, 124–125.

85. How this might happen is a major theme of Gilley, op. cit. See especially Part 2.

86. "A survey by a senior Chinese academic conducted about two years ago among nearly 600 provincial and lower-level party officials in one (unnamed) province found that 85% of the respondents wanted to speed up political reform and more than 60% were dissatisfied or very dissatisfied with the level of democracy in China." Miles, op. cit., 16. An analysis of the different political tendencies within the Chinese Communist Party is in Cheng Li, "The New Bipartisanship within the Chinese Communist Party," *Orbis*, Summer 2005.

87. Gilley, op. cit., 111, 244.

88. "The Party has gradually ceded a good deal of authority to the market, the government, the courts, and other institutions that grapple on a daily basis with the complex decisions and policies required of a rapidly changing society and economy." *China: The Balance Sheet*, 67.

89. "Nearly every Arab government has promoted some type of political reform package. These government-sponsored initiatives vary significantly in scope and intent from country to country. In addition, the Arab League issued the first Arab multilateral pledge for reform in the organization's history." Mona Yacoubian, "Promoting Middle East Democracy II: Arab Initiatives," Special Report 136, United States Institute of Peace, Washington, D.C., May 2006, 1.

90. Steven A. Cook, "The Right Way to Promote Arab Reform," *Foreign Affairs* 84, no. 2 March–April 2005, 96; Barry Rubin, *The Long War for Freedom: The Arab Struggle for Democracy in the Middle East*, New York: Wiley and Sons, 2006, 229.

91. Robert Dahl, *On Democracy*, 189. See also chapter 1, 29–31, and chapter 3, 111–113.

92. Michael Howard, *The Lessons of History*, New Haven, CT: Yale University Press, 1991, 33.

93. According to Egyptian President Hosni Mubarak, "If we open the door completely before the people, there will be chaos." Quoted in Rubin, op. cit., 153.

94. On the history and ideology of pan-Arabism, see Fouad Ajami, *The Arab Predicament: Arab Political Thought and Practice since 1967*, New York: Cambridge University Press, 1981.

95. "Across the Arab world, political power has rested largely with minorities that view democracy as a threat. In Syria, power is concentrated in the hands of the Alawites, a small esoteric sect that many Muslims consider heretical. In Bahrain and Iraq, Sunni Muslims have traditionally dominated Shiite majorities. In other nations, such as Saudi Arabia and Egypt, rulers share the Sunni faith of the majority but are minorities by blood or politics." Andrew Higgins, "After High Hopes, Democracy Project in Bahrain Falters," *The Wall Street Journal*, May 11, 2005, 1.

"The irony is that minorities articulated the most prevalent form of nationalism, Arabism, in order to legitimize their own minority rule. This is particularly true of Alawi rule in Syria (where Sunnis are a majority), Sunni rule in Iraq (where Shiites are the largest group), Hashemite rule in Jordan (imported from Arabia, over a Palestinian majority), and dynastic rule throughout the Persian Gulf (where foreigners outnumber natives)." Martin Kramer, "When Minorities Rule in the Middle East (Part II): Historical Realities," *PolicyWatch* 935, Washington Institute for Near East Policy, Washington, D.C., December 28, 2004, 1.

96. The Sunnis' belief in their right to rule Iraq survived the downfall of Saddam Hussein. According to one observer, "Sunnis don't see themselves as one among many factions. They see themselves as power. They consider themselves the inheritors of the Ottoman Empire. This is not going to change." George Packer, *The Assassins' Gate: America in Iraq*, New York: Farrar, Straus, and Giroux, 2005, 416. See also Fouad Ajami, *The Foreigner's Gift: The Americans, the Arabs, and the Iraqis in Iraq*, New York: The Free Press, 2006, 135.

97. Rubin, op. cit., 70–72.

98. On the anti-democratic effects of oil wealth, see chapter 3, 128–131.

99. Daniel Pipes, *In the Path of God: Islam and Political Power*, New York: Basic Books, 1983, 288. The OPEC members are Iraq, Kuwait, Libya, Qatar, Saudi Arabia, and the United Arab Emirates. The non-OPEC members are Tunisia, Egypt, Syria, Bahrain, and Oman.

100. Fareed Zakaria, *The Future of Freedom: Illiberal Democracy at Home and Abroad*, New York: W. W. Norton, 2003, 138.

101. Thomas L. Friedman, *The World Is Flat: A Brief History of the Twenty-first Century*, New York: Farrar, Straus, and Giroux, 2005, 401. On the economic pathologies of the Arab countries, see Stephen Glain, *Mullahs, Merchants, and Militants: The Economic Collapse of the Arab World*, New York: St. Martin's Press, 2004.

102. Ajami, *Dream Palace*, 275.

103. Rubin, op. cit., 94–95.

104. Amir Taheri, "Bush Is Right: Democracy Is the Answer," in Adam Garfinkle, editor, *A Practical Guide to Winning the War on Terror*, Stanford, CA: Hoover Institution Press, 2004, 6.

105. Bernard Lewis, *What Went Wrong? Western Impact and Middle Eastern Response*, New York: Oxford University Press, 2002, 96–101.

106. In Islam "[t]he state can be called to account for violation of the divinely ordained Law, or for the failure to implement it, but not for some additional requirements imposed by the popular as opposed to the divine will." Ernest Gellner, *Conditions of Liberty: Civil Society and Its Rivals*, New York: Viking Penguin, 1994, 28. Democracy contravenes in particular the Islamic tradition that toleration, but not equality, is to be accorded three categories of people: slaves, women, and unbelievers. In the first decade of the twenty-first century, the second was especially well represented in Arab countries. Lewis, op. cit., 83.

107. Pipes, op. cit., 92–93.

108. This is a major theme of ibid.

109. "When the definition [of democracy] includes protection of individual rights and liberties, it becomes clear that some Islamist parties do not support democracy because they endorse a reduced version of political freedom—namely, freedom from the state at the expense of

the exercise of broader liberties within civil society." Judy Barsalou, "Islamists at the Ballot Box: Findings from Egypt, Jordan, Kuwait, and Turkey," Special Report 144, United States Institute of Peace, Washington, D.C., 10.

110. Pipes, op. cit., 197, 332.

111. Lewis, op. cit., 108.

112. "It would be nice if liberal democrats among the Arab intelligentsia could be the vanguard of political reform, but they are too few and too disconnected from their bodies politic to compel resistant autocrats to open the way for representative government." Amr Hamzawy, "The Key to Arab Reform: Moderate Islamists," Policy Brief 40, Carnegie Endowment for International Peace, Washington, D.C., August 2005, 4.

113. Martin Meredith, *The Fate of Africa: From the Hopes of Freedom to the Heart of Despair*, New York: PublicAffairs, 2005, 461–63. See also Jackson Diehl, "Mubarak Outdoes Himself," *The Washington Post*, December 5, 2005, A21.

114. Meredith, op. cit., 456–61.

115. "[M]ost people would agree that Saudi Islam is rigid and uncompromising, leaving a gap between ideal and practice that provokes accusations of hypocrisy. It is also self-righteous and more than a little xenophobic. The kingdom is the only country in the world, except perhaps North Korea, where the practice of all faiths but one is officially banned. Even other forms of Islam are frowned upon. Max Rodenbeck, "A long walk: a survey of Saudi Arabia," *The Economist*, January 7, 2006, 4.

According to the eminent historian of the Middle East Bernard Lewis,

> The Wahhabi branch of Islam is very fanatical, to the extent
> of being totally intolerant, very oppressive of women, and so
> on. Two things happened in the 20th century that gave
> Wahhabis enormous importance. One of them was that the
> sheikhs of the House of Saud, who were Wahhabis, and their
> followers obtained control of the holy places of Islam—

Mecca and Medina—which gave them enormous prestige in the Muslim world. And second, probably more important, they controlled the oil wells and the immense resources those gave them.

Imagine then that the Ku Klux Klan gets total control of the state of Texas. And the Ku Klux Klan has at its disposal all the oil rigs in Texas. And they use this money to set up a well-endowed network of colleges and schools throughout Christendom, peddling their peculiar brand of Christianity. You would have an approximate equivalent of what has happened in the modern Muslim world.

"What Went Wrong. Bernard Lewis Discusses the Past, Present, and Future of the Middle East," *Princeton Alumni Weekly*, September 11, 2002, available at www.princeton.edu/-paw/archive.

116. The advent of fundamentalist rule in Iran in 1979 created a rival to Saudi Arabia as the beacon of Islam and so provoked greater efforts at spreading Wahhabism, which the sharp increases in the price of oil, and therefore of revenues accruing to the Saudi government, underwrote. Zakaria, op. cit., 146.

117. Lewis, op. cit., 150.

118. Ibid., 3–17; Pipes, op. cit., 74–75.

119. Bernard Lewis, "The Revolt of Islam, *The New Yorker*, November 19, 2001, 50, 53.

120. Osama bin Laden referred, in his pronouncements, to what he regarded as the Muslim entitlement to "al-Andalus"—that is, to Spain. Ibid., 50. See also Rubin, op. cit., 81.

121. Pipes, op. cit., 195. Bernard Lewis, "The Roots of Muslim Rage," *The Atlantic Monthly*, September 1990, 59.

122. See chapter 4, 165–169.

123. Rubin, op. cit., 38, 108, 130; Zakaria, op. cit., 139.

124. The best account of the American encounter with Iraq is Ajami, *The Foreigner's Gift*, which describes it as "a struggle between American will and the laws of gravity in the region." Ibid., 343.

125. Joshua Muravchik, "The Trials of Ayman Nour," *The Wall Street Journal*, May 8, 2006, A18; Bret Stephens, "Bush Betrays Egypt's Democrats. For What?" *The Wall Street Journal*, May 30, 2006, A15.

126. "Daniel Patrick Moynihan, then the American envoy to the United Nations and a former ambassador to India, proclaimed in 1975 that democracy 'increasingly tends to the condition of monarchy in the 19th century: a holdover form of government, one which persists in isolated or peculiar places here and there' but 'which has simply no relevance to the future.'" John Mueller, *Capitalism, Democracy, and Ralph's Pretty Good Grocery*, Princeton, NJ: Princeton University Press, 1999, 214.

127. John Dunn, *Setting the People Free: The Story of Democracy*, London: Atlantic Books, 2005, 69.

128. See chapter 1, 13–14.

129. Gellner, op. cit., 188.

130. Minxin Pei, *China's Trapped Transition*, Cambridge, MA: Harvard University Press, 2006, 209. China also had a very high rate of domestic savings, which permitted unusually high rates of investment, which also contributed to its rapid economic growth.

131. "In the United States, industrial unemployment averaged 37.6 percent in 1933. In Germany and the United Kingdom, the peak had been reached a year earlier, with an average of 43.8 percent and 22.1 percent respectively." Harold James, *The End of Globalization: Lessons from the Great Depression*, Cambridge, MA: Harvard University Press, 2001, 168.

132. Gellner, op. cit., 202–203.

133. Tim Flannery, *The Weather Makers: How Man Is Changing the Climate and What It Means for Life on Earth*, New York: Atlantic Monthly Press, 2005, 191, 205, 291. Jared Diamond, *Collapse: How Societies Choose to Fail or Succeed*, New York: Viking, 2005, 498–99.

134. "[D]emocracy rests on the premise that governments will fail and that hence institutionalized ways have to exist for changing them." Samuel P. Huntington, *The Third Wave: Democratization in the Late Twentieth Century*, Norman, OK: The University of Oklahoma Press, 1991, 262.

INDEX

Afghanistan
anti-Communist insurgents in, 88
governance of, 174
Taliban and, 180
terrorism and, 180
U.S. and, 2, 88, 90, 170, 180, 182–183, 185
Africa
anti-Communist insurgents in, 88
British Empire and, 60–61, 62
corruption in, 132, 133, 269n62, 270n69
dictatorships in, 34
U.S. and, 88
Alawis, 220
Al-Qaeda network, 225
Al-Saud tribe, 182, 225, 226
American War of Independence, 153–154
Andropov, Yuri, 123–124, 125
Angell, Norman, 140, 141
Arab countries
anti-Western sentiments in, 165, 166, 167, 169, 278n67, 68
blaming others for problems of, 165, 278n66, 67, 70
conflict with Israel and 165, 166–167, 168–169, 227, 279n72, 79

future of, 189–190
governance of, 165, 172, 174, 278n67
Islamic terrorism and, 170, 171, 172, 173, 174, 218, 225, 226, 282n96, 99
middle class and, 222
Palestinians, alleged concern for, 167–169, 279n80
See also Petro-states; *specific countries*
Arab countries, potential for democracy in
fundamentalism, threat of, 225–226
heterogeneity of, 219–221, 228, 231–232, 294n95, 96
Islam's power and, 219, 223–227, 228, 281n95, 295n106, 296n115
oil and, 218, 219, 221–223, 226, 228, 296–297n115
overview, 218–219, 218–234, 221, 279n79, 284n12, 295n109, 296n112
political reform and, 218, 293n89
rivalry with West, 219, 226–227, 228
Arab League, 220
Arafat, Yasir, 3, 168–169
Argentina and Falklands, 160

299

Communist Party, potential
for demise of, 217
domestic protests against
government of, 215–216
desire for democratic
government in, 216,
293n86
economy of, 205–208, 209,
212–213, 215, 216, 217,
288n46, 289n49, 50, 51,
53, 292n81, 83
elections in, 210, 291n68
environmental concerns and,
209, 290n60
Internet communications in,
209–210, 211–212, 290n66
legal system and, 210, 290n56
liberty and, 210–211
middle class, creation of, 207,
211, 289n52
pluralism and, 209, 214
political parties and, 210, 211
population and, 207–208
regime's use of the threat of
war, 164–165
Chinese Revolution, 39
Churchill, Winston, 63, 84, 89
Civil society
communism and, 109–110,
267n32
description of, 103, 104, 105,
266n24, 26, 27, 28
free market and, 104–105,
107–108, 109, 110
functions of, 104
government power and, 105
history of, 109
liberty protected by,104, 106
self-government and, 106–110
Civil War (U.S.), 2
Clausewitz, Carl von, 145
Cobden, Richard, 140, 141, 142,
147

Cold War
Catholic Church and, 260n46
danger of surprise attack
during, 156–157
democracy and, 2, 50, 66,
66–67, 72, 84–85, 260n46
description of, 72, 73–74, 79
economic aspect of, 79–82
Germany and, 72–74
Great Britain and, 66
Japan and, 72–74
Nonaligned Movement and,
64
nuclear weapons and, 80, 144,
157
uprisings against communism
during, 77
U.S. and, 74, 84–85, 88–89,
156–157, 184
Communism
civil society and, 109–110,
267n32
coercion under, 33–34
collapse of, 41–42, 49, 63, 70,
77, 81, 87, 88, 123, 124,
198, 203, 212
democratic claims of, 32–33
description of, 69–70, 239
economy under, 95
elections under, 33
fascism, similarities to, 69–70
history of, 32–33, 246–247n15
liberty and, 37, 38–39
post–communist economic
failures and, 126–127,
268n52
power and, 33–34
private property and, 21, 33,
37, 126–127
terrorism and, 175
war and, 164–165
See also Cold War; specific
countries; specific leaders

Pakistan, *continued*
  private property and democracy
    in, 22
  terrorism and, 181–182
Palestinians
  Arab countries' alleged
    concern for, 167–169,
    279n80
  expulsion from Kuwait and
    Saudi Arabia of, 168
  governance among, 221
  Hamas and, 173, 224
Paris Peace Conference, 15, 68,
    69, 87–88, 249n46
Patents, 56–57
Patriotism, use of, 161, 163
Peace and democracy
  compromise and, 152,
    153–154, 158
  democracy, the promotion of
    and, 134, 138, 171
  democratic leaders and,
    151–152
  evidence of association
    between, 134, 137–138,
    176–177, 271n5, 8,
    274n29, 30, 31, 275n41
  liberty and, 151–159, 176
  procedural constraints and,
    152, 154–155, 158
  self-government and,
    146–151, 176
  terrorism and, 169–176
  theories of relationship
    between, 146–148
  transparency and, 152,
    155–158
  trust and, 156–157, 158
Peace and trade, 139–143, 146,
    147, 271n9, 272n11, 12, 14
Peloponnesian Wars, 145
Pentagon attacks. *See* September
    11, 2001, attacks

Petro-states
  democracy and, 128–131,
    133–134, 269n57, 58
  governments' bargain with
    citizens of, 120, 133
  Nigeria as, 133
  Russia as, 201–202, 286n26
  U.S. relations with, 182,
    279n75, 283n7, 284n8
  war and, 133
Philippines, The
  history of democracy in, 3, 41,
    42, 78, 86, 87, 246n15
  U.S. and, 86, 87, 259n38
Poland
  communism and, 76, 77
  history of, 70, 248n27
  post-communist economy of,
    127–128
Political liberty
  communism and, 37
  compromise and, 152–153
  dictatorships and, 38
  history of, 8, 10, 54
Political parties
  description and functions of,
    107–108, 267n41
  free-market and, 107–108, 109
  history of, 107
Popular sovereignty, 12–13
  See also Self-government
Portugal, 3, 41, 58, 76
Poverty
  absence of free-markets and,
    96–97, 263n6
  corruption and, 132–133
Power
  coercion and, 34–35
  communism and, 33–34
  early history of, 34
  military and, 35–36
  motives for holding, 34,
    253n81, 89